Girls
Just Want to Have
Funds

Girls
Just Want to Have
Funds

HOW TO SPRUCE UP YOUR MONEY LIFE
AND INVEST LIKE A PRO

Susannah Blake
Goodman

HYPERION

New York

Contents

Contents

Section III:

Start Investing and
Don't Get Spooked by the Market

Section IV:

Buying Stocks the Smart Shopper Way

Contents

Contents

Section VIII:

Protect What You've Got

Appendixes

Acknowledgments

First of all, this book would not have been possible without the unconditional love and support of my dad, my mom, my brother Mark, my sister (-in-law) Abby, and my boyfriend Tom Miller.

This book would also not have been possible without Carol Mann (for being an awesome, fantastic agent) and my editor Jennifer Lang at Hyperion (for making it all happen and having endless patience and faith!)

There are those who were indispensable because of their special contributions, talents, and gifts: Annie Gaddy (for coaching and believing in the beginning); Doug Gaddy (for coaching); Laura Brown (for editing, hand-holding, research, and catching falling trees); Anne Richardson (for spunky first draft editing); Mary Alma Welch (for being a savior); Tracey Bowen (for book babysitting, Gatorade, Powerbars, and endless generosity, sharing, and love); Heather Boyer (for editing, insight, and "getting the joke"); Jason and Michael Colton (for their brilliant brainstorming and title production); Karen Janis Nozik (for humor, wisdom, sharing, and encouragement); Agnieszka Fryszman (who asked the first questions and somehow always is responsible for my life projects); Stuart Ishimaru (for sitting at my kitchen table); Ellen Taggart and Liz Phillips (ya ya—need I say more?); Jay Bryant (for his expertise and confidence); Janette Robinson (for her encouragement and love); Sacha Millstone (for her sparkle, vision, and expert consulting); Cayte Jablow (for her "can do" spirit); Joan Heckscher (for always believing); Stacey Grundman (for her support); Wendy

Lader (for faith and confidence); Doug Hyde (for editing); Michael Martin (for editing and for his Shakespearean jousting skills); Lixandra Urresta (for awesome fact checking); Ruti Ruela (for all I need to know about taxes); Sharon Nelson Lopez (for love, laughs, understanding, and encouragement); the rest of the Lopez gang (for their spark and light); Janice, Christina, Trisha, and Robert; Miles Brooks (for his friendship and support); Jackie Paulzine (for endless generosity, hospitality, and fun!); Pete Jenner (for his couch and hospitality); Cynthia Brown and Jamie Ingerman (for the workshop of life); Elise and Suzanne Jones (for being the best Great Old Broads Ever); the boy (for his inspiration); the girl (for her encouragement and empathy); the mom (for her kindred spirit); the Sue (for being the Sue); and of course Ernie on the train with Geneva; Julia Hodgson (for constant friendship and the time value of money); Ryan Alexander and Denise Gilpin (for understanding that Francoise needs to learn about money, too); Ayelet Waldman and Michael Chabon (my family and writers extraordinaire); and Billy Parsons (who was there at the start).

A HUGE special thank-you to all my mentors who got me to this place: Joan Claybrook, Pam Gilbert, Mike Waldman, and John and Tony Podesta. And to my co-workers John Canham-Clyne and Nancy Watzman (who deserve an incredible amount of credit because they are such great writers and editors). Also to Mike Casey, Patrick Woodall, and Rebecca Sachs, my fellow foot soldiers.

I'd like to thank the following people for sharing their vision and leadership in the investing world: Amy Domini, Steve Viederman, Jeanne Gauna, Peter Kinder, Steve Lydenberg, Ingrid Saukaitis, Paul Hilton, Lisa Leff, David Schilling, Alice Tepper Marlin, Shelley Alpern, Simon Billenness, Joan Bavaria, Tim Smith, Alisa Gravitz, and Robert Massie.

Acknowledgments

I'd like to thank Paul Wick, Krista Moses, Mauro Farinelli, Maggie Gilliam, Sadia Corone, Sharon Rich, and the smartest of smart shoppers, Warren Buffett, for sharing their wisdom with me personally. Special thanks to Sam Hoyt and Marianne Suscoe for making interviews happen.

Introduction

Have you ever wished someone would give you a "money makeover" the way that models get those makeovers in magazines like *Glamour*?

Do you want to get rid of that skulky feeling in your stomach every time someone mentions the words "401(k)" and "tax-deferred vehicle"?

Or do you just want to feel as brassy and confident about investing in stocks and mutual funds as that gal with the glossy hair on the CNN Financial Network?

If you answered yes to these questions, then this book is for you. The good news is you already have all the mathematical and analytical skills you need to turbo-charge your money life and invest like a pro.

Money and investing may seem difficult because the words are so serious and official-sounding—words like "401(k)" or "tax-deferred vehicle." Don't let that fool you. The concepts are actually very basic.

Think of it this way: Have you ever been on a bus or train somewhere and the people next to you were rattling away in some exotic foreign language? And then later you learned the language and realized that all they were saying was stuff like, "You know, I've been thinking. I've got to do my laundry. I'm totally out of clean socks." Or "Oy. My stomach. I think that tunafish at lunch gave me a stomachache." So it is with investing. The concepts are nothing mysterious, but the language sure makes it seem so.

Finance people love to make up special words to describe simple concepts. This makes me mad. It seems rather deceitful, designed to exclude people, make them think they can't understand what's going on.

For example, in financial-speak, people don't say "big companies" and "little companies." No. That would be too easy. They say "large cap" and "small cap." Why don't they just say "big" and "little?" When they say, "You should dollar-cost-average," what they really mean is "You should put a little bit of money in your account every month."

However, after you read this book, you'll know the language and you'll be ready to invest with the best.

This book is divided into different sections. In the first section, you will learn the three things you *must* do. This stuff is basic. And even if you don't do anything else, YOU MUST DO THESE THREE THINGS! Yes, I am shouting. I am even stomping my feet and saying your *entire* name like your parents did when they'd stopped kidding around. ("Patricia Lee Nelson! Did you hear me? Clean up your room. And invest in your IRA. Now!")

In the sections following that, you will learn the basics about stocks, bonds, mutual funds, and investing. You will learn such vital things as:

◆ What kind of investments are right for your circumstances (After all, one size doesn't fit all)

◆ How to tell the difference between a mutual fund you flirt with and a mutual fund that you bring home to your family

◆ How to learn to do quick and easy research on a mutual fund or a stock you want to buy

◆ How to invest with your values so that your money works to clean up the environment or to pay people fair wages

You've heard of "Fashion Do's and Don'ts"? Well, in this book there are simple but invaluable Stock Market Do's and Don'ts. These tips are discussed in the chapters "What to Do When the Market Crashes" and "Why You Should Ignore Market Mood Swings."

In the section "Creating and Implementing Your Grand Master Plan," everything is put together. In this section, you learn how to do your own "Money Makeover." You know how fashion magazines like to feature makeovers? How with just the right lipstick, cover-up, and eyeliner, a woman's blemishes disappear and her natural beauty is brought out? With a "Money Makeover," it's a woman's debt that vanishes and her financial future that starts to glow—using the "natural beauty" of her current bank balance or retirement plan.

In this section you learn to create a financial plan for yourself and who to go to—financial planners and financial advisors—to get the necessary help.

Also in the section "Money Makeovers," I tell the stories of women who overcame common investment foibles—not saving enough, underearning, getting out of debt, not contributing to a retirement account—to become model money makeovers. These women are inspiring!

HOW TO PUT THIS BOOK INTO PRACTICE

"We, as women, don't like to do things alone. This is not fun. Learning about money can be overwhelming both psychologically and technically." So says Sharon Rich, owner of her own financial planning practice "Womoney" and one of Money Magazine's top financial planners in the United States.

So crack this book with some of your friends. Yes, I tried to write this book so it was readable—but you are bound to have questions. When you went to school, they didn't plunk you down in an isolation tank with a text book and say, "Here! Learn! I'll be back at 5 p.m."

No way. In second grade, you had crayons and clay and games and the occasional math book. And you had a teacher. In twelfth grade, you had papers to write, biology labs, chemistry labs and even language labs. And you had a teacher. And during this whole time you had CLASSROOMS with other people in them. And you got to sneak over to your best friend's house if she was good at math and you weren't and have *her* explain bisecting angles and trigonometry to you. (My thanks to Margaret Brower.)

This book is meant to be the most fantastic teaching tool you'll ever find. But when you're done reading, your job is to go out in the finance world of bankers and brokers, with your best friend for moral support, and ask a million questions. ASK, ASK, ASK. And make sure that half the questions you ask are really, really dumb.

THE BEAUTY OF DUMB QUESTIONS

Afraid of asking "dumb" questions? Of looking stupid? I have something to tell you. There are no dumb questions; only dumb answers.

If you ask a financial professional a question, and you can't understand the answer, it's the professional's fault. *Everything about money is understandable.*

There are only two reasons financial professionals will give you fuzzy answers to your questions. One, they don't really know the answer and they are afraid to say, "I don't know. That's a good question." Or two, they are out to scam you. In either case, run screaming. There are good financial advisors out there and this book tells you how to find them.

But no matter what, you simply must ask questions. You must ask whether you think they are dumb or not. Because, what you don't know about money *will* hurt you.

WOMEN AND MEN, FEAR AND SHAME, AND MONEY

Just in case you are ashamed that you don't know about money issues, I'd like to dispel the myth that you are somehow at fault. First of all, we are all strong capable women (bad hair days notwithstanding). Our professions and responsibilities run the gamut. Some of us raise families. Some practice law. Some run our own organizations. Some of us should just get a darn medal for showing up to work every day! But, we are all smart, cool, and competent. So why don't we know about this very important key to managing our lives?

My answer? **We weren't taught in high school.** None of us were. (And I'll leave the broad sociological formulations as to why this was and is so to feminist historians.) It's not like we all cut class in high school to hang out in the parking lot when they were teaching this stuff. They didn't teach it. I know this because I was too nerdy in high school to be invited to hang out in the parking lot. I went to every class. I swear. It wasn't taught.

In high school they taught driver's ed. They taught sex education. They taught English, physical education, two years of U.S. history, geometry . . . you get the picture. Everything but Money Management 101—answering these simple but vital questions: Why should I put money in a retirement plan when I'm young? What's a stock? What's a bond? What's Wall Street? So there's no reason to be ashamed that you don't know about money. Just throw that sulky feeling out the window right now.

And here's a bit of news. Not only weren't we taught, but neither were the guys who we went to high school with. So the idea that somehow men know this stuff and we don't isn't that valid either. Very few men outside the financial professions have gone through a rigorous training course on all manner of investment vehicles and really have a handle on it. So why does it *seem* like they know these things?

Well, they are just in a different bind than women. Society says they are *supposed* to know. So some men do study and do learn. But others just fake it. They pick up jargon along the way and they may read about business a little more to fulfill the role that society expects of them. But they don't really know.

(You've been in a car when a guy is driving and you both are lost. Will he stop to ask for directions? No. Will he admit that he's lost? Not really. He's just pretending that he knows where he's going; he's faking it. So it also can be with money matters. Passengers and passive investors beware!)

I know about this faking thing because I have spent the better part of two years researching all manner of money in depth. I can tell when a guy is faking it, because the guy will use a lot of jargon to describe something embarrassingly simple. He'll say something like, "Because of sluggish earnings growth in the last quarter, I may have prematurely converted the majority of my equities to cash." You know what he's really saying? "Uh . . . I got spooked. And like an idiot I sold when I shouldn't have."

So if you start to learn about money, will you threaten the egos of the men in your life? No. The truth is, most men like women who have their financial act together. Your knowledge will be welcome. In fact, it will be a relief.

One of my best friends—a guy—bemoans the fact that his live-in girlfriend stubbornly refuses to have a discussion about retirement planning and investing. "I tell her, 'You've got to learn this stuff. How can we plan our future together if you don't know what's going on? How can you have realistic expectations?' " He's frustrated. He'd be psyched if she could be a true partner with him.

Knowing the best aggressive growth mutual fund out there can be downright sexy!

WHY I WROTE THIS BOOK

In another career I was a consumer advocate and spent my time roaming the halls of our nation's capital working to preserve health, safety and consumer banking laws.

But one Thanksgiving I went home to find my brother and my father discussing stocks and mutual funds and interest rates at the kitchen table. It hit me that I had no clue what they were talking about. And it seemed like my brother was about to become very rich and I wasn't. A severe case of sibling envy ensued. When had my brother learned these things? Scandal! He'd majored in psychology, not economics! And more importantly, why didn't I know? He tried to calm me down and told me he'd always been interested in the stock market. But I was still horrified at my ignorance. At that time, I was sure that the reason I didn't know about money was part of a larger conspiracy to keep women in their place . . . part of the whole patriarchal structure where women didn't have the right to vote, and weren't taken seriously as they pursued their careers.

It got me into an advanced stage of paranoia. I began to sincerely suspect that at the age of thirteen lots of middle-class boys were rounded up by accountants, lawyers, and stock brokers, in full voodoo-man regalia. These virile young lads were taken into the woods by their broker-voodoo men, set up around a bonfire, and in a trance-like state were taught to infer how compound interest works, what the best tax shelters are, and how to buy stocks. It seemed to be the only possible explanation.

Well, I decided I would not be outdone by my brother or any other male counterpart. I began to teach myself. Then I took classes. Did it help that my father, the venerable Adam Smith,[1] was a very successful money writer and television host? You bet it did! I grilled the poor man endlessly. He'd come home tired after a week's worth of interviews, writing, and television work and I'd show up on the doorstep of my childhood home with a long list of questions. There was no escaping my endless queries about interest rates, stocks, mutual funds, and market mood swings.

When my good friends found out what I was up to they all had the same reaction: "When you're done learning, you should teach me." So I became a financial advisor to an ever-expanding circle of women. And suddenly it seemed the most logical thing to do was to write a book explaining everything. A book for me and my peers on the topic of money management and investing. That's the book you now hold in your hands.

Whether you are investment-phobic or a stock market sleuth, this book should provide you with useful tools and insight. You'll learn how to analyze retirement plans, mutual funds and stocks with the best of them. You'll realize the ways that you already are a natural investor, saver, and money manager. Once you start reading, you'll be eager to bring out the natural beauty in your financial future. So go for it!

---

[1] Adam Smith, a one-time money manager and the host of the Emmy award–winning television show *Adam Smith's Money World*, is the author of four best-selling books about the stock market and the economy, including *The Money Game*, *Supermoney*, *Paper Money*, and *The Roaring Eighties*.

The

Three

Most Important Things

You MUST Do

Chapter One

Start Early—And Become a Millionaire

Why Investing Early Pays Off, and Hard Work Sometimes Doesn't

What's the best way to retire as a millionaire? Take this pop quiz and find out.

A. Win the lottery.
B. Steal Brad Pitt from his current flame and then sell the secret photos to *Star* magazine
C. Start putting money away NOW—as early as possible—before you have a clue about anything else.
D. Pick the hottest stocks in the market and sell them when the time is right.

You guessed it: Answer C. "Start putting money away NOW—as early as possible—before you have a clue about anything else." In fact, the earlier you start putting money away, the more flexibility you'll have in the future to do what you want, when you want. Check this out.

Sam and Jane are seniors in high school. Sam is dull-witted and slow. Jane is smart and bright.

After high school, Sam goes directly to work in his father's car wash. His father helps him set up an individual retirement account (IRA).

With his father's help, Sam puts away $2,000 a year in the IRA . . . until the age of 28.

At that age, he quits the car wash. He stops contributing to his IRA. He hooks up with one of his shady buddies, Skanky Steve, and heads to Los Angeles. He becomes a total slacker and all he does for the next forty years is smoke pot, drink Wild Turkey, and play bad heavy metal music in dark L.A. clubs.

Jane, on the other hand, goes to college and then to law school. At age 28, she finally feels enough room to breathe between paying back her student loans and managing her other finances. She sets up an IRA and starts to contribute $2,000 per year, and does so continually for the next forty years. She becomes a pillar of her community.

Both Sam's and Jane's IRAs grow at a rate of 10% per year.

Sam has contributed only $20,000 to his.

Jane has contributed $80,000 to hers.

When they both retire at age 68, guess who has more? Sam! Sam's account has grown to $1,442,631. Jane's account has grown to $885,185. Scandalous, you say? Yes.

Sam has almost a million and a half dollars even though *he put in only $20,000*. Jane has less than Sam, even though *she put in $80,000*.

Why? Sam started earlier. Ten years earlier, to be exact. Starting early made all the difference.

Don't believe me? Check out the chart in the Appendix. The numbers tell the story. In fact, if you follow the numbers closely, you'll see that starting at age 27, the *interest* on Sam's account is bigger than Jane's whole first-year contribution of $2,000. That's why Sam stays ahead, even though he completely stops contributing after age 28.

Basically, Sam gets a head start on Jane—and at $2,000 per year, she never, never, never catches up.

You see, there are four factors that make an investment grow: the *interest rate* or "rate of return" of the investment, the *amount you start with*, the *amount you contribute every year*, and the *time* that your investment has to grow. Of all of these, *time is the most compelling*. Time is the magic fairy dust of money. Time is the thing that makes money grow like that crazy beanstalk of "Jack and the Beanstalk" fame. But before focusing on the time factor, let's review the other factors that make an investment grow.

THE RATE OF RETURN OR INTEREST RATE

The rate of return makes a difference—a big difference—in how fast money grows. "What's a *rate of return?*" you ask. Say you put $100 of your money in a bank savings account earning 1.5% interest. Your rate of return is 1.5%. So your money would grow by only $1.50 a year—a paltry sum. But if your rate of return were 11% and you had $100, your money would grow by $11 a year. That's a big difference. I mean you can buy a sandwich and a cup of coffee with $11. Woweee!

So rate of return makes a difference in how quickly your money grows. And for the record, you *should* put your money in a *stock mutual fund*, which I refer to later, if you want it to grow the fastest. (According to careful study by Ibbotson Associates, from 1926 to 1998, large company stocks have had an annualized return of 11.2%. *And that includes all the major stock market crashes.*) But rate of return is not the most important thing.

AMOUNT YOU START WITH

The more you start with, the bigger it will grow. At 10%, your money will double every 7.2 years. If you start with $10,000, it will be $20,000 in 7.2 years. If you start with $20,000, it will be $40,000 in 7.2 years. If you start with $1 million, and it grows by 10%, you will have $2 million in 7.2 years. Even so, the amount that you start with still is not the most important factor.

AMOUNT YOU CONTRIBUTE

If you add to your investment every year, your basic pot of cash will be bigger. It's true. If you keep adding to your stash of cash every year, it will grow. But that's still not the most important component.

In fact, the above three factors are fairly earthly. They are predictable and not magical.

TIME

Yes, time is the most important variable in determining how big your pot of money will get. Time makes money grow exponentially. Think back to the sixth or seventh grade when you learned about exponents. They blew your mind then and they should blow your mind now.

Remember this? Say every day you multiplied the number five by itself. You start the first day with 5. The second day, you'd have 25. The third day, you'd have 125. The fourth, 625. The fifth, 3,125. On the sixth day, you'd have 15,625. On the seventh day, you'd have to rest.

That's how money grows. Exponentially. In a blob-like manner. Oozing out on all sides.

Got it? Okay: read the following story so that you can see exactly how and why starting early makes such a HUGE difference. But the characters this time are not so extreme. In fact, you may see yourself in them.

Once upon a time there were two feisty, independent women

named Heather and Christine. They were best friends and roomed together in college for three of the four years that they went to school together. They both played on the varsity soccer team, both were champions at the drinking game called quarters. At one time, they both had boyfriends named Brian—although Christine broke up with her Brian at the end of junior year, and Heather and her Brian lasted only about two months.

They graduated from college, and their families came to see them, bringing graduation gifts. Christine's older stepbrother, Edward, was a stockbroker for Merrill Lynch. He helped Christine open up an IRA as a graduation gift. He told Christine that no matter what she did, she should always contribute $100 a month to the IRA. That year, Edward died in a mysterious gardening accident.

Meanwhile, Heather, whose mother owned Ye Olde Yummy Bakery in Concord, MA, didn't know from IRAs. She gave Heather a cake for graduation, which Heather ate, and her blessing, which made Heather happy.

Over the years, Christine was less directed than Heather. She flitted from odd job to odd job and eventually found her calling in professional flower arranging. But the death of her stepbrother Edward had made a lasting impact. To honor his name, she kept the IRA as he had instructed. Every month for ten years, she made a contribution to the IRA.

When she stopped contributing to her IRA, she had put in a total of $12,000.

Heather went off into the world and got a degree in urban and environmental planning and became executive director of a group called Recycle or Die. She was 32 when she realized she needed a retirement plan. So she started one. She contributed $100 per month until she retired. In total, she contributed $36,000. They both retired at the age of 62.

Heather put $36,000 into her IRA over thirty years. It grew at a rate of 10%. $100 per month.

Christine put $12,000 into her IRA over ten years. It grew at a rate of 10%. $100 per month.

Overall, Heather put $24,000 more into her IRA.

They both cashed out their IRAs at age 62.

Trick Question: At the end of that time, whose IRA account was worth more?

Answer: Yes. Christine's. (You're catching on.) Christine had $406,359.20 at age 62. Heather had only $226,048.79.

Why? Christine had time on her side.

That's the one thing that Christine had more of than Heather. How much more? Ten years more. And in the world of investing, ten years, at only $100 per month, equals approximately $180,000.

Here's the long version. Just follow along.

1986: Heather and Christine are 22.

Christine and Heather graduate from college.

STARTING SCORE:

HEATHER: 0

CHRISTINE: 0

Christine, waiting tables in Miami, starts to contribute $100 per month to a tax-sheltered account.

Heather, working in Colorado on a campaign to save the environment, is putting nothing away.

1988: Heather and Christine are 24.

SCORE:

CHRISTINE: $2,644.69

HEATHER: 0

Christine is still waiting tables, but she is going to school part-time to study acupuncture. She puts $100 away per month to honor the wishes of her stepbrother, Edward.

Heather is in Berkeley, canvassing for the California Public Interest Research Group. She falls in love with Todd, starts learning how to surf, and still puts nothing away. Her mother sends her cookies.

1990: Heather and Christine are 26.
SCORE:
CHRISTINE: $5,872.25
HEATHER: 0

Heather breaks up with Todd because he has no ambition, and goes back to graduate school to study urban and environmental planning. She wins the local women's surfing competition. She contributes nothing to an IRA.

Christine is still waitressing. She gives up on acupuncture and starts to coach junior high school girls soccer. She still contributes $100 per month to her IRA. She borrows $3,000 from her older brother, Mark, to buy a used Honda Civic.

1992: Heather and Christine are 28.
SCORE:
CHRISTINE: $9,811.13
HEATHER: 0

Heather graduates from her urban and environmental planning school with a master's degree. She goes to work for Recycle or Die, a radical nonprofit environmental organization dedicated to passing mandatory plastic recycling laws in all fifty states. She puts nothing away and starts to pay off her student loans.

Christine decides she wants to go back to school to study plants and flowers. She applies for and receives student loans. She contributes $100 per month to her IRA. Her brother Mark is very nice about the car loan and lets her pay it back slowly, at $50 per month.

1994: Heather and Christine are 30.
SCORE:
CHRISTINE: $14,618.11
HEATHER: 0

Heather becomes executive director of Recycle or Die. She is working sixty-five hours a week and trying to stay on the surfing circuit. She is exhausted. She begins to wonder whether she should start to think about putting money away for retirement, but does not.

Christine gets her first job as a professional flower arranger in a local flower shop. She meets Jimmy and marries him within four months. Then they start fighting all the time, so Christine moves out, even though she is pregnant. Her other best friend, Bernice, comes to live with her. She eats crackers all the time to stop the morning sickness. She racks up $8,000 in credit card debt to get through the hard times.

Throughout all this, she still contributes $100 per month to her IRA. For Christine, putting $100 per month into the IRA has become a ritual way to pay tribute to the memory of her loving older stepbrother, Edward. Her friends urge her to liquidate her IRA to pay off her mountain of debt, but she tearfully refuses.

1996–2006: Heather and Christine grow from age 32 to 42.
SCORE AT AGE 32:
CHRISTINE: $20,484.50
HEATHER: 0

Christine begins the decade $20,484.50 ahead of Heather. She gives birth to a baby boy and names him Edward. She and Jimmy reconcile, and move back in together. Christine goes to consumer credit counseling and gradually pays off her $8,000 in credit card debt. She has another child, whom she names Sheila.

At the beginning of the decade, Christine stops contributing to her IRA every month. Instead, she honors dead stepbrother Edward's memory by opening up a college fund in his name for her two children. But the $20,484.50 inside her IRA still grows by 10% each year. Christine hasn't touched it. She refuses to liquidate it.

Beginning in 1996, Heather begins to contribute $100 to an IRA. She does so every month for ten years. She gets married to Jackie in the year 2000. They have two children named Madison ("Maddy" for short) and Liam.

Even though Heather has started an IRA and Christine has stopped contributing, Christine is still ahead.

2006–2016: Heather and Christine grow from age 42 to 52.
SCORE AT AGE 42:
CHRISTINE: $55,452.39
HEATHER: $20,484.50

The two women grow older and prosper in their careers. Their kids grow up, and they remain friends. Christine still refuses to liquidate her IRA, and it continues to grow by 10% per year.

Heather continues to contribute $100 per month to her IRA. And that money also grows by 10% per year.

2016–2026: Heather and Christine grow from age 52 to 62.
SCORE AT AGE 52:
CHRISTINE: $150,111.92
HEATHER: $75,936.88

In the past ten years, Heather has continued to contribute $100 per month to her IRA. Christine has contributed nothing to her

IRA. Her son Edward and her daughter Sheila go to college. Heather's children are still in high school.

Heather gets the Colorado "Environmentalist of the Year" award. Christine owns her own flower shop. At the end of the decade, they both retire.

2026: Heather and Christine are both 62.
FINAL SCORE AT AGE 62:
CHRISTINE: $406,359.17
HEATHER: $226,048.79

Basically, Christine had a HUGE head start and she never gave up that lead.

Technically speaking, Heather contributed $36,000 over time. Christine contributed only $12,000.

Both of their accounts grew by 10% per year.

That's the thing. The original money—the original $1,200—doesn't grow by 10% only once and then it's done. No. Every year, the original $1,200 gets to grow by another 10%.

That's why, if you start early, you've got it made. You can just sit back and watch your money grow.

AND NOW THE GOOD NEWS

If reading this first chapter depressed you because you haven't started to put money away, don't despair. Few people learn this lesson in their twenties. Most people are just scrambling to try to develop a life and career. So, just heed the lesson and read on. Then get your best girlfriend for support and TAKE ACTION. As soon as you take some action, you will feel better. I promise. You will be empowered. And it won't be too long before you are feeling as savvy about money matters as the glossy-haired gal on the CNN Financial Network.

Chapter Two

Get Paid for Your Work

Max Out Your Retirement Plan

"No, thank you. I don't want to inherit $1,000,000."
"No, thank you. I don't want to win the lottery."
"No, thank you. I don't want to get paid for my work."

When, in your life, have you ever said these things? And if you have, didn't your girlfriends wonder if you were in your right mind? Here's the thing: Maxing out your retirement plan is the next best thing to inheriting a lot of money or winning the lottery. As the L'Oréal commercial says, "You're worth it!"

Here's why.

1. Your taxes will be lower—and lower taxes mean more income for you.
2. Once safely stashed in a retirement plan, your money will grow like it gets dipped in Miracle-Gro every night.
3. *Your employer may GIVE you money to do it.* If your employer has any kind of "matching plan," you are set. You will get additional money on top of your salary.

If you decline to participate in your retirement plan, you will be saying, "No thank you, I don't want to get paid for my work." And please, if you ever say that, I will have to conduct an intervention and send you off to therapy.

Let me explain some important points to you:

1. Your employer may GIVE you money to contribute to your retirement plan. Woody Allen once said, "Ninety percent of life is just showing up." Your employer is giving you this money just for showing up for work. It's part of your benefits package. Many employers have a decent retirement plan and a *matching* program. So they just give you this money in addition to your salary.

Here's how it works: Your employer will deduct a portion of your paycheck and put it in your retirement account each month. Then your employer will contribute something additional, probably a percentage of that contribution. For example, you put in $150 per month. Your employer puts in 50% of that, or $75 per month. And that is *on top* of your regular paycheck.

EXAMPLE:_____

My friend Jill works for the Adopt an Eagle program.

Jill puts $150 of her salary into her retirement plan.

Then her employer *gives* her $150 per month to match it.

That's $1,800 per year—extra—that she gets. It completely offsets the contribution coming out of her own salary.

All Jill has to do is show up for work and sign up for this plan and she receives more money. Money she deserves because she works hard at saving those eagles.

Now, it may be that your employer has chosen a kind of plan in which the company will contribute to an account in your name, no matter what you do. They will just go ahead and contribute a percentage of your salary—whatever the plan provides for.

If that is the case, you should still find out if you can make any kind of contribution yourself, because if you can, you will be adding to your pot o' gold, and you will be reducing your tax liability. Which brings us to the following gem:

2. Your taxes will drop if you contribute to your retirement plan.
When you put your money into your retirement plan, your taxes drop because your taxable income is lower.

The U.S. government is saying, "We think it's so important for you to save money for retirement that we are not going to tax that part of your income that goes toward your official retirement plan." No matter what kind of tax bracket you are in, or what kind of tax form you fill out, you always, always, always will reduce your taxes if you contribute to your retirement plan.

EXAMPLE:

Back to Jill.

She makes $36,000 per year.

She puts $1,800 per year into her retirement account.

Right off the bat, she reduces her taxable income by $1,800. So her taxes are lower. Why? Uncle Sam is ignoring the fact that she makes $36,000 per year. Before she even begins computing her taxes and deducting other things, Uncle Sam will let her say that she only earns $34,200. That $1,800 is subtracted from her taxable income.

And now finally, another big reason your retirement plan is so important . . .

3. Once safely stashed away in a retirement plan, your money will grow like magic. A retirement plan is a protective shield. A shell. An umbrella. What goes inside of it can be any financial instrument—stocks, bonds, options, futures, or a mutual fund, which pools stocks and bonds.

SuperTaxman, faster than a speeding bullet, more powerful than a locomotive, wilts into a limp rag in the face of the kryptonite retirement account.

So any income or profits created inside the protective shell are SAFE. A stock mutual fund, a bond mutual fund, a bond—these all can generate income. If you have bonds, they generate interest income. If you have stocks, and they are sold for a profit, that profit can be taxed. (That profit, incidentally, is called a *capital gain*.) Outside the shell of the retirement plan this profit from the sale of stocks is taxable. Inside the shell of the retirement plan, it is not taxed at all. Any profits or income can just be reinvested into buying more stocks or more bonds for little old you. That means that more cash stays in your account with your name on it.

More money is good.

Technically speaking, this under-the-protective-shell-of-a-retirement-plan growth is called *tax-deferred* growth. Because you don't pay taxes on your capital gains now—you pay them later, much, much, much, later. You *defer* your taxation.

A tax-deferred account grows much faster than a regular account. Here is a practical example. I will use this example over and over again in this book, because I want you to know without any shadow of a doubt that *money grows faster inside retirement plans!*

Joan and Sarah both invest their money in a stock mutual fund called the Blue Chip Stock Fund. This is just a plain old mutual fund that invests in the stocks of about 300 stalwart American companies like the Coca-Cola Company, IBM, the American

Express Company, and Ford Motor Company. They each put $2,000 per year into the Blue Chip Stock Mutual Fund.

The Blue Chip mutual fund grows by 15% per year.

When Joan puts her money into the stock mutual fund, she also puts it *inside* the shell of the retirement account. The return on her money *stays* at 15% because nothing gets taken out for taxes.

Sarah puts her money into the same Blue Chip stock mutual fund, but does not put it inside the shell of the retirement account. Why? Because she doesn't know any better! She has to pay taxes whenever one of the 300 stocks in the mutual fund is sold for a profit. She has to do this every year. The return on Sarah's money, after taxes, is 12%.[1]

Over time, Sarah's money grows much more slowly. Because every year it goes two steps forward with the 15% growth, and one step backward when the Taxman takes a bite out of whatever realized profit or income the mutual fund has made. So the actual growth of the mutual fund is only 12%.

Let's compare the numbers:

BLUE CHIP STOCK FUND

	Sarah's Money NOT Inside the Retirement Account	Joan's Money Inside the Retirement Account
	Grows by 12%	Grows by 15%
10 Yrs.	$35,097.47	$40,607.44
15 Yrs.	$74,559.43	$95,160.82
30 Yrs.	$482,665.37	$869,490.29

[1] This is how it works. Every year, some of the really big company stock is sold for profit and that profit gets taxed. In fact, 10% of the profit and income from the stocks and bonds inside the fund get taxed. The tax liability ends up being 3% of the growth of the whole fund.

So there. Now do you understand why putting money in a retirement account is a no-brainer? You only stand to benefit. You don't really lose any money in the short run, because you make it up in lower taxes and possibly matching contributions. You are creating an empire for yourself, something you can benefit from later.

Still feel like retirement is light years away while your immediate bills are scratching at the door?

Well, Congress, in its infinite wisdom, has finally realized that not all people want to have to wait until they are 59½ to reap some of the benefits of their retirement plans. As such, you may now use the money in certain retirement plans,[2] without penalty, to do the following things:

♦ Pay for the costs of higher education—for yourself or someone in your family. You will have to pay regular income tax on this money when you withdraw it.

♦ Make the down payment on a first-time home purchase (up to $10,000). You will have to pay regular income tax on this money when you withdraw it.

♦ Pay for certain medical expenses. Again, you'll have to pay income tax.

In addition, many retirement plans let you borrow against the amount in the retirement plan. So if you need cash quickly, before you take out an expensive consumer loan, check into whether you can get a loan from your retirement plan—the interest will be a lot lower. The retirement plan administrator at your workplace can

---

[2]These retirement plans include the SIMPLE and the SEP-IRA retirement plans. Money from 401(k) retirement programs may be used, but the account would have to be rolled over to an IRA account first.

help you do this and help you understand what the terms and conditions are. I discuss this in greater detail later.

WHEN CAN I HAVE THE MONEY?

You can have the money *after* age 59½ without being slammed with penalties. When you withdraw it, the IRS will consider it income. You will have to pay regular income tax on it. But the idea behind this setup is that you will be "retired" then (i.e., not working). Your only income will be from sources like Social Security and your retirement plan. So you'll be in a lower tax bracket.

You can have the money before age 59½ for the qualified reasons listed above. However, unless you are taking your money out of your retirement account for these qualified reasons, you will be slammed with a 10% penalty. In other words, the amount you take out will be reduced immediately by 10%. On top of that, you will have to pay taxes on your withdrawal.

WILL I HAVE TO PAY TAXES ON MY RETIREMENT MONEY ONCE I WITHDRAW IT?

The bad news is . . . Yes. Once you take your money out of the protective shell of the retirement plan, it does get taxed.

But, *the good news is . . .* assuming the economy and stock market don't cave in completely, the supergrowth your money experienced inside the shell of the retirement account will more than make up for the taxes you'll have to pay.

HOW BIG WILL THE TAXES THAT I PAY ON MY RETIREMENT ACCOUNT BE?

The money that comes out of the retirement account shell will be taxed as if it were regular income just like your paycheck is taxed today.

If you are still working, the money you take out will be added to your earned income, just as if it were a bonus or a raise. Then the whole package of income will be taxed.

If you are no longer working, you will be taxed according to the tax bracket for your current income level. Chances are you will pay lower taxes because the income you have from your retirement account and other retirement sources (Social Security, etc.) will likely be lower than when you were working full-time. So it goes—if you receive less income, you pay less tax.

WHAT IF I TAKE MONEY OUT BEFORE I AM 59½?

PENALTY! If you needed to take the money out from under the protective shield before age 59½, you'd get socked with a penalty. WHAM! You'd have to pay the IRS an additional 10% when you take your money out. Unless, of course, you have the special circumstances discussed above.

TAXES! On top of that, you'd also have to pay taxes on it as if it were earned income. The money you withdrew would count as a bonus or a raise. That extra income would be counted on top of your earned income—so you could be taxed in a higher bracket.

Now, depending on the rate the money grew inside the retirement account and the number of years you kept it in the retirement account, and of course the continued health of the economy, *the supergrowth of a tax-deferred account may very well offset the penalty and taxes of early withdrawal.*

Moral: Contribute the maximum to your retirement account before you do any, any, any other kind of investing. You win both ways. If you need the money before you retire, you may still have more than if you hadn't put it in a tax-deferred vehicle. If you don't need it . . . you can truly STOP WORKING when you are 59½.

VESTING SCHEDULES: WHEN CAN I QUIT MY JOB AND TAKE THE MATCHING FUNDS WITH ME?

There are three answers to this question because there are three types of what is called "vesting." When you are "vested," that means if you leave the company, you can take with you the money that your company has contributed to your account. There are three basic types of vesting.

There is *immediate vesting*. This means that as soon as you show up to work, you have the right to take whatever your employer contributes to your account with you. Even if you quit after six months, if there's something in your account, you get to keep it.

There is also *cliff vesting*. Your employer will set a time limit, say, two years, within which you won't be vested at all. Then, suddenly you'll be completely vested. Boom. It's as if you hiked up a huge hill and then reached the top of the cliff—and fell off into the money.

The third type of vesting is *graded vesting*. That means that every year you can keep just a little bit more of what your employer contributed. For example, in the first year you'd be able to keep 20% of what your employer contributed to your account in your name. The second year, you could keep 40%. The third year, 60%.

The fourth year, 80%. The fifth year, you would get to keep all of it, 100%.

TIP

Be aware of the *vesting schedule* for your employer's retirement plan. You don't want to quit two months before you become fully vested and give up the free money. On the other hand, I would not recommend staying at a job you hate for five years just because of the retirement plan.

Note: If you do quit your job, you will get to keep the pre-tax money that *you* contributed from your paycheck. That's *always* your money and you get to take it with you. You will not forfeit it even if you quit your job years before you are vested.

EXAMPLE:_____

Consider the Adopt an Eagle organization. Jill contributes 5% of her salary—$1,800—per year to her retirement plan. Every year, Adopt an Eagle contributes $1,800 per year to *match* Jill's contribution. But Adopt an Eagle has one small condition: Jill has to work there for three years before she can take that money with her.

So Jill could leave after two years, but when she left, she would only be able to take the retirement money that *she* contributed from her salary and any profits that it made. So after two years, she would take $3,600 plus any profit she made. But she *would not* be able to take the $3,600 that *Adopt an Eagle* had contributed. She would not be able to keep the gift, or the profit it had generated.

HOW DO I TAKE MY RETIREMENT MONEY WITH ME WHEN I QUIT MY JOB?

When you quit your job, you should transfer the money that has been set aside for you in the company retirement plan to an IRA owned only by you. This is called an IRA roll-over. Any broker, discount or full service, can show you how to do that if you bring them your paperwork. That way the money will then be completely under your control.

BUT WHAT IF I HAVE DEBT?

Even if you have debt, it is very smart to start contributing to your retirement plan now. You get free money, lower income taxes, and tax-deferred growth of your money. Plus, the money you contribute today will grow exponentially over time.

I'm willing to bet that you will get your debt sorted out as you get older and wiser.

In the meantime, contributing to a retirement plan takes minimal focus. You can do this one good thing for yourself *before* you overhaul your other financial behavior. You can do it while you are still playing cat and mouse with your credit card debt. And I recommend that you do it. Later, when you are settled down from your wild ways, or have achieved some sort of financial balance after your big breakup, or career change, or schooling, you can sort your debt out.

HOW DO I BORROW MONEY FROM MY RETIREMENT PLAN?

If you really need money and don't want to pay high interest rates, in most cases you can borrow money from your retirement plan account. Usually you can borrow up to half of the *vested* portion of the money in your retirement plan. The loan will have to be repaid in five years.

Example: Marcelle was deep in credit card debt. She owed $10,000 on a Visa bill and the interest rate was 18% per year! If she made no payments on that credit card debt at all—ten years later she would have owed Visa over $40,000 in interest alone!

Marcelle also had $16,000 in a retirement plan, but she did not want to cash it out to pay her Visa bill. So Marcelle decided to borrow against her retirement plan to refinance some of her debt at a lower rate. So she took a $4,000 loan out against her retirement plan. (That's all that was allowed under the plan.) The interest rate for that loan was 7.5%!

With that money, Marcelle was able to immediately pay off $4,000 of her Visa bill. Even better, as she paid off the debt to her retirement plan, the payments and interest were all going *back into her own account.*

Here's how it worked. Marcelle transferred $4,000 of the $16,000 in her retirement account into an *escrow* account within the retirement plan, which is a special fixed-rate account. Then the retirement plan cut her a check for $4,000.

Now, you must know there are drawbacks as well as benefits to borrowing against your retirement plan.

The drawbacks:

♦ If you miss one of your quarterly payments, the entire loan amount is considered a withdrawal and you get hit with penalties and taxes. In other words, one late payment and your loan automatically defaults! If you are not sure you can make your quarterly payments on time, you shouldn't take out a loan against your retirement plan.

- If you change jobs, you *must* pay your loan back before you transfer your retirement plan anywhere, or it will be considered a withdrawal and you will be hit with penalties and taxes.

- You will lose "earning power" on the borrowed amount of your retirement plan. For example, prior to receiving her loan, $16,000 of Marcelle's retirement plan money was in a mutual fund earning 15% per year. When she took out her loan, only $12,000 of her money was in a retirement plan earning 15% per year; $4,000 had been moved to the special fixed rate escrow account that only earned 5% per year.

The benefits:

- Borrowing against a retirement plan, like taking out a mortgage, is an inexpensive way to borrow money. The rates for the borrower are usually very low. And they are certainly lower than credit cards at 18%!

- Unlike "withdrawing" money from a retirement account, borrowing against a retirement plan does not incur a penalty.

- Also, unlike "withdrawing" money from a retirement account, your money is still actually *in* your retirement account and still growing.

BUT: If you don't start now, you will never ever ever have the opportunity to make up what you have lost in free money, lower taxes, and the exponential growth of your money over time.

If you don't believe me, go back and read the time line about Heather and Christine. Christine incurs a lot of debt and has relationship troubles and career troubles, but she always contributes to her retirement plan. Heather's life is much more smooth-sailing and organized, but she waits ten years to start her retirement plan. In the end, Christine comes out ahead.

WHAT KIND OF RETIREMENT PLANS ARE THERE? I HAVE A 403(B) AND MY BEST FRIEND HAS A 401(K) AND MY DAD HAS A PENSION. WHAT'S THE DIFFERENCE?

There are different kinds of retirement accounts. They all operate under similar principles but are designed differently.

401(k) and 403(b)

The most common kind of retirement plan offered by employers today is popularly known as the **401(k)** plan (used by for-profit corporations) or the **403(b)** (used by nonprofit organizations). The letters and numbers 401 and 403 refer to Sections 401(k) and 403(b) of the Internal Revenue Code. These plans are known as *defined contribution pension plans*.

401(k)

A 401(k) plan will allow *you* to stash away, on a yearly basis, up to $10,000[3] of your salary—coming right out of your paycheck. Remember, this money comes out of your paycheck *before* you are assessed for taxes, decreasing your overall tax bill. Investment earnings are also sheltered from taxation, enabling them to grow at the stated rate without taking periodic tax hits.

---

[3]This figure is for 1999, as are the others in this chapter. With the IRS, things can change yearly.

In this case, your employer may make a "matching" contribution to your account, based on a percentage of your salary. Or they may not, it depends on the generosity and circumstances of your employer.

403(b)

A 403(b) is a retirement plan designed for nonprofit organizations. It is almost identical to the 401(k) and will allow you to stash away up to $10,000 of your salary. Again, this contribution will reduce your taxable income. Your employer can also match your contribution if they choose.

THE SIMPLE PLAN (THE SAVINGS INCENTIVE MATCH PLAN FOR EMPLOYEES)

The SIMPLE plan is the newest and—you guessed it—simplest retirement plan that a small business can offer. Only small businesses with 100 or fewer employees are eligible.

If your employer has a SIMPLE plan, you can defer up to $6,000 of your salary each year to the investment plan. This contribution will be tax deductible. On top of your contribution, your employer can *match* your contribution—dollar for dollar—up to 3% of your salary.

EXAMPLE:_____

You work at Smedley's Food Cooperative. You make $30,000 per year. You contribute $6,000 of that salary toward your retirement plan. Smedley's *can't* match your $6,000 contribution, because that would be 20% of your salary—way over the 3% cap. They *can* put in $900 because that's 3% of $30,000.

If you are a slacker, and don't make any contribution out of your own salary toward the plan, your employer will still contribute 2% of your salary toward the plan. If you made $30,000, that would be $600.

MONEY PURCHASE PENSION PLAN

In a money purchase pension plan, you don't have to invest a portion of your salary. Your employer just invests the money for you based on a fixed percentage of your salary. They can sock away 25% of your salary or $30,000, whichever is less, in an account in your name. This money *does not* come from your salary—it is in addition to your salary.

With this plan, your employer *must* contribute a certain percentage of your salary each year, regardless of the profitability of the business.

When you retire, or reach age 59½, you start receiving fixed payments, called annuities, from the retirement plan, based on how much it has grown.

DEFERRED PROFIT-SHARING PLANS

In this case, your employer will contribute a percentage of company profits each year to be credited to an investment account in your name. You, yourself, do not make any contribution to this plan. If no profits are made by your company in any one year, no contributions are made to your account—or to anyone else's in the company.

SEP-IRA, KEOGH, OR IRA: IF YOU ARE SELF-EMPLOYED OR OWN YOUR OWN COMPANY

If you are self-employed, you may establish the following retirement plans: a SEP-IRA (Simplified Employee Pension—Individual Retirement Arrangement), a Keogh (named for Congressman Eugene Keogh from New York) or an IRA (Individual Retirement Account).[4]

If you open up a SEP-IRA for your own business, the SEP-IRA allows you to contribute up to 13.04% of your self-employment income up to a maximum of $30,000. Income is defined as "business revenue minus expenses." So if your taxes show a "loss" for the year, you can't make a contribution to a SEP-IRA. There is no matching, obviously, because you are the employer.

If you have regular employees, and they have been with you for more than three years, you *must* open up accounts for them, in their name, and contribute the same percentage of their salary as you do of your salary. You can contribute up to 15% or $24,000 if you have employees.

In other words, say you were a seamstress, and had one employee named Stella who worked for you full time. If you contributed 13% of your business income to your SEP-IRA, you would have to contribute 13% of Stella's salary to an account in her name under your SEP-IRA. So if Stella made $40,000 per year sewing for you, you would **have** to contribute $5,200 ($40,000 x 13%) to an account in her name.

However, this plan does not **require** you to make a contribution every year. If you are running your own little business, and you come across some lean years, you don't have to make a contribution to yourself, and, subsequently, you don't have to make a contribution to any of your employees' accounts. In other words, if you contribute to your accounts, you must contribute to your employees' accounts. But there is no *required* contribution.

---

[4]If you work for a small employer, your employer might have already established a SEP-IRA or a Keogh and you may be eligible to receive benefits from it.

KEOGH PLAN

A Keogh plan (pronounced "key oh") is another type of plan for the self-employed. These plans are also used by owners of small companies. The advantage is that they allow you, as a business owner, to put away up to 25% of your business income (revenue minus expenses), or $30,000, per year in a tax-deferred shell.

If you set up a Keogh for your small business, you can also set up a vesting schedule. As stated previously in this chapter, vesting schedules require employees to remain with your company a number of years before they earn the right to take the contributions your company has made to their retirement accounts. If an employee leaves before being fully vested, the unvested portion goes right back into the company coffers. Ah, the joys of being the boss . . .

If you, as a business owner, *do* establish a Keogh plan, it must apply to other people employed by you. Just like the SEP-IRA, you cannot exclude your employees. If you contribute 20% of your business income to your Keogh, and have two employees, you must also contribute 20% of their salaries to accounts in each of their names. This is *on top* of what you pay them.

INDIVIDUAL RETIREMENT ACCOUNT (IRA): IT'S ALL ABOUT YOU

In most cases, your employer has nothing to do with whether you have an IRA. *You* are the person responsible for setting it up. *You* go to a broker, or *you* call one on the phone and they mail you an application, or *you* fill out an online application. *You* pick the stock mutual funds or stocks that go inside it, and *you* make payments into it, $2,000 or less, every year. *You* are the one making the decisions, doing the administrative work, and planning funding. See Chapter 3 (on IRAs) for a much more detailed explanation.

In some cases, your employer will set up an Individual Retirement Account/Payroll Deduction Plan (IRA/PDP). In this case, your employer is just helping you with the administrative work of setting up an IRA. They'll help you fill out the paperwork and then set it up so that the money for your IRA contributions comes right out of your paycheck.

A GOLD WATCH AND A PENSION? BYGONES . . .

The traditional pension plan was more prevalent about 20 years ago. These plans are called "defined benefit plans" instead of "defined contribution plans." That meant that as long as you stayed with a corporation for a number of years, one of your "benefits," in addition to receiving health care or sick days, was a retirement stipend you received each year after your retirement.

These plans are designed to guarantee retiring employees a fixed percentage of their final average salary at retirement—for example, 50 to 60 percent. This fixed percentage is known up front, years before actual retirement.

This is how a pension works. Say you worked at the Paper Mill of America your whole life. When you retired at age 65, you were making $65,000 per year. Paper Mill of America would give you a payment of $39,000 per year (60% of $65,000), and they would give you that payment until you keeled over and died.

Paper Mill of America would have to begin investing money on your behalf when you first started working there. They would have to invest money each year for you to ensure that enough money was available to fund your retirement and give you $39,000 per year for the rest of your life. If you lived for twenty years (till age 85) after you retired, Paper Mill of America would be responsible for doling out a grand total of $780,000 to you during your golden years ($39,000 x 20 years).

Pension planning was and is a tricky business, involving a lot of administrative and guess work. The pension plan managers have to assume responsibility for your retirement once you are vested. So they have to plan for your career advancement, to account for your successful climb up the corporate ladder, and they have to plan to be able to give you your yearly pension payment no matter how long you live.

If the pension fund were mismanaged, you would have *no* retirement income other than Social Security. Then you would have to sic your pack of carnivorous lawyers on Paper Mill of America for breach of contract. The whole thing could get really messy.

Because of this risk, pension funds are heavily regulated under the Employee Retirement Income Security Act (ERISA). They are also expensive to maintain. Consequently, fewer and fewer companies are establishing them.

These plans were originally designed to encourage employees to remain with the company for their entire working careers. That was back in the day when you got a job, and stayed at that job. If you were lucky and worked hard, you got promoted through the ranks, and when you retired you got a gold watch and a pension. The nature of jobs in America has changed radically since then. People don't usually stay at one job for more than three or four years, and companies don't want to assume the risk for managing all that retirement money.

So don't you tell me something like, "No, thank you. I don't want to get paid for my work." No. You go out there and soak up every benefit that your employer offers you.

STEPS TO TAKE

1. Sit down with the person at your workplace who handles benefits and ask about your retirement plan.

2. Ask if the company will match your contribution, and by how much.

3. Contribute the maximum you can—even if your employer won't match the maximum. Your income taxes will be lower. The money will grow faster than the Blob in that science fiction movie. AND you won't have to pay tax on your investment until you're much much older.

4. Find out if you can put this money in a stock mutual fund. Conventional wisdom says stocks are the way to go in the long term. According to careful study by Ibbotson Associates, from 1926 to 1998, large company stocks have had an annualized return of 11.2%. That includes the great stock market crash of 1929 and the stock market "mood swing" of 1987. That's better than any other investment out there.

5. If your employer does not have a retirement plan, you can set one up yourself (see Chapter 3, "Start Building Your Empire Now . . .") and have your money automatically taken out of your checking account. You won't get the benefit of the free money/matching contribution, but your income taxes will be lower, and again, that money will grow like an orchid in a greenhouse.

Chapter Three

Start Building Your Empire Now—And Still Save for Your Ski Trip

Open up a Roth IRA

Does locking up your hard-earned cash in a retirement plan that you can't have until you're a knock-kneed 59½ sound like a buzz kill? Want to be able to use that money to send your kids to college or buy a house? Or better yet, take a dream vacation?

If retirement planning doesn't appeal to you, you're not alone. In fact, you are probably fairly typical. You wonder: What if I put money away for years and then am run over by a truck? What if I die of some dread unforeseen illness? Can't I wait until I'm richer, like *next* year?

Well, get this. The individual retirement account (IRA) has now been made very flexible for the likes of you and all your life desires. You can invest your money in a mutual fund and then stash the mutual fund inside an IRA. You'll pay *no* tax on a yearly basis while that money is growing. If you need it before you are 59½, you can have it. If that money is in a Roth IRA, you can take it out at any time, for any reason, including going on a ski trip.

So what exactly is an IRA? And how is a Roth IRA different from the traditional IRA?

POCKETFUL OF KRYPTONITE: AN IRA DEFINED

An IRA is a protective shield that protects your investment from SuperTaxman. You can put any type of investment under that shield—stocks, bonds, mutual funds, certificates of deposit. You name it. You will not have to pay yearly tax on any profit that is made from the sale of stocks or the interest of the bonds or CDs while your investment is under the IRA shield.

The IRA shield is kryptonite to SuperTaxman. He is defenseless. He can't get to it.

That's a good thing, because money grows faster under the protective IRA shield. Here is a practical example. If you already read the chapter on retirement plans, it will sound familiar, but it's so important that I'm putting it here again. This is why your investment will grow faster inside the protective shield of an IRA.

Joan and Sarah both invest their money in a stock mutual fund called the Blue Chip Stock Fund. They both put $2,000 per year into the Blue Chip Stock Fund. The Blue Chip Stock Fund grows by 15% per year.

When Joan puts her money into the Blue Chip Stock Fund she *also* puts it *under* the shield of an IRA. The return on her money *stays* at 15%, because Joan doesn't have to pay taxes on it.

On the other hand, Sarah puts her money in the Blue Chip Stock Fund, but she *does not* put it under the IRA shield. Every year, she has to give up a chunk of this money to SuperTaxman. Why? Because SuperTaxman says that if you sell stocks or bonds or other property for a profit, the IRS gets a slice of that profit. It's very simple really.

Anyway, the return on Sarah's money, after SuperTaxman takes a bite out of it, is 12%.

Let's compare.

BLUE CHIP STOCK FUND

	Sarah's Money NOT Inside the IRA	Joan's Money Inside the IRA
	Grows by 12%	Grows by 15%
10 years	$35,097.47	$40,607.44
15 years	$74,559.43	$95,160.82
30 years	$482,665.37	$869,490.29

Joan has almost twice as much money as Sarah, thirty years later, just because she put her Blue Chip Stock Fund under an IRA.

ROTH IRA VS. THE TRADITIONAL IRA

So just how are a traditional IRA and a Roth IRA different? I discuss this below. But you can refer to the chart at the end of the chapter for a quick comparison.

The traditional IRA was invented in case your employer was too stingy or too small to offer a retirement plan. It has all the features of a regular retirement plan, except there will be no matching contributions.

- Your contributions are tax deductible, i.e., "pretax."
- Your retirement money can be put into an investment that will not be taxed while it is in the retirement plan.
- You can't touch the money until you are 59½. (There are some exceptions: Please see the chart.)
- When you withdraw the money from the IRA, it is taxed as if it were regular income.

The Roth IRA was invented for a different purpose. It was invented to encourage people, all people, those with retirement plans and those without, to save money for retirement. It's generally a better deal, with only one down side: Your contributions are not—I repeat *not* tax deductible. This is the only drawback.

♦ Your retirement money can be put into an investment that will not be taxed while it is in the retirement plan.

♦ You *can* withdraw some of the money *before* you are age 59½! And here's the best part:

♦ When you withdraw money from the Roth IRA, *AFTER you reach age 59½, it won't be taxed!*

PAY THE TAXES NOW OR PAY THE TAXES LATER: HOW SUPERTAXMAN TREATS THE ROTH IRA AND THE TRADITIONAL IRA

SuperTaxman always gets his share; pay him now, or pay him later. With a traditional IRA, you pay him later. With the Roth IRA, you pay him now. There's no free lunch. Sorry.

Taxes and the traditional IRA

A traditional IRA *may* reduce your income tax up front if the conditions are right. In tax language, that means your contributions are *tax deductible*, meaning you can *deduct* the contributions from the income you report to the IRS.

EXAMPLE:_____

Say you make $40,000 per year and you contribute $2,000 per year to your IRA. You won't have to pay income tax on that $2,000. The $2,000 contribution is deducted from your income for tax purposes. You can start calculating your income tax as if you'd only made $38,000. Your income taxes will be less.[1]

But aha! No free lunch! With a traditional IRA, because you don't pay now, you pay later. All the money taken out of a traditional IRA after age 59½ will be taxed as if it were regular earned income. At age 60, you'll be forking over a chunk of your retirement money to SuperTaxman.

Taxes and the Roth IRA

The Roth IRA does not reduce your income tax because you can't deduct the $2,000 from your reported income. Example: If you make $40,000 per year, you must start to calculate your income tax on the full $40,000, even if you put $2,000 into a Roth IRA. *Your yearly contributions to the Roth IRA are not tax-deductible.*

The good news is, since you pay taxes up front on your $2,000, you don't pay later. *Because it has already been taxed, all money taken OUT of the Roth IRA after age 59½ IS NOT TAXED.* This is the polar opposite of the regular IRA. Imagine how psyched you'll be when you're 59½. People with regular IRAs and retirement plans will be losing a large chunk of their money to taxes—and you won't!

THE ZAP FACTOR: YOU CAN'T TOUCH THE MONEY INSIDE A TRADITIONAL IRA

The traditional IRA is expressly intended for retirement. If you try to put your little hands under the IRA shield to peel off some of your investment before you have reached age 59½, you get zapped

---

[1] One caveat: If you also have money in a employer-sponsored retirement plan, you may not get this tax reduction. That will depend on what your annual income is.

with a 10% penalty. The government would want 10% of the chunk of money you peeled off your investment, right away. On top of that, when April 15 rolled around, you would have to count the IRA money that you peeled off as earned income. You'd have to pay taxes on it in addition to your regular income.

You can avoid the 10% penalty only if you take your money out of a traditional IRA under the following special circumstances:

- No penalty if you can prove that you are using the money for a *first-time home purchase*. In this case, you can only withdraw up to $10,000, and you still have to pay income tax on the withdrawn money.
- No penalty if you can prove that you are using the money for *higher education* purposes for yourself or someone in your immediate family. You still have to pay income tax on the withdrawn money.
- No penalty if you can prove that you need the money because you have become *legally permanently disabled*. You still have to pay income tax on the withdrawn money.
- No penalty if your beneficiaries can prove that you are *dead*. They still have to pay income tax on the withdrawn money.

Even under the special circumstances, you will still have to pay taxes on the withdrawn money as if it were part of your regular income, like a paycheck or a bonus.

THE ZAP FACTOR: YOU CAN TOUCH THE MONEY INSIDE A ROTH IRA

The *Roth IRA*, on the other hand, allows you to get at your money in the following five ways.

1. You can have some of the money at any time. The Roth IRA allows you to take your *contributions* (i.e., not the profits, interest, or earnings) out at any time, tax-free and penalty-free. That's the money you scrimp and save to put in every year. Those are the hard-earned wages that *you* put in and have already paid taxes on.

   Here's the MATH: If you put $2,000 into a Roth IRA every year for ten years, you could take $20,000 at the end of that time out tax-free and penalty-free. (That's ten years multiplied by $2,000 per year.)
   Any profits your contribution made (i.e., interest or earnings) you would *not* be able to take out tax-free. So if you put in $2,000 per year for ten years and it grew at a rate of 15%, the grand total in your Roth IRA would be $40,607.44 after ten years. You could take $20,000 of that money out *tax-free* and *penalty-free*. That's the money *you* put in, so *you* can take it out. But you couldn't withdraw the rest of the $20,607.44 without paying a penalty and a tax.

   That's why the Roth IRA is the "live-for-today" IRA. You can use the money to finance your dream vacation, your rock-and-roll band, an addition to your house. They are your contributions. You can take them out.

2. You can also use your Roth IRA money for higher education expenses penalty-free: You can take money out of the Roth IRA to pay for college expenses. You won't get slammed with a penalty. But you will have to pay income tax on some of your withdrawn money.

   Combined with number 1 above—tax-free and penalty-free withdrawal of your own contributions—this is a pretty good deal.

Here's the MATH: If you put in $2,000 for ten years and it earned 15% annually, it would have grown to $40,607.44 after ten years. You can take out $20,000 for college with no penalty or tax, because that's money that *you* put in. The last $20,607.44 could be taken out for college expenses and you would only have to include it as part of your income and pay income taxes on it. You wouldn't have to pay the penalty.

3. You can use your Roth IRA money to buy a house—tax-free and penalty-free. As with the traditional IRA, you can take $10,000 out of your investment if it's been under a Roth IRA after five years—for a down payment on a house without getting zapped by a penalty. This withdrawal is *tax-free*—but only up to $10,000.
4. If you've held the Roth IRA for more than five years, and you become legally disabled, you can take the money out tax-free and penalty-free.
5. If you've held the Roth IRA for more than five years, and you die, your beneficiaries can withdraw the money tax-free and penalty free.

Still not convinced? Want to live for today just one more year—even though the Roth IRA is such a win-win deal? I'll tell you why that's not such a good idea.

If you are age 33 and you save $100 per month until age 65, earning 10% per year, your account will be worth approximately $278,000.

If you wait just one year, beginning your savings at age 34 instead of age 33, your account at age 65 will be worth approximately $250,000.

So, the cost of not saving $100 per month for just one year could be $28,000 or more. Too much to throw away. Better get started today.

THE ROTH IRA

	DREAM SCHEME (Ski trip, tour in Italy, summer off painting sunsets in the desert)	FIRST-TIME HOME PURCHASE (but only for withdrawals up to $10,000)	HIGHER EDUCATION
Roth IRA **Cashed in before age 59½**	Contribution$ that come out first are TAX-FREE and PENALTY-FREE Earnings are taxed as ordinary income 10% PENALTY	Contribution$ that come out first are TAX-FREE and PENALTY-FREE Earnings are taxed as ordinary income NO PENALTY	Contribution$ that come out first are TAX-FREE and PENALTY-FREE Earnings are taxed as ordinary income NO PENALTY
Roth IRA **Cashed in after the ripe old age of 59½**	All money is TAX-FREE and PENALTY-FREE WAHOOO!	(No $10,000 cap) All money is TAX-FREE and PENALTY-FREE WAHOOO!	All money is TAX-FREE and PENALTY-FREE WAHOOO!

Data obtained from the Senate Finance Committee

THE TRADITIONAL IRA

	DREAM SCHEME (Ski trip, tour in Italy, summer off painting sunsets in the desert)	FIRST-TIME HOME PURCHASE (but only for withdrawals up to $10,000)	HIGHER EDUCATION
Traditional IRA **Cashed in before age 59½**	All money is TAXED as ordinary income plus 10% PENALTY	All money is TAXED as ordinary income NO PENALTY	All money is TAXED as ordinary income NO PENALTY
Traditional IRA **Cashed in after the ripe old age of 59½**	All money is TAXED as ordinary income NO PENALTY	(No $10,000 cap) All money is TAXED as ordinary income NO PENALTY	All money is TAXED as ordinary income NO PENALTY

Data obtained from the Senate Finance Committee

One Size Doesn't
Fit All
—You Have to
Mix and Match

Chapter Four

Identify Your Money Goals

and Find the Financial Product to Match

Let's face it. Sex, money, and the love lives of our favorite movie stars—now that's interesting. Stocks, bonds, and debt instruments—they are just boring abstractions . . . until you realize that they are the keys that can unlock your very bright future. Whether that means an awesome house with plenty of windows, three dogs, three children, and one husband, or a suite in the city that never sleeps, understanding basic financial terms will help you get there.

In fact, for each of your dreams and goals, there's probably a financial product (i.e., mutual fund, stock, certificate of deposit) to match. But unless you know what the financial products are and how they behave, you might not be maxing out on your money potential.

It's helpful to group your different dreams, goals, and needs into categories. This will determine what kind of financial products you'll want to use. I've identified four categories of money and matched an investment vehicle for each goal.

Immediate Needs Money: This is the money you need to meet your basic short-term needs every month. This includes things like groceries, food, underwear, rent, gasoline, car payment, child care, utilities, and mortgage.

Financial Product: The bland, boring checking account

Emergency Reserves: You need to have three to six months living expenses stashed away. This is the proverbial rainy-day money, for when a big expense hits you and you need money right away.

It's money that's there "just in case" you lose your job, you become injured or ill, your car breaks down, your best friend cracks up, your spouse has a midlife crisis, or you get sick and your HMO won't pay for the expert doctor you need to see.

Financial Product: Checking account, savings account, or money market mutual fund

Short-Term Goal: This type of money is useful to have when you know you'll need a big chunk of change on a certain date within the next *two* years such as paying for college or grad school, buying a house, or having a baby.

Financial Product: Money market mutual fund or certificate of deposit

Long-Term Goal: This is "empire building money." You put this money away so that it will grow. In the future, it should spell financial freedom for you: freedom to quit working when you want, send your kids to college, or buy that dream house.

Financial Product: Stock mutual funds or individual stocks

In the next chapters, I will go through these goals and matching financial products in detail.

Chapter Five

Immediate Needs Money: The Bland and Boring Checking Account

A Great Idea for the Short Term; A Lousy Place for the Long Term

A checking account is a great place for your immediate needs money. It's great because your money is there for your monthly expenses—rent or mortgage, groceries, train pass or car payment, child care or elder care, bills and clothes (especially if there's a killer sale on!). Hooray for the boring checking account. Yawn, stretch, thank you very much.

CHECKING AND SAVINGS ACCOUNTS ARE GREAT FOR THE VERY SHORT TERM . . .

When your money is in a checking account at an FDIC-insured bank or a credit union backed by the National Credit Union Share Insurance Fund (NCUSIF), it is insured up to $100,000. It's safe.

Why? Let me explain.

Back in the 1930s, during the Great Depression, many banks failed. People who kept their money in banks lost their life savings. So Congress passed a law establishing the Federal Deposit Insurance Corporation. It is called *Federal* because it was established by the national government; *Deposit* because all money deposits are insured; *Insurance* because all the money deposits up to $100,000 are backed by an insurance fund, which is in turn backed by the government.

The National Credit Union Share Insurance Fund (NCUSIF) is the federal fund created by Congress to insure credit union deposits up to $100,000. If your credit union fails, and the NCUSIF goes bankrupt, Uncle Sam will bail you out to the tune of $100,000 . . . if you had that much stashed away.

BUT CHECKING AND SAVINGS ACCOUNTS ARE LOUSY FOR STORING MONEY LONG TERM . . .

There is no growth opportunity for your money when it's inside a checking account? None. Sorry. The interest rate, if you do have one, is much too low. If your savings are in a checking account, they are not your savings—they are your *losings*.

I called my bank today. There was no interest on checking, and only an interest rate of 1.49% on the savings account offered.

"So what," you say? "I'm not greedy. It's more important to me that my money be there in the end than that I make money on it." Well here's a factoid that will send chills up even the yoga-toned spine. If I kept my money in a savings account earning 1.5%, like my bank offers today, and the inflation rate were 2.3%, as it has been calculated to be since last April, I would be *losing* money.

Why? Because the price of things—coffee, bread, gasoline, rent, diapers, tomatoes—will go up by 2.3%, but my money will grow in value only by 1.5% each year. Here's a little story to prove it.

Say I had $3. That's how much it will cost to buy a double skim latte in the year 2000. (For those of you who are non–caffeine heads—a double skim latte is a really yummy coffee drink.) Say I put that $3 into a savings account earning 1.5%—as my savings account earns today.

Then say I went to sleep for ten years, and say the savings account rate stayed at 1.5% for those 10 years, and also say that the inflation rate stayed at exactly 2.3% for ten years.

When I woke up from my ten-year nap, I wouldn't have enough for my double skim latte—even though when I went to sleep I had enough. Why? Because the price of coffee, milk, and cappuccino machines will have gone up 2.3% but my money would have only grown by 1.5%.

Here's a snappy little chart to show you this awful truth.

	Year 1999	**Year 2009**	
Coffee (Tall Skim Latte)	$3.00	$3.77	increased in price by 2.3% per year because of inflation
Money in FDIC insured Savings Account	$3.00	$3.48	increased in value by 1.5% per year

Understand?

In econo-speak that is: "The return I get on my money (1.5%) is not equal to the rising costs of goods and services (2.3%)." In English, this means I don't get my latte when I really need it.

This is what they mean when they say, "A dollar ain't what it used to be."

That's why, in a world where the inflation rate is higher than the return on your savings or checking accounts, these accounts are your *losings* accounts.

So: If you have a large chunk of change, say $2,000 or more, and you intend on parking it somewhere for a while, say more than two years, whatever you do, don't park it in an FDIC-insured savings account. You won't get the return you'll be able to get elsewhere. You may not even keep up with inflation rates.

This brings us naturally to a discussion on savings, and the best place to save your money for emergencies.

Chapter Six

Rainy Day Reserves: Where to Stash Your Cash for Emergencies

You'll want to try to stash away three to six months' worth of living expenses, to be there just in case you need a chunk of cash. This is crisis money, and it has to have one very important characteristic—accessibility. It must, must, be accessible so you can get your hands on it whenever you need it.

You *don't* want this money tied up in something you'd have to sell to get the cash you need, like real estate, a certificate of deposit, or a bond. You *don't* want to put it in an investment that will go up and down in value like stocks, bonds, and real estate, because you don't want to be forced to sell them in a down period.

You want to take your three to six months' living expenses and put it somewhere boring and safe and accessible.

PLACES TO STASH YOUR EMERGENCY CASH

As a place to store your emergency cash I suggest one of the following: a *checking account, savings account,* or *money market account* at your insured bank or credit union. You can also safely save your money at a *money market mutual fund* offered by a brokerage service. You will get a higher return there than at your bank or credit union.

(Yes, there *is* a difference between a money market account offered at your bank and a money market mutual fund offered at a brokerage service. That was not an error. A money market account is, in fact, a savings account with a fancy name. The return you get on a money market account will be lower than the return on a money market mutual fund.)

The advantage of using all of the options offered at your bank or credit union is clear: It's very simple to do. Often, all it takes is a phone call and a signature. You can get money directly deposited from your checking account into your savings account every month so your emergency cash stash grows without any hassle.

This money is readily accessible by check or ATM card. And above all, it's safe. Even if your bank or credit union fails, the government will step in and make sure you get every last penny of your emergency money back. That's not just a promise, it's the law.

If you do want to branch out, you can put your savings in a money market mutual fund offered by a brokerage service, and that will give you a better return.

WHAT IS A MONEY MARKET MUTUAL FUND?

Well, first of all, a *mutual fund* is just a fund that lots of people mutually contribute to. A *mutual fund manager* is the person selected to take the money from the fund and invest it. Mutual fund money can be invested in all kinds of things—stocks, bonds, certificates of deposit, even gold and silver.

A *money market mutual fund* is a mutual fund, but the mutual fund manager invests only in the world's most boring, completely safe investments. All of the investments are very short-term, extremely stable, government, quasi-government, or corporate bonds.

ARE MONEY MARKET MUTUAL FUNDS A SAFE INVESTMENT?

Yes. They are designed to be safe. They have cushions and air bags and everything. Money market mutual funds are tightly regulated to keep their risk level practically at zero. Although they can invest in corporate bonds, these are super stable, solid bonds—and they are very short-term. Also, most money market mutual funds invest in short-term bonds like U.S. Treasury bills, government agency bonds, and FDIC-insured CDs. All of these bonds (except the corporate ones) are backed implicitly or explicitly by the U.S. government. That means that Uncle Sam will make good on them if for some reason they go into default. That's one reason why money market mutual funds are so risk-free.

WHY IS A MONEY MARKET MUTUAL FUND SO GREAT?

A money market mutual fund is a great place to stash away a small nest-egg of money, say, anything over $1,000, for emergency reserves.

First, your money is very *safe*. Like I said, the operators of the mutual fund will take your money and only put it in extremely safe boring investments, many of which are backed by the government in some form.

Secondly, just like a checking or savings account, you have *access* to your money whenever you want it. There is no waiting period or redemption penalty. In fact, with some of the money market mutual funds offered today, you can receive an ATM card and check-writing privileges.

Thirdly, you will get a *bigger bang for your buck* in a money market mutual fund offered at a brokerage service than you will in a checking account, savings account, or money market account offered at your bank. That is because money market mutual funds simply reflect the going rate of U.S. Treasury bills and government agency bonds and the other investments they hold.

The savings account at your bank will usually have lower interest rates because the constraints on FDIC-insured accounts are higher than brokerage services offering money market mutual funds.

WHERE CAN I FIND A MONEY MARKET MUTUAL FUND?

You can find a money market mutual fund at *any* brokerage house—whether it's a discount broker, such as the Charles Schwab Corporation, The Vanguard Group, T. Rowe Price Associates, or full service brokers, like Raymond James Financial, Merrill Lynch, or Morgan Stanley Dean Witter. You can walk into an office and sign up in person, or go online and do it, or do it on the phone and through the mail. (See Chapter 20, "Choosing a Broker to Implement the Grand Financial Plan.")

Lately, to remain competitive, many large banks are creating brokerage services of their own. Banc of America, for example, is closely affiliated with Bank of America Investment Services Inc. First Union Corporation also has a brokerage service. Some sales people at these banks are trained to explain both the FDIC-insured options and the non-insured (but safe) money market mutual fund options to their customers.

WHAT IS THE MINIMUM I NEED TO PUT MY MONEY IN A MONEY MARKET MUTUAL FUND?

With most money market mutual funds, you need $1,000 to open an account. Among the great exceptions to that rule are the money market mutual funds offered by the discount broker T. Rowe Price Associates (1-800-638-5660 or http://www.troweprice.com). As long as at least $50 is being electronically transferred into the T. Rowe Price Money Market Mutual Fund of your choice each month, you can keep whatever balance you want in that account. You can get that $50 transferred from your checking account or from your paycheck. (Basically, T. Rowe Price wants you to have *some* sort of commitment to keeping your money invested in its funds, and they know that not all of us have $1,000 handy to stash away.)

Below is a chart comparing the rates of six money market mutual funds.

In most money market mutual funds, the rate of return will fluctuate a little bit. This is because the rate is simply a reflection of all the items mutually held in the fund—certificates of deposit, Treasury bills and government agency bonds, and the like. Their rates of return fluctuate with inflation.

Shares of money market mutual funds generally cost $1. As money comes into the money market mutual fund through interest payments or other profits, a pro-rated percentage goes into your account and is invested in more shares.

So now you know where to stash your emergency cash.

Check out the chart and review your options.

A SAMPLE OF MONEY MARKET MUTUAL FUNDS AND THEIR FEATURES

Name of Fund	Type of Fund	Return[1]	Minimum	Checkwriting/ ATM card
Fidelity Cash Reserves	All instruments	5.46%	$2,500	Yes, only checks for large amounts, $500 and up
T. Rowe Price Prime Reserve Fund	All instruments	5.46%	$2,500 minimum is waived if $50 a month goes into account through electronic transfer	Yes, only checks for large amounts, $500 and up
T. Rowe Price U.S. Treasury Money Fund	Over 90% U.S. Treasury bills and notes	4.8%	$2,500 minimum is waived if $50 a month goes into account through electronic transfer	Yes, only checks for large amounts, $500 and up
Schwab One Taxable Interest	All instruments	4.8%	$10,000	Yes, no minimum to amount of check
Schwab Money Fund	Treasury bills only	4.83%	$5,000 minimum is waived if $250 a month goes into account through electronic transfer	Yes, if inside Schwab One Taxable Interest

[1] These returns are annual percentage rates, compounded monthly. All rate data was collected on February 4, 2000.

EMERGENCY MONEY OPTIONS

Emergency Money Vehicle	Advantages	Disadvantages
FDIC Insured Bank: Checking account or Savings account or Money Market account	Money is accessible all the time Money is safe because it is insured by the FDIC Easy to open Money is accessible all the time	Interest rate will be low compared to money market mutual fund below Interest rate will lag behind inflation rate Minimum checkwriting and ATM privileges with savings account and money market account
Brokerage service: Money market mutual fund	Money is safe because much of it will be invested in boring, safe, very short-term bonds backed implicitly or explicitly by the U.S. government Rate of return will be above inflation rate and higher than checking or savings account	Have to go through a brokerage service (a process you should learn to weather anyway) Minimum checkwriting and ATM privileges

But what about non-emergency cash? What about cash for a short-term goal, say two to five years away? Well, read on!

Chapter Seven

Money for Your Short-Term Goals

Okay: Let's say within the next two to five years you'll need a large amount of money for a near-term goal, like paying for graduate school, a big trip to Italy, buying a house, or having a baby. Say you've been saving up and you've got about $2,000 to $5,000 or $10,000. Lucky you. You're going to need a place that will maintain the value of your savings. You need a place that is very safe, and will give you a decent return.

But if you put that much money in a checking account or savings account, the money will lose value because of inflation. So I recommend either a **money market mutual fund**, or a **certificate of deposit.** In rare cases, when you have a whole lot of cash, at least $10,000 or more, you can invest your short-term goal money in an **investment-grade bond**. Let's review why these financial products are so appropriate.

The **money market mutual fund** was described in the previous chapter. It's an ideal place to put money that you will need for a short-term goal. If you are interested in that option—great! It makes a lot of sense. Why?

1. You may withdraw your money from the money market mutual fund when you want.

2. Your investment is safe. Money market mutual funds are tightly regulated to keep risk at a minimum. Most money market mutual funds invest in short-term bonds that are backed by the U.S. government, either implicitly or explicitly.

3. You are getting a decent rate of return and one that will likely keep pace with inflation and will certainly beat the return you can get at your bank savings account.

In certain situations, a *certificate of deposit* can be a good place to invest money when you are storing it for a short-term goal. It may get an even higher rate of return than a money market mutual fund. But you have to make sure you won't need the money before a certain date. That, of course, can be an advantage, if you don't want the temptation of touching it before a certain date.

CERTIFICATE OF DEPOSIT: GOOD FOR SHORT-TERM GOALS ONLY

A *certificate of deposit* (CD) is really only good for a short-term goal and when you know you will need the money *after* a certain date, but not before. For example, if you know you'll need money in exactly six months or a year because you are going to start school, have a baby, or put a down payment on a car, a house, or mobile home, you can invest in a certificate of deposit. A CD can be a great way for you to hide money from yourself, so that you won't be tempted to spend it.

WHAT IS A CERTIFICATE OF DEPOSIT?

A certificate of deposit is simply money you deposit in a special account at your bank. You are actually lending your bank this money; usually in $1,000 increments for a specific period, say, six months, one year, two years, five years, etc. The catch is that you can't have the money back until that period is up unless you pay a stiff penalty and give up some of the interest you've earned.

In return for this inconvenience, the bank will give you a higher interest rate than it would if you put your money in a savings account or a checking account.

When you make this special kind of deposit, the bank will give you a loan agreement called a *certificate of deposit*, certifying that you have deposited a certain amount into a special account, that you expect to have access to your money after a certain period, and that you expect to receive a certain interest rate.

Example of a Certificate of Deposit:

On February 28, 2000, Martha lent Confidential Bank $1,000.
Confidential Bank owes Martha $1,000 due on February 28, 2002.
Confidential Bank also owes Martha 4% interest per year on $1,000.
Total Confidential Bank Owes Martha: $1080[1]

WHERE CAN I GET A CERTIFICATE OF DEPOSIT?

You can get a certificate of deposit at any bank. There is no fee associated with buying one. In fact, if you have more than $1,000 in your bank, you could probably call them up today and simply purchase the certificate of deposit over the phone. They would make you the actual "certificate of deposit" later on. But use some care in choosing a CD. There will be a penalty if you try to withdraw your money early.

---

[1] Note: Interest on some certificates of deposit is compounded monthly, which means the total amount you receive at the end of the CD term will actually be a little bit higher.

ARE CDS SAFE?

Yes. Certificates of deposit are safe, if they are issued by your FDIC-insured bank or a federally insured credit union, which insure certificates of deposit up to $100,000.

INVESTMENT GRADE BONDS: GOOD FOR SHORT-TERM GOALS

Like the CD, an investment grade bond can be used to invest your money if you are going to want it in two to five years because that's when you think you're going to go back to school or buy a house. However, it's really only worth it if you have a huge chunk of change, like $10,000, because the majority of bonds must be bought through a broker-dealer and that means there will be a transaction cost.[2]

Like the certificate of deposit, a bond is a loan. You lend your money to the U.S. government, state and local governments, or a corporation for a period of years. Let's say you lent General Automakers of America $10,000. They agree to pay you, say, 7%, on that $10,000 each year for a certain number of years, say, five years. So every year, for five years, you would receive $700. (The total would be $3,500). Then, at the end of that five-year period, you would receive your $10,000 back. That's the amount of money that you originally lent.

So with a bond, you can park a large chunk of money for a while, you can receive a percentage on that money, and then you can have your original amount back. In a nutshell, a bond can be a way to store more than $10,000 worth of cash and lock in a higher

---

[2]At Charles Schwab, for example, that transaction cost would be approximately $40.

interest rate than you could get with a CD or a money market mutual fund. The minimum is high because you have to go through a broker to buy the majority of bonds. (Only about 20% of corporate bonds can be bought through the Internet.)

HOW WILL I BE TAXED ON A BOND?

Hey! Wake up! I caught you falling asleep there as soon as I mentioned taxes. Yes it's all very tedious—but I would be remiss if I did not inform you of the tax consequences of your investment decisions.

If you own a bond, when tax time comes, you will need to fill out a Schedule B to declare your interest income.

If you sell a bond prematurely, and make a profit on the sale, that you will have to pay a capital gain tax on that profit and fill out a Schedule D.

Now, of course, I highly urge you to read the next chapter, because depending on the bond, the tax situation can be complex. For example—drum roll, please—in some cases the interest you receive is taxable on the state and federal level. In some cases it's only partially taxable. In some cases it's tax-free. Who? What? When? Where? Huh? I'll explain it to you in the next chapter.

ARE BONDS A SAFE INVESTMENT?

Some bonds are the safest investment money can buy, and some are the riskiest. It all depends on who is offering the bond, and the type of bond it is. Again, see the next chapter for the nitty gritty details.

WHERE CAN I BUY A BOND?

As of this writing, only about 20% of bond offerings were available through the Internet. The other 80% were available only through a live human being.

In other words, to buy a bond, you will likely have to go through a full service or discount broker. That means you will have to set up a brokerage account, and then place the order with a live person.

In summary, there are different options for your short-term money goals. I have drawn up a chart to lay out all your options at once.

Short-Term Goal Money Vehicle	Advantages	Disadvantages
FDIC Insured Bank: Certificate of Deposit	*Money is tied up.* You can't dip into it prematurely *Money is safe* because it is insured by the FDIC Easy to open No cost to purchase it	*Money is tied up.* You can't get to it prematurely unless you pay a stiff penalty Money market mutual funds might have better rates Investment grade bonds might have better rate
Brokerage Service: Money Market Mutual Fund	*Money is accessible* all the time *Money is safe* because much of it will be invested in boring, safe, very short-term bonds backed implicitly or explicitly by the U.S. government *Rate of return will be above inflation* rate and higher than checking or savings account	Have to go through a brokerage service (a process you should learn to weather anyway)
Brokerage Service: Investment Grade Bond	*Money is tied up.* You can't dip into it prematurely Higher rate of return than with a money market mutual fund or certificate of deposit Interest is distributed every year (can be spent or reinvested automatically in money market)	Have to go through a brokerage service (a process you should learn to weather anyway) Must have at least $10,000 to be cost-effective (will incur a fee in purchasing the bond) May not be able to sell it for a good price if you have to cash out before due date Have to read next chapter on bonds to understand the options

Chapter Eight

Bonding with Bonds

Ever heard this before? "Diamonds are a girl's best friend." Who said that? If your best friend is a rock, you're in serious emotional trouble! However, I don't knock diamonds per se. They can come in handy. So can bonds, at certain very specific times in your life. So go ahead, bond with them.

Now, for the average woman like you and me, bonds may not ever come in handy. If we do have a huge chunk of cash, usually it should be in stock mutual funds or stocks. Remember, the return on bonds has historically paled compared to stocks. So just be forewarned, a bond is a good place to *store* money. *Not to grow money.*

That being said, a bond can make a good solid short-term investment, as long as it is "investment grade" and as long as you have a big chunk of change, $10,000 or more. Here's why. If you buy a bond for $10,000, you can lock in a good rate of return. When the bond comes due, you can get your $10,000 back.

It's also important to mention here that some folks, especially retirees, have all of their investment money in bonds. That's because bonds kick out coupon payments twice a year. If you own *enough* bonds, you can actually live off those coupon payments. But I don't go into that practice here. Why? This isn't a book for people who are retired. Even for young people who are retired. This is a book for people who are still building their empires! In this chapter, I'm assuming you are buying a bond, or bonds, because you want a steady safe place to stash *a lot* of cash for a short-term goal.

Enough intro. Let's get down to basics.

WHAT IS A BOND?

Quite simply, a bond is an IOU certificate.

Say General Automakers of America wanted to make good on its promise to make super-clean driving machines, and it needed money to build a new manufacturing plant because it was starting up a line of electric cars. Instead of simply going to a bank to borrow the money, GAA could appeal to individuals and institutions.

GAA could come to you and say, "I'd like to borrow $10,000. I'll pay you back in 5 years."

Then you'd say, "Okay, but what's in it for me?"

GAA would say, "I'll give you $700 per year on that $10,000 for five years, and then I'll give you the full ten grand back." Then GAA would give you a *bond certificate* that says basically two things.

First it would state the *principal* of $10,000. That's the original amount that you lent to GAA. Then it would state the *coupon rate* of 7%. In this case the coupon rate would be 7% of $10,000, or stated simply, $700. (It's called the *coupon* rate, because back in the early days, bonds literally were pieces of paper with little coupons attached to them. When the date stamped on the coupon arrived, you'd take the coupon to your broker and exchange it for cash. The coupon rate is also referred to as the **interest rate**. I use coupon rate here because it presents a more visual picture.)

The total bond would look like this.

You Lent GAA:

February 28, 1999	$10,000

GAA Owes You:

Principal

February 28, 2004	$10,000

Coupon Payment

February 28, 2000	$700
February 28, 2001	$700
February 28, 2002	$700
February 28, 2003	$700
February 28, 2004	$700

(For the record, most payments are made to you twice a year, so you'd get $350 twice a year.) If you just held onto this GAA bond, you would receive a total of $13,500 over a period of five years. That would include both the coupon payments and the principal.

That's $10,000 + $700 + $700 + $700 + $700 + $700 = $13,500.

WHO CAN ISSUE BONDS?

Bonds can be issued by the following entities:

◆ Corporations
◆ The U.S. government
◆ State and local governments

- Quasi-private agencies of the United States government—such as Fannie Mae and Freddie Mac

THERE'S NO "RISK" RATING FOR PEOPLE, BUT AT LEAST THERE IS FOR BONDS. HOW TO DISCOVER BONDS TO BUY AND BONDS TO AVOID BUYING.

There's no official risk rating for people. Don't you think that would come in handy sometimes? Then you'd know if it was safe to date a certain guy, or work for a certain boss, or even if your mother-in-law was as bad as she seemed. Fortunately there *is* a risk rating for bonds.

You decide to lend your money to a corporation in the form of a bond. The first thing you worry about in lending your money to anyone or anything is—will you get it back? What if you lend your hard-earned money to GAA and then GAA suddenly crumbles, goes bankrupt, and is unable to pay you your $700 per year and/or your principal of $10,000. Yikes!

Fortunately, you're not the first person to worry about how reliable a corporation is when it issues its bonds. Most people are worried about that. So here is something to help put your worries aside.

There are four separate rating services for bonds. It is their job to determine how risky it is for you to buy a particular bond. They are *Standard & Poor's*, *Moody's*, *Duff & Phelps*, and *Fitch Investors Service*.

They give bonds ratings based on the bond issuer's ability to pay its debts; that is, its ability to make all coupon and principal payments in full and on schedule.

Bonds rated BBB or higher by *Standard & Poor's*, *Fitch*, and *Duff & Phelps*, or Ba or higher by *Moody's* are considered investment-grade. This means it's unlikely the entity selling you the bond will welch on the deal. You will very likely get your principal back along with the coupon payments promised. In investment speak, that means "the quality of the securities is high enough for a prudent investor to purchase them."

These are the nice, boring bonds. Because they are so safe and steady, the interest rates they offer will not knock your socks off, but you'll get everything you were promised.

[Note: If investment-grade bonds were guys, they'd be just the type of boyfriend you'd want to bring home to your parents for dinner. Nice. Clean. Tidy. Boring, maybe. Predictable, maybe. But then your folks wouldn't worry about who you were seeing and they'd stop asking you if that guy with the earring was still hanging around.]

Bonds with a rating of BB (Standard & Poor's, Fitch, and Duff & Phelps) or Ba (Moody's) or below are speculative investments. They are called high-yield, or junk bonds. Such bonds are issued by newer or start-up companies, companies that have had financial problems, companies in a particularly competitive or volatile market and those featuring aggressive financial and business policies. They pay higher coupon rates than investment-grade bonds to compensate for the extra risk.

[Note: If junk bonds were guys, they'd be moody, brilliant, highly unstable, and insecure musicians. They'd have the glimmer of promise—but not a whole lot of backup in terms of financial stability. Of course, by the time you've got a CCC bond or a D boy, we are no longer talking about a prospective boyfriend here. We are talking about a guy whose drug problem clearly has a hold on him and whose musical career has taken a huge dive.]

Below is a chart of two of the different rating services with some corporate bond examples.

CREDIT RATINGS

Credit Risk	Moody's	Standard & Poor's	Corporate Example[1]
Investment-Grade			
Highest quality Capital Corp.	Aaa	AAA	General Electric
High quality (very strong)	Aa	AA	Wal-Mart Stores
Upper-medium grade (strong)	A	A	PepsiCo
Medium grade Co.	Baa	BBB	Quaker Oats
Non-Investment-Grade			
Lower-medium grade (somewhat speculative)	Ba	BB	Kmart
Low-grade (speculative)	B	B	Nextel
Poor quality (may default)	Caa	CCC	
Most speculative	Ca	CC	
No Interest being paid or bankruptcy petition being filed	C	C	
In default	C	D	

[1]Each of the investment-grade corporate examples was taken from Standard & Poor's Bond Rating Guide, issued in February 1999. These ratings may have been upgraded or downgraded since then. Non-investment-grade corporate examples were provided by Merrill Lynch on October 9, 1999. These ratings also may have been upgraded or downgraded since then.

THE FOUR QUESTIONS YOU WANT TO ASK BEFORE MARRYING YOUR SPOUSE OR PURCHASING A BOND

I lied. I don't know the four questions to ask a prospective spouse. People are tricky. Bonds are also tricky—but at least I know a thing or two about them. When it comes to buying bonds, you'll need to get answers to a number of different questions. Here are four to start with.

1. How safe is the bond? A bond is a loan. You want to make sure you'll get *all* your money back—and that *all* the interest payments will be made to you on time.
2. How high a coupon rate will you get for the bond? Will you have to trade off safety for the high coupon rate?
3. How will you be taxed on any money you make from owning this bond?
4. Where can you buy this bond?

So let's review the different types of bonds and ask the preceding four questions about each one.

UNITED STATES GOVERNMENT BONDS

When the U.S. government needs to raise money for roads, schools, AIDS research, or B-1 bombers, it can do two things. It can tax, or it can borrow money by issuing bonds. Our government does both. So just like GAA above, the U.S. government issues bonds. Because the Treasury Department of the United States issues these bonds, they are called **Treasuries.**

There are three types or classifications of Treasuries you can buy:

- Treasury Bills: these will all be paid back to you, the lender, within one year.
- Treasury Notes: these will all be paid back to you, the lender, within one to ten years.
- Treasury Bonds: these will all be paid back to you, the lender, within ten to thirty years.

Now the four questions:

1. How Safe Is It to Buy a U.S. Treasury Bond? All Treasuries are backed with "the full faith and credit of the United States Government." That means that Uncle Sam thinks paying off its debt to you is one of its biggest priorities. For that reason, a Treasury is the safest investment you can make. Furthermore, because of the seriousness of this "full faith and credit" promise, the U.S. government has NEVER defaulted on its debt to anyone ever. If it ran out of money, and couldn't pay, it could actually just print money (and then later raise taxes) to get the money to pay you back.

The U.S. government has NEVER defaulted on its debt.

Put it this way: If the U.S. government defaulted on any of its debt, an international crisis the likes of World War III would ensue. To avoid that, Congress and the President would go to all kinds of completely extraordinary measures to make good on all outstanding Treasury payments. In fact, throughout the world, U.S. Treasury bonds are known for their reliability.

2. How High Will the Coupon Rate Be for Each Type of U.S. Treasury Bond? Your Uncle Sam is dull. The down side of this super-safe investment is that because it is so super-safe, the coupon rate offered by Treasuries is usually not very high. It doesn't have to be. People still want a safe place to put their money.

The yield you get with a Treasury can vary a little. Generally speaking, the more time you give the government to pay back the bond, the higher the coupon rate you'll get.

The following chart illustrates the yield-to-maturity rates that U.S. Treasury bonds were going for when bought for their face value.

Treasury Type	Term (How Many Months/Years)	Maturity Date	Yield To Maturity
Treasury Bill	3 Months	6/4/99	4.51%
Cost: $ 10,000		Bought: 3/4/99	
Treasury Note	2 Years	2/2/2001	5%
Cost: $1,000		Bought: 3/4/99	
Treasury Bond	30 Years	2/20/2029	5.25%
Cost: $1,000		Bought: 3/4/99	

Source: Charles Schwab Customer Hotline as of March 7, 1999.

3. Will You Be Taxed on the Coupon Payments You Receive From U.S. Treasury Bonds? Good question. You will have to pay federal taxes on any coupon payments you receive. But you won't have to pay state and local taxes on the coupon payments you receive (at least in most states).

4. Where Can You Buy U.S. Treasury Bonds? You can buy U.S. Treasury notes, bills, and bonds through brokerage firms, government securities dealers, and some banks. You can also place them directly with the Federal Reserve. The Treasury Department offers new bills, notes, and bonds at regularly scheduled auctions throughout the year.

You can also buy Treasury notes and bonds that have been previously held by someone else in what is called the "secondary market." You can buy these through a brokerage firm or through some banks. The advantage of buying Treasuries on the secondary market is that you have a wider choice, and you don't have to wait for auction time.

GOVERNMENT "AGENCY" BONDS

There is a class of bond known as "government agency" or "government-sponsored enterprise" bonds. Government-sponsored enterprises are quasi-private—not government—corporations. However, these corporations are "quasi-private" because they have been chartered by Congress for good public ends like helping aspiring college students get student loans or helping people get home loans. Government-sponsored enterprises generally raise money to fund these good public deeds by—you guessed it—issuing bonds. Below I have listed and described five of the major government-sponsored enterprises.

Federal National Mortgage Association (Fannie Mae)

Banks make loans to home owners. Fannie Mae buys home mortgages from banks. Banks sell the mortgages to Fannie Mae, and this frees their money up to lend to new homeowners. Fannie Mae will worry about collecting mortgage payments.

Government National Mortgage Association (Ginnie Mae)

This agency does essentially the same thing as Fannie Mae—but it is actually directly part of the government and is run through HUD.

Federal Home Mortgage Loan Corporation (Freddie Mac)

This agency does essentially the same thing as Fannie Mae.

Federal Agriculture Mortgage Corporation (Farmer Mac)

This organization buys farm loans from banks and services them, creating an incentive for banks to make farm loans.

Student Loan Marketing Association (Sallie Mae)

This agency buys student loans from banks and services them, creating an incentive for banks to make student loans.

1. How Safe Are Government "Agency" Bonds? All of these bonds are extremely safe. Because these bonds are issued by government-sponsored enterprises chartered by Congress, they have a special status. While they are not direct obligations of the U.S. government, like Treasuries, the government still has a practical obligation to honor the debts these agencies incur should they go belly up. Ginnie Mae bonds are the exception to this rule. They are direct obligations of the U.S. government and so they are as safe as Treasury bills.

2. How High Will the Coupon Rate Be on Government "Agency" Bonds? Well, like Treasuries, because these bonds are backed up by the government for all practical purposes, they are very safe. Because they are safe, they do not offer very high coupon rates. In fact, the coupon rates they offer are only slightly higher than the rates of Treasury bills, notes, and bonds of comparable time lengths.

3. Will You Be Taxed on the Coupon Payments You Earn on a Government Agency Bond? Some of these bonds, like Treasury bonds, are exempt from state and local taxes in most cases. Below is a list of which are exempt from state tax and which aren't:

Coupon payments NOT taxable on state and local level

Federal Home Loan Bank Bonds
Federal Farm Credit Bank Bonds
Sallie Mae Bonds
Resolution Funding Corporation Bonds
Federal Farm Credit Assistance Corporation Bonds

Coupon payments taxable on the state and local level

Fannie Mae Bonds
Farmer Mac Bonds
Freddie Mac Bonds
Ginnie Mae Bonds

4. Where Can You Buy Government Agency Bonds? You need to have a brokerage account set up to buy bonds. You can buy government agency bonds from any broker—a discount broker, a full-service broker, or through an online brokerage account.

MUNICIPAL BONDS

When your state and local governments need to raise money to pay for roads and schools, they also issue bonds. There are two types of municipal bonds:

1. General obligation bonds: The government pays you the coupon and principal on these bonds with the money it receives from taxes.

2. Revenue Bonds: The government pays you the principal and coupon back on these bonds with money generated by certain projects such as highways (the toll booth) and airports (the airport tax).

1. How Safe Are Municipal Bonds? Municipal bonds are all ranked by the different rating services. To determine their safety, you can just look up this rating on the Internet or in *Standard & Poor's Stock and Bond Guide*.

General obligation bonds generally are very safe. They are also known as "full faith and credit" bonds because the issuing state, city, or town is putting its good name on the line when issuing these bonds. To make good on them, if they run out of money, these governments must raise taxes or sell off assets such as land.

Revenue bonds are considered less safe than general obligation bonds because their issuers will pay you back only if the income stream stays positive from the projects they finance. For example, New Jersey Turnpike bonds will remain good as long as those tolls keep rolling in.

Overall, there is a wide range of municipal bonds, from prime quality investment-grade bonds to lower-rated speculative bonds.

Some municipal bonds are covered by bond insurance, which will cover the coupon and principal payments if the city or state issuing them goes bankrupt. Bonds with bond insurance from the Municipal Bond Investors Assurance Corporation (MBIAC), the American Municipal Bond Assurance Corporation (AMBAC), the Financial Guaranty Insurance Corporation (FGIC), and Financial Security Assurance Incorporated (FSA) will receive the highest credit rating and are perceived to have the least amount of risk.

2. What Kind of Coupon Rate Can I Get With a Municipal Bond?
Aha! Now that's an interesting question. Municipal bond coupon
rates are generally low because the coupon payment you receive on
municipal bonds is not taxed by the federal government.

**3. Will I Be Taxed on the Coupon Payments I Receive? How Will
I Be Taxed on Any Money Made by a Municipal Bond?** As a rule,
the coupon payments on municipal bonds are exempt from federal
taxation.

See, there is an agreement between the state and federal government that reads, "Don't tax me; I won't tax you." So Treasury
bonds are exempt from state and local income tax, and municipal
bonds are exempt from federal income tax.

If you are going to compare municipal bonds to, say, corporate
bonds, you need to factor in the tax break you will be getting to
determine if it is worth it for you to invest in municipal bonds.

The general rule is that if you are in a high income tax bracket
(above 28%), municipal bonds are worth investing in. The tax
break you will receive from investing in a municipal bond will
more than offset any gains you could make by investing in a corporate bond. (If you want to see how this works mathematically,
check out Appendix II.)

4. Where Can You Buy Municipal Bonds? You can buy municipal
bonds with any full-service, discount, or online broker.

CORPORATE BONDS

When big corporations, like our fictional General Automakers of
America or real corporations like IBM or Nike or McDonald's,
need money, they can also borrow it by issuing bonds.

Corporate bonds come in any time length.

A short-term corporate bond with a term of nine months or less is called *commercial paper*. Generally speaking, since commercial paper is so short-term, it is considered NOT to be as risky as longer term corporate bonds.

Corporate bonds with a duration of one year or more are simply called *corporate bonds*.

1. How Safe Are Corporate Bonds? Corporate bonds run the gamut. Some are dull and boring and so safe you could go to sleep for twenty years and nothing would have happened. You'll get your coupon payment and your principal back and nothing will happen. These are the investment-grade bonds discussed previously. Pretty much everything rated BBB or better by Standard & Poor's is a safe corporate bond.

Some corporate bonds are exceedingly risky because the company issuing them is on very shaky financial ground. Again, you can find out the degree of risk by looking at Standard and Poor's or Moody's ratings. You can find out why they are so risky by reading their financial statements.

2. How High a Coupon Rate Will I Get With a Corporate Bond? Generally speaking, the credit rating of the bond is the biggest factor in determining its coupon rate. (You thought you were the only one who needed a good credit rating to get an affordable loan.) If the credit rating of the bond is high, for example, investment grade, then the bond is considered safe, but the coupon rate can be low. It won't have to be very high to attract investors.

If the credit rating is low, the coupon rate will make up for it.

EXAMPLE: HIGH CREDIT RATING, LOW COUPON RATE

Pharmaco, the drug company that invented and marketed Zipzap—a miracle cure for the common cold—is issuing bonds. Its profit stream is so healthy from selling Zipzap that it doesn't *need* to issue bonds to raise money, but it issues them anyway. Its credit rating is AAA because of its excellent financial health, so it can offer a relatively low coupon rate; people will invest in the bonds because they know they're safe and reliable.

EXAMPLE: LOW CREDIT RATING — HIGH COUPON RATE

Billy Bob's Hair Salon could issue bonds to finance its expansion. Billy Bob is selling his bonds for $1,000 apiece.

Now, Billy Bob could promise to pay the bonds back, but if you looked at his credit rating, you'd see that it was only a CCC. A closer examination of Billy Bob's Hair Salon's finances would tell you why. Billy Bob's Hair Salon doesn't even turn a profit. It's more likely that Billy Bob will declare bankruptcy before he turns a profit and pays you back your principal, let alone your coupon payments.

So Billy Bob has to make his bonds appealing somehow, because he still wants to issue them. Billy Bob has to jack up his coupon rate to 18%. Enough to get your greedy juices flowing and lure you into crossing that line from "investment grade" to "speculative"—from "humdrum" to "high roller."

3. Will I Be Taxed on Coupon Payments I Receive from Owning a Corporate Bond? You absolutely will be taxed on the coupon payments you receive from owning a corporate bond. You will be taxed on the state level and on the federal level. There's no sneaking out the back way like with all the preceding bonds.

You will have to declare your coupon payment income on your taxes.

4. Where Can I Buy Corporate Bonds? You can buy corporate bonds from any full-service, discount, or online broker.

DON'T BE FOOLED BY BONDS IN HIGH HEELS

You may be out there in the financial supermarket and browsing over the bond section. Suddenly, you'll see a bond with an A rating, and a coupon rate of 14%, and you'll say, "Hey. I'm a genius! I really found something here." Well, unfortunately, this bond is wearing lifts in its shoes. It's really not that tall, dark, and handsome.

You have to realize that over the past thirty years, inflation has gone way up and gone way down again. The government has needed to raise money during this time. They've needed to compete with the crazy inflation rates, so they've had to offer really high coupon rates on their Treasury bonds. The same is true for corporations.

So if you see a bond with a coupon rate of 13%, chances are it's a really old bond; and anyone who's going to sell you an A rated bond that yields 13% in this economy is going to jack up the price of that bond to make it worth their while to sell it to you. Instead of selling it to you for the original $10,000 that they bought it for, they are going to sell it to you for $10,000 plus maybe another $1,500. It's going to go for a *premium*.

Sometimes, the reverse is true. A bond will have a low coupon rate—like say 4.75%—and then inflation will spike for some reason. New bonds issued will come out with higher coupon rates, and guess what? The original bond will have to sell at a *discount*. So instead of selling for $10,000, it will sell for $9,600.

Getting fuzzy? Sorry. Here's a story.

Say you gave GAA $10,000 for a GAA bond that pays a 7% coupon for five years and will eventually yield you $13,500. (Just like the one we mapped out at the beginning of the chapter.) What if you want to sell it before your five years is up? Well, you could try. You could stand there ringing your metaphorical bell on your metaphorical street corner saying:

"Bond here. I got a bond here! I bought it for $10,000! I'll sell it to you for $10,000. It's an 'A' rated bond. Yes, it is. Investment-grade. Check it out! Bond here. Good bond here. It pays 7% on $10,000. Seven hundred dollars a year this bond pays! Yes, it does!"

Suzy Snafu could walk up to you and say, "Honey, put down that darn bell. Nobody's going to buy your bond. Inflation rates have been rising and so Cable & Television Inc. is selling bonds down the street. They cost $10,000 just like your bond, they have an 'A' rating, but *they* are paying 8% And that makes your 7% bond look bad."

What has happened here? Your decent GAA bond has become a victim of a rise in interest rates. It has lost value in the market. Although you bought your bond for $10,000 and it pays 7%, things have changed. It's lost its sex appeal.

Now, if you want to sell your bond, you have to sell it for $9,000, instead of the $10,000 you bought it for, because there already are bonds out there for $10,000 and they pay 8%. So you sell your bond for $9,000. That's called selling at a *discount*. In bond-speak, your bond would be selling at 90%—that is, 90% of its $10,000 value.

When interest rates rise, bonds already out there seem dull and boring. They have to be sold at a discount.

The buyer of your bond is buying at a discount—*less than its original purchase price.*

Now, say the reverse happened. Say there you were on the street corner, ringing your bell and you said, "Bond here! Got a bond here! Pays 7%. I'm selling it for $10,000 because that's what I paid for it."

And then Suzy Snafu ran up to you. And then thirty other people ran up to you, and they all said, "I'll buy it!" "Shut up! No! Let me buy it!" "Shut up! No, let me!"

And then you looked at all of them.

And then Suzy Snafu said, "Look, sell it to me and I'll pay $11,000 for it. Pretty please?"

What has happened here?

Well, **inflation has dropped, so interest rates have dropped.** Suddenly, you are the only kid on the block with a bond that is paying as high as 7%. All the new bonds being issued are paying a lot less then 7%. Cable and Television is issuing its new bonds with a coupon rate of 6%.

Well, it's kind of like having a glass of water in the desert. So, although you originally paid $10,000 for it, people are willing to pay you $11,000 for it. In fact, some people might offer you $12,000 for it. Then your bond would be selling at a *premium.* In bond-speak, it would be selling for 120—meaning 120% of its original price.

When interest rates drop, bonds already out there in the marketplace become very appealing.

Now, of course, you don't have to sell your bond. If you just hold onto it, it will keep on paying out its coupon payments and at the end of its term, you'll get your money back.

Most bonds that you might buy have been issued and bought by someone at least once before you come into the picture, and they now sell at either a discount or a premium—either more or less than the original cost of the bond. One last thing: If a bond is selling at face value, it's selling at *par*.

So there. Now you've had a great beginner's lesson on bonds. Remember, bonds are not a good long-term investment. But they are useful for storing short-term goal money. If you don't want to "risk" selling your bond for less than you paid for it, just make sure its last payment and return of principal will occur right around the time that you need it.

Note: Some publications and people like to tout bond funds for the purpose of saving for a short-term goal. But substituting a bond fund for a bond is not adequate in my book. Here's why. Investment-grade bonds are great because they are safe, predictable, and boring. But bond funds, even those made up of investment-grade bonds, are not as safe, predictable, and boring. For one thing, although interest rate fluctuations can affect the value of a bond fund, they won't hurt a bond that you bought and just plan on holding on to until its term is up. Also, you usually have to pay capital gains taxes with a bond fund, because the bonds inside the fund are bought and sold. If you just buy a bond and plan on holding it until its term is up, then you won't have to pay any capital gains taxes. So that is why I don't recommend bond funds.

Chapter Nine

Meet the Best Little Investment in America

Stocks and Stock Mutual Funds: An Overview

WHY INVEST FOR LONG-TERM GOALS?

Why invest for long-term goals? There's a one-word answer to that question. Freedom. Once you make your little pot of gold, you'll have the freedom to quit working when you want. Or to send your kids to the college of their choice. Or to buy that dream house. Or maybe to live in a cabin in the woods somewhere painting nature scenes. Only you know what you'll want to do—but it will take financial security to do it without worrying about bills and expenses and health care costs.

Hey. I know you don't want to call your kids on the phone in the future and say the following:

"Uh, Billy? This is Mom. Can I borrow a $20? Your father and I want to go to the movies. Oh. And can we borrow the car?" That's why you need to invest for the long term.

Now, you don't *have* to ever stop working—but you'll be glad to have the option. You don't *have* to pay for your kids' college education—but you'll be glad to have the option.

And remember, for long-term investing it is important to *start early*; if you don't believe me, go back and read chapter one.

Enough said.

WHY ARE STOCKS AND STOCK MUTUAL FUNDS SO GREAT FOR YOUR LONG-TERM GOALS?

When you invest for the long term, I recommend that you put your money in individual stocks or stock mutual funds. Why? Because stock ownership had been the most lucrative way to invest for the long term. Looking backwards can provide some encouragement.

According to careful study by Ibbotson Associates, from 1926 to 1998, large company stocks have had an annualized return of 11.2%. Long-term corporate bonds grew by a rate of 5.8%.[1]

Let's see what that looks like with real money.

Say you had $2,000 in 1926, and you put $1,000 of it in large company stocks and $1,000 of it in long-term corporate bonds. This is what you would have ended up with:

Investment Vehicle	1926	1998
Large Company Stocks	$1,000	$2,087,107
Long-Term Corporate Bonds	$1,000	$57,939

[In the meantime, inflation rose by only 3.1% per year. Inflation measures how the prices of goods like eggs, cars, and computers grew from year to year.]

By 1998, the stocks would have yielded you almost forty times more than the bonds. And that *includes* all the major stock market

[1] Ibbotson Associates 1999 Yearbook.

disasters. That *includes* the stock market crashes of 1929 and 1987. That *includes* the huge drops of 1973 and 1974. That *includes* the whole decade of the 1970s when stock growth, if you factored in inflation, went backwards.

That's why, if you are investing for the long term—putting away money that you won't use for twenty or forty years—investing in stocks is the way to go. Better than bonds. Better than your checking account for sure.

DON'T FREAK OUT: YOU PROBABLY ALREADY INVEST IN THE STOCK MARKET

Before you get too freaked out, just remember: Owning stock is nothing new to you. You probably own some now and don't even think about it.

In fact, when I sit down with my girlfriends and tell them about stocks, the first thing I say is: "Go get your retirement plan; let's look at the mutual funds you're invested in and see what stocks they own."

When I did this with my friend Stacey, she was pleased to discover she owned stock in Microsoft. She'd owned it for two years as part of the mutual fund inside her retirement plan.

Overall, it helped demystify the process of owning stock. It kind of made her feel like a swashbuckling Wall Street tycoon.

So, what exactly is a stock?

WHAT'S A STOCK?

A stock is a slice of ownership of a company—ownership in everyday companies like The Gap, Ann Taylor, PepsiCo, General Electric, and Gillette, and ownership in tiny obscure companies like, say, Tropical Sportswear International Corporation, a wee clothing manufacturer based in Florida.

When you own stock in a company, you own a piece of that company. If you owned *all* of the stock in the company, you'd own the whole company. If you just own some of the stock, you own just some of the company.

HOW DO YOU MAKE MONEY BY OWNING A STOCK?

Simple. You make money in the stock market like this. Buy a stock for a low price. Wait. Sell the stock for a high price. Make a profit. There. You just made some money in the stock market. It's just as if you bought a painting for $50, waited for the artist to become well-known, and sold it for $500 ten years later. The same principle applies.

Say you bought a share of stock in Jill's Cool Clothing Company for $15. So you owned a piece of the company, Jill's Cool Clothing Company. Not a big piece, but a piece nonetheless. Then say Jill's Cool Clothing Company became really successful and made lots of money selling clothing. Say over the next three years, the company quadrupled in size and opened five new stores. At that time, the company would be worth much more—four times more, because it quadrupled in size. Then your tiny little piece of the company would be worth much more—four times more—because it, too, would have quadrupled in size. In fact, your tiny share would now be worth $60.

If you wanted to, you could sell your tiny share for $60. You would have made money—$45, to be exact—and that's how you make money by buying, owning, and selling stock.

DIPPING YOUR FINGERS IN THE PIE: WHEN A STOCK PAYS A DIVIDEND

The goal of most companies is to make a profit. Many companies take that profit and just reinvest it right back into the company. But some companies, especially large ones that have been around for a while, will take some of that profit and kick it out to you, the stock owner.

For example, in 1998, IBM earned $6.3 billion in *profits*. IBM kept a lot of those profits, but also distributed some of them to its shareholders. If you owned just one share of IBM, you would have received $0.43 in 1998.

Now that may seem nice, but keep in mind that if the company is giving you the money, then they are not spending it on themselves and trying to grow. So younger companies rarely ever pay out dividends. It's just the older ones that do it.

WHY SIZE MATTERS

When you are considering a stock, you want to look at the size of the companies that are issuing them. The conventional wisdom is that the stocks of larger companies grow slower, but are very stable, and the stocks of smaller companies grow faster, but are much riskier.

For example, take a large company like General Electric. GE is the prototype "large" company. It is one of the largest, most diversified companies in the world. It's involved in a huge range of industries—aircraft engines, appliances, broadcasting, industrial systems, and power generation. As of this writing, it was a $380 billion company. If GE were to double its size and become an $800 billion company, that would be quite an accomplishment. That could take a long time, and your stock would take a long time to double its price.

The up side is that large companies are seen as very stable. Take GE again. It is so big, so diverse, and has so many assets, where is it going to go? The likelihood of a large company in good financial health going bankrupt overnight is almost nil.

The complete opposite is true for smaller companies. It would not be much of a stretch for a healthy $30 million company to double its size and become a $60 million company within a year. And the good news is that if you owned stock in that company, your stock price would double too. Are your greed meters rolling?

Moreover, if you owned $10,000 of a tiny company, and its share price doubled in a year, you would own $20,000 the next.

Of course, the *risk* that the company will hit a glitch and become unable to sustain itself is also *much* higher. There is no huge international array of assets for a small company to fall back on. You might just as easily see your $30 million company shrink down to a $3 million company, and you might lose *all* your money with it.

Now, as you know, coffee used to come in three sizes: small, medium, and large. But because of Starbucks, that's all changed. It's now short, tall, grande, and vente. Go figure.

Well, there's insider jargon for stocks too. In investment-speak these companies are called small cap, mid-cap, and large cap. What's all this "cap" business?

"Cap" is short for "capitalization" meaning how much "capital" or "money" a company is worth. Below I've listed the dollar breakdown for each of the capitalization levels.

Small capitalization: less than $1 billion
Mid-capitalization: between $1 billion and $5 billion
Large capitalization: $5 billion and up

But you really need to know only the basic mantra. *Small company* = risky, fast grower. *Big company* = stable, slow grower.

There are always exceptions to these rules. For example, Microsoft is big **and** a fast grower. But that is an exception.

HOW MUCH DOES A SHARE OF STOCK COST?

Most companies, no matter how big they are, sell their shares in bite-size pieces—within the $4 to $130 range. So usually, the more a company is worth, the more shares it will have available for purchase.

For example, on May 21, 1999, The Limited cost $48 per share, but it had 226 million shares available for purchase. On the same date, CDW Computer cost $49 per share—roughly the same price—but it only has 43 million shares available for purchase. The Limited is worth $10.8 billion; and CDW Computer is worth $2.1 billion, but their share prices are almost the same.

Think of cake. One is a really big cake—like a wedding cake at some movie star's wedding. One is a smaller cake, like the kind you used to cook in your EZ-Bake oven. The pieces of the cake are roughly the same size. It's the cakes overall that are different sizes: One is big and one is small.

WHAT'S A STOCK SPLIT?

When the cake grows, because the company gets bigger, the pieces of the cake will be split in half. That's what a *stock split* is. That way, the cake pieces remain bite-size, in the $4 to $130 range. If you own a stock and it goes from $30 to $140 per share and then splits in half to $70 per share, you'll have two pieces. Your total investment will still be worth $140, as before the split, but you'll have two shares instead of one.

Note: Some people think that if a stock splits, it becomes more valuable. The reverse is true, a stock that splits has *already* grown in value to the point where it had to split. A stock split is a symptom of growth, not the cause.

WHEN I BECOME RICH OFF OF MY STOCKS, HOW WILL I BE TAXED?

While you own your stocks, you won't be taxed. If you sell your stocks and make a profit, you will be taxed on that profit. The profit is called a *capital gain*. The tax on it is called a *capital gains tax*.

Now, if your stock kicks out a dividend, you will be taxed on that payment whenever you get it, right along with all the other goodies you get during the year like a bonus from work or your basic paycheck.

WHAT'S A STOCK MUTUAL FUND?

Are you sick of my dessert analogies? How about pie? Yummy, ooey, gooey pie? Well, here's one more pie analogy. Envision a fruit pie.

A stock mutual fund is a big fruit pie of stocks. Think of a pie with many different types of fruit—peaches, apples, oranges, and pears. You get maybe a couple of different pieces of fruit in each slice.

So it is with a mutual fund. It's a pie of the stocks of different companies—like AT&T, Ben & Jerry's, Microsoft, and The Gap. When you get a share of the mutual fund, you don't get all the shares of the company. You get a couple slices of all the different companies. (Not as ooey-gooey as the real pie, but it holds up better in the long term.)

Investing in a mutual fund is a great way to invest if you are just starting out. When you invest in a mutual fund, someone else picks the stocks—the mutual fund manager. There are lots of stocks, so if one stock does poorly, it won't ruin your whole investment. Later, I devote a whole section to mutual funds.

WHAT IS "THE STOCK MARKET?"

"The Stock Market" is the entire panoply of all the stocks that are available for purchase. As of this writing, there were more than 7,400 companies that have offered up their stock for purchase by the public in the United States alone.

WHERE ARE STOCKS TRADED?

The actual buying and selling of stocks occurs on stock "exchanges." There are quite a few well known stock exchanges in the United States, including the New York Stock Exchange, the American Stock Exchange, the Philadelphia Stock Exchange, and the National Association of Securities Dealers Automated Quotation System (NASDAQ). They should call the NASDAQ the Virtual Exchange, because it doesn't live in any one particular place but stock trading occurs on computer and via telephone.

There are many other successful stock exchanges. These include exchanges in large cities in the United States, such as Chicago, Boston, Los Angeles, and San Francisco, and around the world, including London, Tokyo, Paris, and Toronto. (See Appendix III for a list and description of some of the major exchanges.)

WHEN THEY SAY, "THE MARKET IS UP" OR "THE MARKET IS DOWN," WHAT DO THEY MEAN?

When they say, "The market is up," or "The market is down," what do they mean? They don't mean the entire universe of stock prices has soared. "They," meaning the financial press, usually are referring to one of the indexes of the stock market—some subsection of the market—some average of the prices of stocks or the prices of whole companies. The popular media most frequently refer to the following indexes—the *Dow Jones Industrial Average*, the *NASDAQ Composite Index* and the *Standard & Poor's 500 Index*. An index is a tool you can use to find out how your investment is doing relative to the rest of the market. When your stocks and mutual funds *beat* the indexes, you'll be psyched. When they lag behind, you'll be worried.

The Dow Jones Industrial Average is made up of the stocks of thirty U.S.-based large industrial companies. The Standard & Poor's 500 measures the price movements of 500 large U.S.-based companies. The NASDAQ Composite Index measures the price movements of the companies on the NASDAQ exchange discussed above—this is mostly small stocks and technology stocks.

THE DOW JONES INDUSTRIAL AVERAGE

The Dow Jones Industrial Average is the most widely cited index. (It was created over a hundred years ago by two actual guys named Mr. Dow and Mr. Jones.) You may have seen headlines of the major papers read "Dow Soars Above $10,000" or "Dow Plummets 508 Points." Well, the Dow Jones Industrial Average is an average of the stock prices of thirty major industrial companies in the United States.

As of September 18, 1999, the Dow Jones Industrial Average list included the following companies:

AT&T	Exxon	Minnesota Mining and Manufacturing Company
Alcoa	General Electric	
Allied Signal	General Motors	J.P. Morgan
American Express	Goodyear	Philip Morris
Boeing	Hewlett-Packard	Procter and Gamble
Caterpillar	IBM	Sears Roebuck
Chevron	International Paper	Travelers Group
Coca-Cola	Johnson & Johnson	Union Carbide
Disney	McDonald's	United Technologies
DuPont	Merck	Wal-Mart
Eastman Kodak		

Below, I've created two charts with the other major indexes and their definitions. Unlike the Dow, the values of these indexes are computed with the bigger companies getting the most weight. They are called "market-value weighted" or "capitalization weighted" indexes. Back to the old pie analogies. Let's go for some pumpkin pie imagery. Okay. With the Dow Jones Industrial Average, each of the 30 companies is represented by an equal-size slice of the pumpkin pie. Even though General Electric is a bigger company than J.P. Morgan, the General Electric piece of the pie is the same size as the J.P. Morgan piece of the pie.

Now, with a market-value weighted index, like the Standard & Poor's 500 Index, the pumpkin pie is sliced differently. In that case, because General Electric is a bigger company than J.P. Morgan, the

General Electric piece of the pie is much bigger than the J.P. Morgan piece of the pie.

Got that? In a "market-value weighted" index or a "capitalization weighted" index, the bigger the company, the bigger the piece of the pie. The smaller the company, the smaller the piece of the pie that it represents.

The Standard & Poor's 500 Index

The Standard and Poor's Index, known more popularly as "the S&P" index, is a market value–weighted index of the 500 large U.S.-based companies that are leaders in major U.S. industries. In a market-value weighted index, the value of the whole company is taken into account—not just the prices of the stocks it owns.

If you invest in *large* companies, you should compare their progress to this index.

The Domini Social Equity Index

This 400-company index has proven that socially responsible investing can be just as profitable as other types of investing. The index creators started with the S&P 500 index described above. It was modified to *exclude* companies that invested in alcohol, gambling, tobacco, and companies with a bad track record on the environment, employee relations, diversity, and product safety.

Moreover, the index *includes* large companies that exhibit an outstanding record on the environment, product safety, employee relations, or diversity.

If you invest in *large* companies, you can compare their progress to this index, regardless of whether you invest in a socially responsible manner.

The NASDAQ Composite Index

This is a market-value weighted index of the prices of all the stocks trading on the National Association of Securities Dealers Automated Quotation exchange. Generally, the stocks traded on the NASDAQ are smaller, newer companies. As of June 18, 1999, there were almost 5,000 companies listed on the NASDAQ exchange.

If you invest in *smaller, newer companies*, you should compare their progress to this index.

The Russell 2000

This index is comprised from a list of 2,000 smaller company stocks from various industries and it is a market-value weighted index.

If you invest in *small companies*, you should compare their progress to this index.

The Wilshire 5000

This market-value weighted index is the most comprehensive index for measuring the performance of the whole U.S. stock market. It includes all the publicly traded stock of U.S.-headquartered companies. As of December 1998, there were 7,234 stocks in the Wilshire 5000.

The progress of all U.S.-based companies can be compared to the growth of this index as this factors in the whole stock market.

Worldwide Indexes:

Different countries track the performance of their own stocks. For example, Japan, the U.K., Germany, France, Canada, and Hong Kong all have stock indexes that rank the performance of their own stock markets. Here are some examples:

Nikkei 225: measures the growth of the top companies on the Tokyo exchange

Financial Times Stock Exchange 100 Index: measures the growth of the top 100 companies on the London exchange

TSE 300 Composite Index: measures the growth of the top 300 companies on the Toronto exchange

Morgan Stanley EAFE: measures the growth of major companies in Europe, Australia, and the Far East

WHAT MAKES THE PRICES OF STOCKS GO UP AND DOWN?

The basic rule of thumb here is to remember that stocks are just parts of companies. When a company is perceived to become more valuable, because it sells more cars, opens more factories, makes more profits, and generally grows, the value of the company goes up. When the value of the company goes up, the price goes up. When the price of the whole company goes up, then the price of the individual pieces of the company—individual stock shares—go up. So, in a nutshell, the price of a stock will go up when a company becomes more valuable.

Later, I'll go into greater depth about what makes the price of stocks go soaring up and down in such extreme ways, because they sure can act like manic depressives, but what I have just described is the general rule.

WHAT'S THE BEST WAY TO INVEST IN STOCKS?

There's no right way to invest in stocks, but there are generally three options available to you as the average investor.

1. You can buy a "mutual fund" of stocks as described above. I teach you how to do that later.

And guess what? There are over 50 "socially responsible" mutual funds available. They urge the companies they own to improve their environmental records, labor relations, and overall corporate citizenship. So you don't have to check your values at the door.

2. You can buy an "index" fund. An index fund is a mutual fund that mirrors the stock composition of a particular index like the ones discussed above. You can buy an index mutual fund that mirrors the S&P 500 Index, the Domini Social Equity Index, or even the Wilshire Index—which is like buying the whole U.S. stock market.

In this way, you are literally investing in tiny slices of hundreds of different companies. It's a great way to go if you have trouble making up your mind about which stocks to buy. And it has been profitable, too.

3. You can learn how to choose individual stocks yourself. This book includes a chapter explaining how to do that, where I review some key things to track down, like a company's profits and size.

Now, after you learn the basics of "how to" buy a mutual fund and "how to" buy stocks and stock mutual funds, you are likely to have a fit of anxiety. "Yikes!" you might think. "What if the market crashes and I just put all that money into it?" That's dealt with later in the book as well. We'll discuss why the market goes up and down so much, what to do when the market crashes, and why to hang on for the roller coaster ride. In many ways, learning how to hold on to stocks in tough times is the most important part of the deal.

The way to make money in the stock market is to invest in stocks and/or stock mutual funds that are sound and have room for growth, stay invested, and then fold your arms and look the other way while the market goes up and down.

Start
Investing
and Don't Get Spooked by
the Market

Chapter Ten

Make Investing a Snap with a Mutual Fund

So you're psyched and ready to go. You're going to open up an IRA or just plain start investing. You don't have the time or patience to pick and monitor individual stocks. The answer? Buy a stock mutual fund.

WHAT IS A MUTUAL FUND?

Have you ever packed for a trip to a friend's wedding and brought along two outfits when one would do? Did you do this "just in case?" Just in case something happened to one of the dresses and you needed to have another one?

Usually, when people invest in stocks, they invest in more than one. This is based on "just in case" reasoning. No investor is going to tell you that she is buying a bad stock. No. Most investors think that the stocks they invest in are going to do well. However, "just in case" one of the companies does poorly, they'll still be invested in the others. It's the old "not all your eggs in one basket" theory. But researching all those stocks can be time-consuming. It can also be expensive—buying lots of shares of single companies.

Enter the *stock mutual fund.* Remember, a mutual fund is just a *fund* that a lot of people *mutually* contribute to. In a stock mutual fund, the fund manager chooses the stocks that go in the portfolio. The manager is the shopper at the big grocery store of stocks. She chooses companies to invest in and then buys the stock in those ten or twenty or 100 or 200 different companies. The fund manager pushes her mutual fund cart down the grocery store aisles of domestic and foreign companies, and chooses stocks to put in the cart—maybe some Gap this week, some Limited, some AT&T . . . oh, and don't forget the Microsoft.

You come along and buy a "share" of the whole basket. When the basket gets bigger because the companies grow, your "share" gets bigger. You are richer. If the basket gets smaller because the companies are doing poorly, your "share" gets smaller. You are less rich.

WHEN DO YOU BUY A STOCK MUTUAL FUND?

When you have to choose a mutual fund to invest in, you may be doing it for one of the reasons below.

- ◆ You have to pick a fund for your retirement plan. Your human resources person has made an announcement that everyone has to fill out their retirement plan paperwork by Friday. You are given some promotional materials and a form to fill out and it all looks like a bunch of gobbledygook.
- ◆ You want to set up a Roth IRA.
- ◆ You have a chunk of money and you want it to stay invested but you also want it to supplement your income.
- ◆ You want to diversify into some riskier companies that have potential for huge growth (and you can afford to take some losses).

WHAT ARE THE BENEFITS OF A STOCK MUTUAL FUND?

Benefit One: Diversity

This is the old "just in case" theory at work. Say your stock mutual fund, the Big Bang Blue Chip Fund, invested in Starbucks Coffee. Then, over a three-year period, the nation suddenly and collectively put coffee drinking in the category of smoking. (For example, "If you are going to drink coffee please do so outside." "I can't date him, he drinks coffee." "Don't kiss me—you've been drinking coffee again! I can smell it!") Starbucks, because its staple sale is coffee, might see a huge dive in its sales and profits and subsequently in its stock price.

On the other hand, say your Big Bang Blue Chip Fund also owned Colgate-Palmolive, and that Colgate had come out with this great mouthwash called "Bean Ban" designed to "rid the mouth of the icky taste of coffee," and guilty coffee drinkers were buying so much of the mouthwash that storekeepers couldn't keep it on the shelf. The nationwide swing against coffee would be a boon to some of the sales of Colgate-Palmolive. The subsequent lift in the stock price of Colgate-Palmolive would offset the losses you might see in Starbucks.

This kind of diversity is a hedge against unforeseen events in the world and against mistakes that stock pickers make.

Benefit Two: Liquidity

No waiting around for real estate ladies here. Selling shares in a mutual fund is not like selling a house. You can buy and sell your shares in a stock mutual fund whenever you want or need to. All your transactions happen very quickly. You just call your mutual fund, retirement plan administrator, or broker and say, "Sell!" You can even do it online if that's how you opened your account.

Benefit Three: Simplified Book-Keeping

You will receive handy-dandy up-to-date monthly statements on the progress of your investment. (Hey—your bills come every month—why shouldn't you get some news on the progress of your empire as well?)

Benefit Four: Simplified Tax Record-Keeping

During the year, your stock mutual fund manager may buy certain stocks and sell others for profit. Because *you* are the one that benefits from the profit, *you* have to pay the taxes on it. Fortunately, your stock mutual fund company will keep track of all that for you. They will send you a 1099-DIV in January.

But remember, if your mutual fund is *inside* an IRA or part of a retirement plan, you don't have to pay taxes.

Benefit Five: You Don't Have to Have a lot of Money

You don't have to be rich to start investing. Some funds allow you to start with as little as $50, as long as you sign up for an automatic investment plan. For the rest, the minimum ranges from $1,000 to $2,500.

Benefit Six: You Can Be a Socially Responsible Investor with No Fuss and No Muss

Choosing companies that are going to succeed financially is a lot of work. It's even more work to monitor those companies for their environmental, labor, and human rights practices. A socially responsible mutual fund will do that for you. And with the clout of millions of investors behind them, the mutual fund managers can confront those companies about their environmental records or manufacturing policies. All you have to do is be proud that you are part of that process. (Huge corporations have radically improved because of this kind of relationship with their shareholders; see Chapter 17, "How to Invest Without Checking Your Values at the Door.")

Benefit Seven: Simplified Investing and Withdrawal

You can sign up with a mutual fund company and arrange for them to send you a check every month. You can specify a dollar amount or a percentage of the total amount you have in the fund. That way, if you need it, you can have income from your fund and still have the advantage of the strong return of stocks.

THE DOWNSIDE OF OWNING A STOCK MUTUAL FUND

Downside One: One Home Run Can't Make Your Whole Game

My friend, Bill, has worked for America Online for the past eight years. Part of the way he gets paid is in stock. That one stock has made him very, very rich.

That's not going to be the case with a stock mutual fund. You can't quit working at age 35, just because one of the stocks in your mutual fund shot through the roof. Sure, it might help the overall return of the mutual fund, but just as one stock isn't going to kill you, one stock isn't going to make you rich.

Downside Two: No Control Over Individual Stocks

Alas . . . you can see with your eyes but not your hands. As an owner of a stock mutual fund, you are entitled to know which companies your fund chooses to invest in, but if you don't like the fact that your fund, Big Bang Blue Chip, invests in Hayseed Typewriters, you can't do anything about it. You can't call the fund manager up and say, "You idiot! What are you doing in typewriters for goodness' sake? What do you think this is, the 1920s? Sheesh!"

Downside Three: Costs

Although you may save money because you won't have to pay for the buying and selling of individual stocks, there are costs associated with buying a mutual fund. These costs come from the basic work of running a company. It's good to know what they are—and the following pages teach you how.

Downside Four: Taxes

Unless your mutual fund is in a tax-deferred account, you are going to have to pay capital gains taxes and income taxes. Sometimes these can be very small, and sometimes they can be substantial.

As you can see, there are substantial benefits to buying a mutual fund, but where do you start? How do you choose one?

Chapter Eleven

How to Choose a Mutual Fund

There are basically three ways to choose a mutual fund.

1. You can go to a broker or financial planner and seek a recommendation about which fund to choose.
2. You can just buy an index fund.
3. You can read up on funds and pick one yourself. It's not hard to do. There are some helpful hints later in this chapter for researching funds yourself.

Let me elaborate on these three options.

OPTION ONE: CONSULT A BROKER

If you feel you don't have the time or expertise to choose a mutual fund, you can go to a full-service broker or a fee-only financial planner and have them make a recommendation for you. Working with a broker or a fee-only financial planner to choose a mutual fund is a perfectly valid course to take. The financial world can be intimidating, and it always helps to have another human to work with. Moreover, we women don't like to do things alone. It's always good to have a helping hand.

The catch here is that you want to be sure that the hand you are reaching out to for assistance belongs to a wise and well-intentioned person. So for a step-by-step process on how to find a good full-service broker and a good financial advisor, you should skim Chapter 18, "Creating Your Grand Financial Plan and Finding a Financial Advisor," and Chapter 20, "Choosing a Broker to Implement the Grand Financial Plan." These chapters tell you how you can find someone that you can truly trust.

If you want a financial consultant to help you choose a mutual fund, you should still read the rest of this section so you will be able to evaluate the fund that your financial advisor recommends *yourself*. After all, I'm assuming you are reading this book because you want to be an **empowered** woman. In the end, it's your money and your future. And even if you want someone else to do your homework for you, you should know what they are doing.

OPTION TWO: JUST BUY AN INDEX FUND

Don't want to go to a broker, but want a simple way of choosing a mutual fund? Buy an "index" fund. An index fund? What's that? An index fund is designed to mirror the performance of a particular index such as the Standard & Poor's 500 Index, or the Russell 2000 Index, or the Domini Social Equity Index. The job of the fund manager is simply to make sure that the mutual fund has a proportional slice of each of the companies in the index.

There are two big benefits to investing in an index fund.

◆ **Instant diversification:** You are literally invested in the stock of hundreds of companies.
◆ **Very low costs:** Only a very small portion of the money that you put into an index fund will be used for administrative costs.

The fund manager doesn't have to spend time or money choosing the companies—all she or he has to do is make sure that the stock portfolio is similar to the index. That means your dollars go right to the stocks in the fund.

One of the most highly recommended index funds to buy of late has been the Vanguard 500 Index. Why is the Vanguard S&P 500 Index so popular?

First, the S&P 500 Index provides diversification among large growth companies. The S&P 500 Index is made up of 500 large U.S.-based companies. There are over 100 specific industry groups in the S&P 500 from airlines, to beverages, to computers, to foods, to gas and oil, to retail (clothes). The object of the index is not just to come up with the biggest companies in the U.S. economy, but to come up with, and I quote, a list of 500 of the "leading companies in the leading industries."

(Once the list of 500 is made, the companies are ranked according to size and are represented in the index proportionally. As a consequence, the fifty largest companies in the index make up almost half the index. So it's not like all 500 companies are represented equally. Because of this, during a time when large companies are doing well, the index will boom. However, at a time when large companies become sluggish and little companies grow, the index fund will lag behind.)

The second reason the Vanguard 500 Index is such a popular mutual fund is that the S&P 500 Index is made up of "the leading companies in the leading industries" according to the good people over at Standard & Poor's. Now, I like the sound of that. If you are a company and you make it onto the S&P 500 index, you've been anointed. You are on the Dream Team of U.S.-based companies. You do your job well, and more importantly, people notice and drive your stock price up. That doesn't mean S&P 500 companies are invincible. If there were, say, a huge hike in oil prices, some of the businesses in the S&P 500 would falter.

Overall, an index fund is fine for a retirement plan, an IRA, or just plain socking money away. Don't take it from me, take it from the world's greatest investor, Warren Buffett. He's the third richest man in the United States because of his investing savvy. He endorsed index funds. I know this because on one occasion I got to meet the man. A close family relation of mine was interviewing him and I tagged along and tried to stay out of the way. Toward the end of the meeting, I piped up and asked him how people should decide where to put their retirement money. Here's our conversation:

> SUSANNAH: You know you've got a situation where most people put money in their 401(k). They have to pick a mutual fund. So what mutual fund should they pick?
>
> WARREN BUFFETT: They should buy an index fund. If they are going to buy equities [stocks] for the next 25 years, they should just buy an index fund and just keep on.
>
> SUSANNAH: Really?
>
> WARREN BUFFETT: Yeah.
>
> SUSANNAH: Even though . . .
>
> WARREN BUFFETT: Let's just say if they are going to stick with it and they are in their twenties now. And they are going to save for thirty years—just go on straight through. They'll pay too much some of the time, and they'll get some bargains some of the time. Overall the compound will be reasonable.

So there you have it. Warren Buffett said, "Buy an index fund." So it can't be that bad of an idea.

On the other hand, it's good to remember that this world's greatest investor did not make his billions investing in index funds.

He researched and bought companies, looked over their shoulders and nursed them along, and found every tax advantage he could.

Furthermore, there are good mutual funds out there that post better returns than the Vanguard 500 Index. Check it out. As of this writing, the Vanguard 500 Index had a return of 18.66% over the past ten years. But the Sequoia fund had a total return of 20.46% over the past ten years. Sequoia still beat the Vanguard 500 Index after adjusting for taxes. (Incidentally, Sequoia invests almost 30% of its capital in Berkshire Hathaway, which is Warren Buffett's company.) So an index fund will serve you well, but you might want to do some more research.

OPTION THREE: DECODE THE FINANCIAL PAGES AND CHOOSE YOUR OWN MUTUAL FUND

Okay. But what if you don't "just" want to buy an index fund? What if you want to see what other mutual funds are out there? There are basically two steps to researching mutual funds and choosing the right one for you. First you need to decide what *type* of fund to get. That is, you need to know why you want the fund: Do you want your fund to grow slowly, safely, and steadily over time so that you can meet your retirement goals? Or do you want to try to triple your money in five years by investing in some big risk/big reward venture? Second, you need to learn how to read the mutual fund guides out there. These guides will give you the information you need to choose a good mutual fund.

Step One: Choose the Type of Fund You Want to Buy

There are many different types of funds out there. And they are designed to meet different financial goals you may have. Here's a handy chart you can refer to as I review the different types of funds and their matching strategies.

Fund Type	Grows Slowly and Steadily Over Time	Grows Steadily Over Time but Also Kicks Out Income	Grows Rapidly but Fund Value Also Goes Up and Down a Lot	Reflects Growth in One Geographic Place or Economic Sector: Very Risky, but Also Can Reap Big Rewards
Growth Fund	X			
Growth and Income Fund		X		
Balanced Fund		X		
Aggressive Growth Fund			X	
International Fund				X
Sector Fund				X
Socially Responsible Fund (fund type can vary)	X	X	X	X

Growth Funds

Goal: You want your investment to grow over time. These funds are good for a retirement plan, IRA, or just plain socking money away for the long term.

Generally, growth stock mutual funds buy companies that are solid, have a track record of high growth, and are dedicated to still more growth. These companies should become more valuable over time and their stock prices should eventually reflect that value.

One example of a good growth company is Williams-Sonoma— you know, that store that sells all kinds of awesome kitchen and dining items like glasses, table cloths, napkins, flatware, and cutlery. (Perfect place to buy a wedding present.) Williams-Sonoma is considered a growth company because, as of August 1999, the company's profits had grown at a rate of 23.5% per year in the past ten years, and their stock price has climbed up nicely as well. Now, Williams-Sonoma *has never declared a dividend.* They've used all of their profits to continue to expand.

Another example is Microsoft. It's a large company committed to becoming larger. All the money that it makes in profits—it keeps and pours back into more Microsoft products. There's no cash kickback for you. But it sure does grow. Its profits grew 41.5% per year in the past ten years—so it looks like Microsoft put that money to good use.

A stock fund that holds these stable, growing companies is good for a retirement plan, because that's what you want in the long term: reliable good growth from strong companies.

Growth & Income Funds

Goal: You want to have your investment grow over time, but also want it to kick out money to you in the form of monthly or quarterly payments.

Growth and income stocks come from huge companies like IBM, General Electric, and Coca-Cola. They are called *growth* companies because their aim is to continue to grow every year— sell more computers than previous years or more Coca-Cola—and subsequently make more money.

The stocks of these companies are also called *income* stocks because they return a portion of the profits that they make each year to you, the investor, in the form of a *dividend*. So the point of owning these stocks is to have your invested money grow slowly but surely—and also generate a little kickback for you.

When you are young and capable of working, the dividend should be of less concern to you. You should be most interested in a company that will grow over time, so that *you* can make more money over time.

Balanced Funds

Goal: You want to have your investment grow over time, but also want it to kick out money to you in the form of monthly or quarterly payments. Like growth and income funds, these funds provide income for their shareholders on a regular basis.

Balanced funds are so named because they hold both stocks *and* bonds. They generate income from stock dividends and from the coupon payments of bonds that they hold. These funds are not good for an IRA or retirement plan because they generally do not grow as fast as the growth funds. However, during bad economic times, they tend to hold up a little better. My advice? Check into owning a balanced fund when you are sixty-five. In the meantime, growth is the way to go.

Aggressive Growth Funds

Goal: You've already invested in some large growth companies and you want to focus on some faster-growing segments of the market. You need to have a long time horizon for these mutual funds and the discipline not to sell in a panic, because the value of these funds often fluctuates more than your average growth fund.

Aggressive growth stock mutual funds choose stocks that have the "potential" to post very high returns and are high risk. They are either really small companies capable of becoming really big (Starbucks ten years ago) or businesses that have hit hard times but have big turnaround potential (Chrysler emerging from the brink of disaster in the 1980s).

This fund area is a catch-all category. So you really need to look at the individual fund, the track record of the manager, and the economics of the time. It can be frustrating.

For example, for a while I owned an aggressive growth fund called Stein Roe Capital Opportunities. It was a roller coaster ride. In 1993, it posted returns of 27.51% and everyone praised it. Then in 1994, it posted no growth. Yep. Zero. Then in another manic phase in 1995, it posted a return of 50.72%. Boy was I smart to own such a fund, huh? But in 1998 it posted a return of -1.51%. Go figure. It made me seasick.

Sector Funds

Goal: These funds are great if you really want to concentrate in a certain industry, like banking, technology, medicine, gas and oil, or telecommunications, because you believe that there will be exceptional growth. Don't put your whole retirement plan in one of these. It's too risky.

Entire industries can boom or bust because of changes in the world and local economy, interest rates, or government regulation. For example, in the early 1990s, a drop in interest rates and a merger mania in the banking industry pushed bank stocks from very low prices to high prices in a matter of years. The mutual fund John Hancock Regional Bank B—which bought up the stocks of these medium-sized banks—posted a return of 47.56% in 1995,

28.43% in 1996, and 52.83% in 1997. Crazy right? But as of this writing, higher interest rates and a reduction of mergers have crushed small and medium-sized bank stock prices. The fund posted a return of 0.73% in 1998. Ooops. In a word, when you invest in only one sector of the economy, be prepared for volatility.

International and Global Funds

Goal: These funds allow you to invest in certain countries or regions of the world if you believe that growth will be exceptional there. Global funds refer to funds that invest in both the U.S. and foreign stocks, whereas international funds invest strictly in foreign stocks. For example, T. Rowe Price Latin America is an international fund which invests in stocks of companies based in Mexico, Brazil, Argentina, Chile, and Peru.

Investing in international funds can be risky business. But it can pay off. For example, in the early 1990s, the Mexican economy was in a crisis. And it looked like the Mexican government was going to default on its debt, which would have set the whole country reeling and had a ripple effect throughout South and Central America. Then the United States government stepped in and helped restore confidence in the Mexican government. A couple of savvy investors bought mutual funds of Latin American country stocks at depressed prices, and got to see their investment pay off nicely when the stock prices returned to normal after the U.S. government intervention. Risky? Yes, but it's an option.

Socially Responsible Funds

Goal: With these funds, you don't have to check your values at the door. Whatever those values may be.

These funds come in all different types from aggressive growth to growth and income. Many of these funds screen out "sin" stocks like tobacco, alcohol, and gambling. They may also proactively choose companies that focus on creating recycled products or that have progressive labor and human rights policies. The mutual fund manager, or her staff, is also responsible for communicating with the leadership of the companies they choose and voicing concerns about company manufacturing, labor, environmental, and human rights policy. Contrary to previous criticism, these funds can be just as profitable as non-screened funds.

That about sums it up for the different types of funds. So, you need to choose the type of fund you want to invest in, and then go out and select the best one for you.

Step Two: Research and Choose a Specific Fund

After you choose the type of fund you want to invest in, you need to choose a specific fund, the same way you'd choose a skirt or a blouse. Check it out. Compare and contrast a couple of different funds, and choose the one that suits your needs the best.

Say you are looking for a fund to go in your IRA and you've decided that you want a growth fund that specializes in medium-size or large-size growth companies. Where do you go to find this fund?

Well, one of the best resources for fund analysis is a company called Morningstar. Morningstar writes up reports on different mutual funds in their monthly Morningstar-Fund Investor newsletter. This should be available in your public library. Morningstar also posts these writeups on the World Wide Web at www.Morningstar.com. And finally, you can buy a book called the Morningstar Mutual Fund 500, which is a select group of mutual funds that Morningstar chooses to profile.

If your retirement plan administrator gives you a list of several mutual funds and tells you that you need to choose one for your 401(k) money, ask him or her for the Morningstar data on the fund. There may not be a full page writeup of the fund, but Morningstar does track a ton of data for each fund.

What are the things that you want to be mindful of when perusing the data and choosing a fund? I've created a list for you, and provide a sample of a Morningstar page on a highly successful socially responsible fund, called the Domini Social Equity Index Fund (see page 131). As I go down the list, follow along with the Morningstar page on the fund.

1. Prospectus Objective. This is the first thing you should peruse when researching a fund. You want to make sure you're in the right place! As you can see, the prospectus objective for the Domini Social Equity Index Fund is "growth and income," and that the fund "seeks long-term return that corresponds with the performance of the Domini Social Index, which consists of approximately 400 companies that meet certain social criteria."

2. Total Return by Calendar Year. There are two places on a Morningstar page where you can check out how well a fund has fared over time. The first is in the box called *History*, near the top. Morningstar prints out the calendar years and the total return for the fund in that calendar year. You can see that the Domini Social Equity Index Fund has posted returns since 1991. Right under the total return box, you can see how well the fund fared against the two benchmarks, the S&P 500 and the Wilshire Top 750. Looking at this row, you'll see that the Domini Social Equity Fund has generally kept pace with S&P 500. That's a good thing, if you were wondering.

3. Total Return Averages. The second place to check out total return is a box called *Trailing*. There you can see what the average returns of a fund have been over a five, ten, and fifteen year period.

Domini Social Equity has had an average annualized return of 25.39% in the past five years. That's very good. In the last column in the "performance" section, you can see that Morningstar has calculated what the growth of $10,000 would be. According to them, if you had invested $10,000 in the Domini Social Equity Index five years ago, you would have $30,992 today.

A word on total return: It's good to make sure that a fund has a long, steady track record. Any fund can have one good year. You want to see consistency. So it's good to look at total return over a ten-year period if you can.

However, total return is only *one* indicator that the people at the fund know what they are doing. All mutual funds have a disclaimer, "Past performance is no guarantee of future results," and that's true. It's true everywhere in life—on the job, in sports, in relationships. Certain economic conditions can prevail to harm the returns of your fund.

Remember, lots of different factors can affect total return. One of my favorite funds other than this one is called Seligman Communications and Information A. It's had a spectacular ten-year return of 25.11% as of this writing, but that has to do with a lot of factors. First, the fund was very small when it started out, and so a couple of wise choices by fund manager Paul Wick went a long way. Second, the decade of the 90s has been an incredible boom time for technology—the sector that the fund concentrates in.

All that being said, total return can still help you find a good fund. It can also help you avoid buying a bad fund. If a fund has returned only 8%, while every other fund in its class has returned 24%, chances are, that's a fund you want to avoid.

4. Portfolio Manager. The fourth box you want to look at is the *Portfolio Manager*. Why? Well, think of it this way. The Chicago Bulls were the NBA champs six out of seven years when Michael Jordan played and Phil Jackson ran the team. After those two left Chicago, the Bulls finished near the bottom of the league and didn't come close to making the playoffs.

So it can be with a fund manager. Choosing companies is an art and a science. Moreover, if the manager who led the fund to success leaves the fund, then you may want to evaluate whether you want to stay there or not.

Now, with an index fund, such as Domini Social Equity, the fund manager has a smaller role because the criteria for choosing the companies is already set. So you don't have to worry as much when the manager of an index fund changes.

5. Portfolio Analysis. You'll want to look at the *Portfolio Analysis* section. This section is cool. It lists the top twenty-five companies that the mutual fund owns stock in. So you can see which companies you own slices of.

Also, under *Sector Weightings*, you'll be able to see which industries the fund manager invests in. As you can see, the Domini Social Equity Index is spread across the board—and that diversity will help keep the fund's return stable if one of the sectors, "financials" for example, starts to do poorly.

Under *Market Cap*, you'll be able to see the size of the companies that the fund invests in. Over 85% of the Domini Social Equity Index is in large companies and 12% is in medium-sized and small companies. Under the rule of thumb "large companies = slow-growth but solid companies," this fund should continue to climb.

6. Tax Analysis. *Note*: Remember that if your mutual fund is inside of a retirement plan or a 401(k), you do not have to pay taxes on any realized growth year to year. For mutual funds outside of retirement accounts, there are taxes.

Say your mutual fund manager bought stock in a company called Joe's Comic Books and sold it three years later, subsequently making a profit of, say, $35 per share. The profit of $35 a share would be made in *your* name, so *you* have to pay *capital gains* taxes on *your* portion of the profit.

Because those tax dollars come from you, they eat into your total return. That's why Morningstar gives you a figure that accounts for taxes. This is called the *tax-adjusted return*. As you can see, it does affect how much money you get to keep. The total return for the Domini Social Equity Index Fund over a five-year period is 25.39%. But the tax-adjusted return for that same period is 24.88%.

In some funds, the disparity is much higher. For example, in my other fund, Seligman Communications and Information A, the ten-year *total return* of the fund was 25.11%. And the *tax-adjusted return* was 20.7%. Now that's a fund that you'd want to have under the shell of a retirement account.

TAX TIPS

Hold on to your tax returns and a copy of your 1099-DIV statements. In January of every year your mutual fund will send you the information you need to pay any taxes you may owe. The form is called a 1099-DIV. When you finally sell your mutual fund you'll want to make sure you're not paying your taxes twice. Because you pay taxes on a mutual fund every year, your overall tax bill should be pretty small when you finally do sell the fund. So hold onto those 1099-DIVs and tax returns.

Never buy a fund in late November or December. That's when the fund managers credit shareholder accounts with any capital gains distributions—i.e., profits the fund made during the year from the sale of stock (like Joe's Comic Books). If you buy a mutual fund at this time, you will be credited with receiving the profits and be taxed on them—even though you weren't even invested in the fund at the time of the stock purchase and you didn't get to experience the gain.

---

7. Expenses and Fees. When you buy a fund you should be mindful of the costs associated with running the fund. These expenses include a *management fee*—salary money that goes to the women and men choosing your companies; *administrative costs*—record-keeping, mailings, customer service lines, etc.; and the *12b-1 distribution fee*, which covers marketing, advertising, and distribution services.

Every fund has these costs, and will sum them all up for you in something called the "expense ratio." All of these costs are subtracted from the total return of the fund.

Now check out the Domini Social Equity Fund. Up in the top righthand corner, you can see the *expense ratio*, and it totals 1.17%. That's the amount that is deducted from every dollar that goes into the fund, to pay for salaries and upkeep.

The conventional wisdom is that you want more of your money going directly into the stocks of the fund and less going into fancy conference rooms and luxuries at headquarters. At 1.17%, the Domini Social Equity Fund is criticized by Morningstar as being too high.

8. "Loads" or Sales Commissions. The "load" refers to a sales commission given to the full service broker selling you the fund.

Take the Smith Barney Concert Social Awareness Fund A. That fund has a "load" of 5%. Say I bought that fund from a Smith Barney broker. If I gave her $10,000 to invest in the fund, she would get, as her commission, 5% right off the top. So $9,500 would go to the fund and $500 would go to her.

Now keep in mind that not all funds have loads. In fact, the model fund that we are looking at, the Domini Social Equity Fund, does *not* have a load. So, if you look on the chart at #8, under Sales Fees, you will not see an "L" for load. See? And that means that a broker will not make a commission if she sells you this fund. Your full $10,000 will go right to the fund and be invested.

When is buying a fund *with* a load a good idea?

With all this talk of commissions, you may wonder if buying a mutual fund with a load is ever a good idea. I mean, who wants to lose $500 out of $10,000 right away? Well, that's a good question.

But the truth is that sometimes buying a fund *with* a load is still a good idea. Here are two rules of thumb.

1. Buy a fund with a load if you really want to buy that particular fund. Some funds are only available with loads. And sometimes they perform so well that they more than make up the cost of their "loads."

   For example, the Fidelity Select Health Care Fund, a fund that invests in pharmaceutical, medical device, and health care delivery services, posted a 22.47% annualized return over the past ten years. If you adjusted for the load of 3%, the return was 22.10%. That still beats the no-load Vanguard 500 Index fund, which had a 17.85% annualized return over the past ten years.[1] So sometimes, even with losing $500 of your $10,000 off the top, you still come out ahead.

2. Buy a fund with a load if you want to work with a full-service broker. Most full-service brokers are only allowed to sell you funds with "loads" because that is how they make their commission. Sometimes $500 is a cheap price to pay for a long-term financial plan.

When is buying a fund *without* a load a good idea?

Sometimes it's good to buy a fund without a load. And, again, there are two rules of thumb that can tell you when buying a fund without a load is a good idea.

---

[1]Ten-year annualized returns calculated as of August 31, 1999.

1. Buy a fund without a load if you really want to buy that particular fund. There are some terrific funds out there that just don't have a load. A relatively new socially responsible fund comes to mind. It's called the IPS Millenium fund. It posted a 36.7% three-year annualized return.[2] Again, that beat the Vanguard 500 Index fund for the same period. That fund is only available *without* a load. And it looks like a good buy.

2. Buy a fund without a load if you don't want any of the benefits from working with a full-service broker, and the idea of "paying" someone $500 to do something you can do yourself seems unnecessary.

What kind of "load" will save you the most money?

There are different kinds of loads. The most common ones you'll see are "A" loads (also called front loads), "B" loads (also called back loads), and "C" loads. Yikes! What does all this mean? Basically, these three types of loads are different ways of structuring the commission that the broker gets paid. When you need to decide between an A load, a B load, and a C load, there are two easy rules to remember:

1. If you plan on buying your mutual fund shares and holding on to them for five years or more, you should buy a fund with an A load or B load. As long as you are going to hold on to your mutual fund for the long run, it doesn't matter whether or not you buy your mutual fund with an A load or a B load.

   With the A load funds, you will be charged up front. Five hundred dollars of your $10,000 will come out right off the top. With the B load funds, you will be charged a smaller amount

2. Three-year annualized return calculated on September 30, 1999.

right off the top, say $100, but the costs will be spread out and hidden as you go along. If you do the math and compare the overall numbers, you will see that there is no difference between A loads and B loads.

2. If you plan on selling your fund before five years is up, you should buy a fund with a C load. In that case it will be cheaper for you to buy a fund with a C load.

With a C load, the up-front costs are low, but expenses of the fund are higher all the way through. After about six years in a fund with a C load, you will be wishing that you had bought a fund with a B or an A load. Again, if you crunch the numbers you will see that this is true.

Got that? Buy a fund with an A or a B load if you plan to buy and hold. Buy a fund with a C load if you plan to buy and turn around in three years or so and sell it. And you can find out what kind of load your fund has, and how much it's going to cost you, just by looking at the little box at the bottom of the page called Sales Fees.

9. Load-Adjusted Return. Is all this conversation about loads making you wonder how much money you will actually make in the fund? Morningstar has an answer for that, too. In the box labeled *Risk Analysis*, Morningstar calculates what your return would be, adjusted for the load. That's where I got the figures about Fidelity Select Health Care. Morningstar data showed that Fidelity Select Health Care posted a *total return* of 22.47% over the past ten years and a *load-adjusted return* of 22.10%. Because the Domini Social Equity Index Fund has no load—the load adjusted return is the same as the total return.

10. Size of the Fund. One other item you may want to notice when choosing a mutual fund is the size of the fund itself. This is not as important when dealing with a large company mutual fund like the Domini Social Equity Fund or the Vanguard Index 500. However, it can make a difference when you are looking at a fund that made its fortune by buying up medium-sized companies or small companies.

When the pool of money that a fund manager has is small, one or two companies that jump in value can pull up the average return of the whole fund. When the pool of money is big, just one company doing well is more of a drop in a bucket. I asked Paul Wick, manager of the successful Seligman Communications and Information A fund, about this problem. His fund grew from a tiny $40 million fund to a fund with over $6 billion in it by investing in medium- and small-sized companies. When I asked him if having such a large fund made a difference, he replied that the size of the fund definitely made his work more challenging.

> SUSANNAH: Time was you could find a couple great companies and put your position in that and it would move the whole fund forward.
> PAUL WICK: And now we can't. So we own more stock. And when we do own small cap stocks we own huge positions in them . . . So yes. It does make it harder. We can't own anymore shares of Orboteck at this point.

Now this mutual fund is doing fine, but Paul's job is more difficult than it was ten years ago.

11. Analysis. Finally, in the box called Analysis, a staffer at Morningstar shares her analysis of the Domini Social Equity Index Fund. While she gripes about the expense ratio of the fund, she does state that the fund "helped salvage the reputation of socially responsible investing," and that "high fees and all, it's still one of the best screened choices around."

So. Those are some of the fundamental tools you can use when choosing a fund. As you can see, there are many ways you can do well in the mutual fund world, whether you buy a fund with a load, a fund without, an index fund, or an actively managed fund. As a rule, stick to growth funds for your IRA and retirement plan.

As for research resources, there are many, especially on the Internet and they are growing all the time. Value Line also has very complete materials like Morningstar. Here are some Web sites that you should check out.

SocialFunds	www.SocialFunds.com
Co-op America	www.socialinvest.org
The Motley Fool	www.fool.com
Yahoo! Finance	quote.yahoo.com
Big Charts	www.bigcharts.com
Dow Jones	www.dowjones.com
Nasdaq	www.nasdaq.com
Value Line	www.valueline.com

Published October 7, 1999. Reprinted by permission of Morningstar.

Domini Social Equity

	Ticker	Load	NAV	Yield	Total Assets	Mstar Category
	DSEFX	12b–1 only	$35.90	0.1%	$1,105.8 mil	Large Blend

Prospectus Objective: Growth ___ ome

Domini Social Equity Fund se___ ___ ___ total return that corresponds with the performance ___ ___ ___ ___ Social Index, which consists of approximately 400 com___ ___ that meet certain social criteria.

The fund invests substantially all assets in stocks in the index. To construct the index, the advisor selects companies in the S&P 500 based on social responsibility and on its requirements for industry diversification, financial solvency, market capitalization, and minimal portfolio turnover. The index also includes companies not included in the S&P 500.

Prior to Oct. 26, 1993, the fund was named Domini Social Index Trust.

Portfolio Manager(s)

John O'Toole. Since 12-94. BA U. of Pennsylvania; MBA U. of Chicago. A senior vice president and portfolio manager with Mellon Equity Associates, O'Toole is also responsible for the research and development of the company's asset-allocation process. He joined Mellon Bank as a junior portfolio manager in 1979 and has gained extensive experience in portfolio management and quantitative application. Other funds currently managed: Dreyfus Basic S&P 500 Stk, Dreyfus S&P 500 Stk, Dreyfus Prem Midcap Stk, Devcap Shared Return, Domini Inst Social Eqty.

Performance 09-30-99

	1st Qtr	2nd Qtr	3rd Qtr	4th Qtr	Total
1995	9.59	9.28	7.22	5.28	35.17
1996		4.32	3.89	7.49	21.84
1997		17.31	7.70	4.32	36.02
1998		3.75	-9.83	24.82	32.99
1999		6.47	-6.36		

Trailing	Total Return%	+/- S&P 500	+/- Will Top 750	% Rank All Cat	Growth of $10,000
3 Mo	-6.36	-0.13	0.20	80	53	9,364
6 Mo	-0.30	-0.67	0.13	57	64	9,970
1 Yr	30.09	2.30	2.37	22	20	13,009
3 Yr Avg	26.62	1.53	1.99	3	3	20,298
5 Yr Avg	25.39	0.37	0.83	3	2	30,932
10 Yr Avg						
15 Yr Avg						

Tax Analysis	Tax-Adj Ret%	%Pretax Ret	%Rank Cat
3 Yr Avg	26.31	99.9	2
5 Yr Avg	24.86	98.0	2
10 Yr Avg			

Potential Capital Gain Exposure: 22% of assets

Analysis by La___ ___ 12-07-98

Domini Social ___ ___ ___'s place seems secure, but it sh___ ___ get too cocky.

This fund has helped salvage the reputation of socially responsible investing, a concept sneered at by investing cognoscenti just a few years ago. The performance of the Domini Social Index (which this fund tracks) and the record of its competitor Citizens Index have gained SRI a grudging acceptance. Both large-cap indexes have given the S&P 500 a run for its money. But all three can't run this fast forever. Market watchers are waiting for a smaller-cap catch-up any day now (though "any day" has been many days in coming).

Thus, it's disheartening to see the fund's expenses remain high, even as its assets have grown by more than two thirds in 1998. In fact, fees rose to 1.17% as of the most recent annual report, reflecting a one-time payment to a former administrator. They should fall back to 98 basis points, but that's still high for an index fund. It isn't as vexsome as Citizen's

1.59% charge, but at least that fund's fees have trended down. High price tags won't be as easy to overlook when mega-cap stocks lose steam: Much of this fund's lead on its peers owes to its huge median market cap.

The fund may still be a formidable foe for the S&P 500. Its differences will keep it interesting. The fund's social screens skew it toward consumer goods, services, retail, and tech, giving it a growth bias that has served it in good stead in 1998. (The index spurns firms involved in tobacco, alcohol, gaming, weapons, or nuclear power, and favors those with progressive environmental, labor, and other social policies.) But while such industries should outperform stodgy sectors such as utilities in the long run, the fund might fritter away its edge with high expenses.

As more socially screened choices come to market, this fund will also face stiffer direct competition. But high fees and all, it's still one of the best screened choices around.

Address:	11 West 25th St 7th Floor
	New York, NY 10010–2001
	800–762–6814
Web Address:	http://www.domini.com
Inception:	06-03-91
Advisor:	Domini Social Investments
Subadvisor:	Mellon Equity
NTF Plans:	Jack White , Schwab , Waterhouse

Minimum Purchase:	$1000	Add: $50	IRA: $250
Min Auto Inv Plan:	$500	Add: $25	
Sales Fees:	0.25%B		
Management Fee:	0.20%, 0.50%A		
Actual Fees:	Mgt: 0.19% Dist: 0.12%		
Expense Projections:	3Yr: $31 5Yr: $54 10Yr: $120		
Avg Brok Commission:	— Income Distrib: Semi–Ann.		
Total Cost (relative to category):		Below Avg	

M✩RNINGSTAR Mutual Funds

Historical Profile
Return	High
Risk	Average
Rating	★★★★★ Highest

97% 99% 100% 98% 99% 99% 100% 100%

Investment Style
Equity
Average Stock %

▼ Manager Change
▽ Partial Manager Change

Fund Performance vs. Category Average
▦ Quarterly Fund Return
+/- Category Average
— Category Baseline

Performance Quartile (within Category)

	1988	1989	1990	1991	1992	1993	1994	1995	1996	1997	1998	1999	History
NAV				10.72	11.87	12.43	12.10	16.11	19.35	26.22	34.40		
Total Return %				8.37	12.10	6.53	-0.36	35.17	21.84	36.02	32.99		
+/- S&P 500				-1.08	4.49	-3.52	-1.67	-2.36	-1.10	2.67	4.41	-0.09	
+/- Wilshire Top 750					3.91	-3.20	1.99	-2.49	0.29	2.72	3.94		
Income Return %				0.63	1.17	1.18	1.62	1.25	0.95	0.31	0.06	0.03	
Capital Return %				7.74	10.93	5.35	-1.97	33.92	20.89	35.72	32.93	4.36	
Total Rtn % Rank Cat					14	80	44	31	38	4	4		
Income $				0.06	0.13	0.14	0.20	0.15	0.15	0.06	0.02	0.01	
Capital Gains $				0.00	0.02	0.07	0.08	0.06	0.12	0.03	0.45	0.00	
Expense Ratio %				0.75	0.75	0.75	0.75	0.90	0.98	0.98	1.17	0.98	
Income Ratio %				1.48	1.53	1.41	1.67	1.38	1.01	0.62	0.07	0.06	
Turnover Rate %				—	3	1	4	8	5	1	5		
Net Assets $mil				3.6	10.3	27.0	33.7	69.4	115.3	301.4	715.8	1,105.8	

Risk Analysis

Time Period	Load-Adj Return %	Risk % Rank All	Morningstar Return Risk	Morningstar Risk-Adj Rating
1 Yr	30.09			
3 Yr	26.62	67 64	2.40 0.90	★★★★★
5 Yr	25.39	65 52	1.96 0.83	★★★★★
Incept	18.14			

Average Historical Rating (65 months): 4.0★s

1=low, 100=high

Category Rating (3 Yr)		Other Measures	Standard Index S&P 500	Best Fit Index S&P 500
① ② ③ ④ ⑤		Alpha	0.4	0.4
Worst Best		Beta	1.06	1.06
		R-Squared	98	98
Return High		Standard Deviation		22.59
Risk Average		Mean		26.62
		Sharpe Ratio		1.07

Portfolio Analysis 07-31-99

Share change since 01-99 Total Stocks: 401

		PE	YTD Ret%	% Assets
⊕ Microsoft		83.8	30.60	9.26
⊕ Intel	Technology	35.1	25.45	4.84
⊕ Cisco Sys	Technology	NMF	47.74	4.20
⊕ Lucent Tech	Technology	43.3	18.14	4.18
⊕ Wal-Mart Stores	Retail	42.9	17.19	3.98
⊕ AT&T	Services	18.4	-12.70	3.50
⊕ Merck	Health	28.3	-11.00	3.38
⊕ Coca-Cola	Staples	37.7	-27.40	3.15
⊕ American Intl Grp	Financials	28.1	12.64	3.04
⊕ Johnson & Johnson	Health	38.0	10.51	2.62
⊕ Procter & Gamble	Staples	36.2	3.68	2.54
⊕ SBC Comms	Services	23.5	-3.02	2.38
⊕ Hewlett-Packard	Technology	27.6	33.58	2.25
⊕ Dell Comp	Technology	64.8	14.26	2.19
⊕ Bell Atlantic	Services	31.9	27.17	2.09
⊕ Home Depot	Retail	53.2	12.36	2.00
⊕ BellSouth	Services	25.7	-8.64	1.92
⊕ Ameritech	Services	23.5	6.85	1.70
⊕ Schering-Plough	Health	33.6	-20.40	1.53
⊕ Fannie Mae	Financials	18.2	-14.50	1.50
⊕ Wells Fargo	Financials	28.1	-0.75	1.36
⊕ Bank One	Financials	12.1	-30.00	1.36
⊕ EMC/Mass	Technology	79.3	67.94	1.36
⊕ American Express	Financials	26.6	32.47	1.26
⊕ PepsiCo	Staples	21.0	-24.50	1.22

Current Investment Style

Style Value Blend Growth		Stock Port Avg	Relative S&P 500	Rel Cat
	Price/Earnings Ratio	35.1	0.97 1.04	1.06
	Price/Book Ratio	9.2	1.03 1.12	1.20
	Price/Cash Flow	24.6	1.02 1.07	1.09
	3 Yr Earnings Growth	19.5	1.19 1.07	1.10
	1 Yr Earnings Est%	18.3	1.00 —	1.05
	Med Mkt Cap $mil	71,735	1.0 1.0	1.57

Special Securities	% assets 07-31-99		Sector Weightings	% of Stocks	Rel S&P	5-Year High Low
Restricted/Illiquid Secs	0		Utilities	1.0	0.4	4 1
Emerging-Markets Secs	0		Energy	1.6	0.2	6 1
Options/Futures/Warrants	No		Financials	15.9	1.1	21 15
			Industrials	4.1	0.3	8 4
Composition % assets 07-31-99		**Market Cap**	Durables	1.4	0.7	4 1
Cash	0.0	Giant	54.9	Staples	10.2	1.3	17 10
Stocks*	100.0	Large	29.9	Services	17.3	1.3	23 15
Bonds	0.0	Medium	10.7	Retail	10.7	1.8	19 8
Other	0.0	Small	1.3	Health	8.3	0.8	11 5
		Micro	0.2	Technology	29.6	1.3	30 6
*Foreign (% stocks)	0.0					

Chapter Twelve

What to Do When the Market Crashes

It's Monday night. The stock market crashed today. The value of your retirement plan has gone from $80,000 to $40,000 in one day. What should you do?

A. Take a bubble bath. Consider painting your nails.
B. Take your best friend, your kids, or your spouse to the park and play on the swing set.
C. Call your broker and/or your retirement plan administrator and leave a message to "SELL EVERYTHING!"

Well? The answer is either A or B. If you answered C, you have just flunked Investor Training School. Why? Consider the following story.

Tuesday, September 1, 1998. The Washington Post read "*Dow Plunges 512.61 Points; 6% Drop Erases Year's Gains as Global Economic Woes Continue.*" My phone rang. It was my longtime friend Beth calling.

"I'm selling my mutual fund," she announced. Beth wasn't a big investor. The only money that she did have invested was in her retirement plan. She had seen that meager amount in her retirement nest egg shrink way down over the course of the month, and then tumble in value in the one day in which the Dow Jones industrial average fell over 500 points.

"You're what?" I asked in disbelief.

"I'm selling my mutual fund. I'm getting out."

"NONONONONONONONONONONONONONO! Don't do it, Beth! Please don't." I felt like I was coaxing her back in from the window ledge where she stood twenty flights up threatening to jump.

First I tried reason. "Remember way back when we had our financial discussion? I told you that the stock market does this. It goes way up. It goes way down. It's a manic depressive. Pay no attention to it. The economy is strong. The economy is doing okay. The businesses that your retirement plan owns are still good businesses. They will grow. Their stocks will catch up. Please, please don't sell."

"Yeah," she said. "But the market dropped 512 points yesterday. The stock market is going down. I can tell. The economy is going down. The stock market is going to plummet further. This is the beginning of a recession. I know it."

And the conversation continued like this, with me telling her not to sell, everything was going to be okay, and her telling me that she was going to sell, because she knew it wasn't.

ME: But you don't *know* that a recession is starting. You don't *know* that. You just feel that way. That's not a fact. There is a difference.
BETH: But I do know.
ME: No you don't. How can you know?
BETH: I just know. I have a feeling.
ME: Beth, there is only thing for certain here. If you sell your mutual fund now, you will have done the one thing you are never supposed to do.
BETH: What's that?

ME: You'll be buying high and selling low.

BETH: Huh?

ME: Look if I bought a new car for $40,000 and then turned around and sold it to my neighbors the next day for $5,000, you'd say I was crazy. I would have just thrown away $35,000. You'd say I was a lunatic and needed to have my head examined. *That's buying high and selling low. That's dumb.* AND THAT'S WHAT YOU WANT TO DO!

If you sell your mutual fund now, right now, just because there is a crash and a panic, the only thing that is certain is that you'll be buying high and selling low. You'll be losing money.

BETH: Yeah. But I just KNOW the market is going to drop some more. It will. You'll see. I am going to sell my fund and then buy back in when it drops even lower.

ME: But you *don't know.* Nobody knows. What information do you have that no one else has?

BETH: I have a feeling.

That morning, Beth sold off her entire retirement fund, taking a huge loss.

The next day the stock market rebounded. By mid-September, it had regained almost the whole 512 points. Beth's "feeling" turned out to have led her astray. By following her "feeling," she lost quite a lot of money.

Moral: When the market plummets from dizzying heights and crashes, don't sell. You may not "feel" good. You may have an "urge" to sell. But don't.

WHAT TO DO

1. Imagine you are Warren Buffett, the third richest man in America. Go on. Close your eyes. Imagine that you are the greatest investor of all time. Feel the tweed jacket on your back. Think of your house in Omaha, Nebraska. When you open your eyes, POOF! You are Warren Buffett. Warren Buffett would not sell stock in companies that he owned because the market crashed.

Warren Buffett, billionaire, knows that the stock market has wild mood swings and that the mood swings don't reflect the true value of the stocks in the company he owns. He has been known to say that *if the stock market closed for two years, he wouldn't care.* Warren says:

> We own parts of businesses when we own stocks. And the New York Stock Exchange being open has nothing to do with whether *The Washington Post* [the business] is getting more valuable over a 5-year or a 10-year period. What we want to do is be right on the business. If we're right on the business, the stock market will take care of itself.
>
> The stock exchange closes on Saturday and Sunday and I don't break out in hives. So if it closed for a couple of years and the businesses were doing well, we'd do very well.

Warren says to keep faith in your original investment in the stocks you picked, or the index fund you picked, or the mutual fund you picked. You did research it, right? You did your homework. So calm down, settle down, and you will succeed. He compares being in the stock market to being in a poker game with an idiot, or as he calls it, "a patsy." Warren says:

> Well, in the market, if you think the market knows more about your business than you do . . . in other words, if your stock goes down 10% and that upsets you, it obviously means that you think the market knows more about the company than you do . . . then you're the patsy. If it [your stock] goes down 10% or more, and *you want to buy more* because you know the business is worth just as much as

when you bought it before, perhaps a little bit more with the passage of time, they're the patsy.

2. Consider buying more stock at the bargain basement prices. If you get $50 taken out of each pay check for your retirement plan, don't change that course of action if the market crashes, even if it stays crashed for a long time. Remember, you are in it for the long term.

Consider this. When the market was high, your $50 bought only a few shares in your retirement plan mutual fund. When the market is low, your $50 may buy twice as many shares or three times as many shares as when it was high. *You are getting bargains.*

For example. Say you give yourself a clothing allowance of $200 per month. If you go out to Jones New York and you buy that sassy navy blue vest and matching skirt at the beginning of the season, you pay full price. (Not to mention probably going over your clothing allowance.) However, if you wait until the middle or the end of the season, you can probably get that sassy navy blue vest and matching skirt for one-third less! Are the clothes any less valuable? No. Not at all. And I don't want to see you turn up your nose and say in your best Alicia Silverstone voice, "Oh my God—I couldn't do that—that would be so last season."

The same is true for stocks. When the market crashes, all it's doing is putting perfectly valuable stocks out on the clearance rack. [*But remember!* Just because a stock is on sale doesn't mean it's a good stock. I'm sure you've had the experience of buying a sweater because it was on sale and you "might wear it some day." I used to do that. Then I learned that "some day" never comes. If I don't want to wear the thing out of the store, I'll never wear it. And that, too, is money down the drain.]

Before the market takes a tumble, or a rise, or anything, manage your money well.

- Always keep three to six months' pay in a money market account as backup, in case you get fired or come upon hard times.
- Make the maximum contribution to your retirement plan.
- If you know that you are going to *need* money in the short term (one to five years), *do not buy stocks or a mutual fund made up of stocks*. That is too risky. You risk needing to cash out your stocks to pay for car repair, medical expenses, or to tide you over until you find that new job. Then you'll have to sell your stocks. You may have to cash out your stocks at half their value. You'll be buying high and selling low—losing hard-earned money in the process.
- Before you invest in stocks, understand the following: When you own stock, you own a piece of a company. In the long run, the stock will go up if the company does well. It will go down if the company does not do well. In the short run, the stock will act like a manic depressive. It will be low when the company is doing fine. It will be soaring super-high—when the company is doing just average. Eventually, in the long run, the price of the stock will catch up to the value of the company. But you don't know when that will happen. No one does. One thing is for sure: You will not be able to "time" when the stock goes up. It certainly will not go up when you want it to. So you need to hold on to it for the long term.

So what do you do when the market crashes? Stay the course.

THE FLYING ANALOGY

Sometimes when pilots fly, they experience vertigo. Up feels like down. Sideways feels like upright. It all has something to do with the inner ear, which keeps your body oriented. That's why instead of flying according to "how they feel," pilots have to fly according to how the instruments on their control panels tell them to fly.

The instruments tell them which way is up, which way is north, which way is south, and where they are in relationship to things around them. If a pilot doesn't experience vertigo, she feels like her instruments are correct. However, if she does experience vertigo, she'll "feel" like her instruments are lying to her. Like the compass is broken. She'll "feel" that she should be coming down in elevation, when, in fact the instruments are telling her to climb. If she does what she "feels" like doing, she will probably crash the plane and kill herself.

If she does what she has "learned," not what she "feels" like doing, she will be able to land the plane, and realize later over a cold drink that all her "feelings" amounted to a very bad case of vertigo.

Moral: The wild and crazy mood swings of the stock market can cause vertigo. Vertigo can impair the judgment of even the most seasoned expert. As someone who is putting money in the stock market, whether through a retirement plan mutual fund or through purchasing individual stocks, remember to stay your course: The course that you drew up when you were sane, when you didn't have stock market vertigo, when you chose your investments carefully and wisely, and when you understood that the markets were crazy—not you.

Chapter Thirteen

Why You Should Ignore Market Mood Swings and Stock Price Panics

Here's the first thing that you need to learn about the stock market and never forget: It's run by people. Never forget that. People are not Vulcans. They are not rational. Well, not all the time. Certainly not all the time where money matters are concerned. Or where Beanie Babies are concerned. Or that Tickle Me Elmo doll. So if your stocks are going up and down in price, or your mutual funds are making you seasick, you might gain some insight here. So why do stock prices go up and down?

SOMETIMES STOCK PRICES GO DOWN FOR "ECONOMIC REASONS"

A downswing in the price of a stock can reflect something real. For example, a war, or inflation, or a huge hike in oil prices can make it much harder for the average corporation to do business, make profits, and grow. Subsequently, its stocks may have a hard time growing. As the growth of the company slows, the stocks lose value, and the prices of the stocks go down and sometimes "crash."

Furthermore, sales and profits from a corporation may continue to drop off year after year. The company can shrink in size and become less valuable.

Smith Corona: An Example of a Company Whose Stock Price Dropped for "Real Reasons"

Smith Corona used to be the king of typewriters. If you had a typewriter, you had a Smith Corona. Based on this success, the company grew and diversified. The introduction of the personal computer and home word processors was a death knell for the typewriter division of Smith Corona. The company continually lost sales and value until it had to declare Chapter 11 bankruptcy in 1995. The stock price plummeted to the ground along with the decline of the company. This is a classic example of a stock price reflecting the value of a company.[1]

SOMETIMES THE STOCK MARKET GOES DOWN BECAUSE PEOPLE ARE PANICKY

A downswing in the stock market can also be caused by simple "fear" alone. A chain of events can lead investors to "think" that there is going to be high inflation or high oil prices. This is important. Pay attention.

When I was six years old, I woke up in the middle of the night. My coatrack had turned into a vampire. I knew it. I could see the gleaming white teeth, the long black cape. I screamed. My brother rushed into my room to see what was wrong and turned on the light. The vampire disappeared. In its place was the coatrack, upon which hung my long navy blue winter coat.

Take heed: Stock market investors can easily become steadfastly

---

[1]After the Chapter 11 bankruptcy, Smith Corona is still in the consumer electronics business today.

certain that coatracks are vampires. One three-month period of lower housing sales than normal can mean that the big fearsome ghoul of economics, the Great Depression, is lurking under the bed. Frightened investors can scream "Sell! Sell!" in an effort to preserve their stocks in the face of the boogie monster Great Depression.

This, of course, is like letting a six-year-old have a gun in the drawer of the bedside table. One nightmare, one vampire, and blam! blam! blam!—you've got a coatrack full of bullet holes.

So it is with investors. Before anyone can turn on the light, they can spook themselves into selling perfectly good stocks for stupidly low prices. When their neighbors see them unloading, they become afraid, too. The neighbors start unloading their stocks as well. Because maybe someone knows something they don't.

If enough investors get spooked at the same time, they all try to sell, and there are no buyers. So prices go lower and lower and lower until finally, they are so low that there are some buyers.

The bottom buyers get away with a sweet deal.

Platinum Technology: An Example of Panicky Selling

You don't believe me? Let me a tell you a story about a company called Platinum Technology. The company provided more than 160 software products and related services that helped corporations manage their computer networks and database systems by automating and managing operations. Platinum Technology grew through acquisitions—it bought more than sixty companies in a four-year period. Mind you, the company itself was doing okay, growing and expanding, suffering a little bit of growing pain here and there. But overall, doing okay.

The coatrack vampire: Because of the spending activity, there was one three-month period where the sales of the company were way down and their profits were way down. Egad! You'd think a meteor had struck.

The investing public, the mutual fund managers, and everybody *freaked out*. They all shouted, "Sell! Sell!" (Blam! Blam! Someone kill the coatrack!)

They all tried to sell the stock as fast as they could. That's why the stock dove from around $30 per share to $10 per share.

Doesn't sound too bad, eh? Well, just multiply that $20 per share loss by 101 million shares and you are talking real money. Real money like *two billion dollars!* I mean, you try borrowing that kind of money from your mom or kid brother when you run into hard times. Ha! Good luck.

Seriously, that's the kind of damage a little stock market panic can do. Platinum Technology saw its purchase price go from $3 billion to $1 billion in a matter of weeks. But here's the irony: All those panicky investors were wrong. Dead wrong.

Turning on the lights: Not too long after the big tumble, Computer Associates decided to buy Platinum Technology. They bought it for $29.25 per share—not the $10 listed price. Why not $10 per share? *Because Platinum Technology was worth much more than $10 per share.* Everyone who knew anything about the business knew it. The "price" of the company may have tumbled overnight, but the "value" of the company was still the same.

Paul Wick, manager of the flagship technology fund, Seligman Communications and Information Fund A, commented on it this way:

> They [Platinum Technology] stumbled a couple quarters ago—the December quarter. And the stock went from like 30 to 10. This was a software company with reasonably good profit margins that had a near term glitch.

And yet no one wanted to own the stock—no one in the analyst community was recommending the company. But it was announced last week that they were getting bought by Computer Associates for $29 per share in cash. *So the discrepancy—the gulf between what a corporate buyer in the know would pay and what the investment community would pay is crazy.*

There you have it. He said it first. And he's one of the most successful mutual fund managers in the business. Let me repeat that so that you don't forget it. Because it's often true. *The gulf between what a corporate buyer in the know would pay and what the investment community would pay is crazy.* In other words, the investment community will sell a perfectly good company. A coporate buyer in the know is a corporation that is looking for a valuable corporation. The execs at Computer Associates knew that despite what the investing community thought of Platinum Technology, the company was very valuable.

Computer Associates: Another Example of Panicky Selling

These types of examples just abound. This one is about Computer Associates. The company that bought Platinum Technology.

The coatrack vampire: In June 1998 the company had lower profits—officially called "earnings"—than expected. On July 21, 1998, the company announced that the rest of the year might be difficult because of problems in Asia and Y2K compliance. Overnight, the stock went from its high of $61.94 to a low of $37.13. So the price of the company went from around $33 billion to $20 billion *in one night.*

Nothing had really changed—at least, not that drastically. Had the company lost $19 billion in value overnight? Where did it go? Did aliens invade? Did a fire burn down the company? Did everyone up and quit? No. Everyone ignored it and went on quietly working. And like a foreboding dark cloud, the threat passed overhead and went away.

Turning on the Lights: After a while, everyone realized that it was just a bad scare and the company was really as valuable as it had been all along. Today—September 9, 1999—the stock price was at $61 per share at its high. Just about the same as its all-time high.

STOCK PRICES CAN GO UP FOR "REAL" REASONS

Of course, the stock market can go up for real reasons. In the '90's, we've had incredibly low inflation, low unemployment, as a result we also have booming businesses, booming profits, and booming stock prices. Most notably, the technology and information companies have been making mad profits and growing in value.

All the numbers reflect that. The inflation rate of the past ten years (1989–1998) was 3.8%. And the annual rate of return for the S&P 500 was 19%. So if you were invested in large stocks during this time, you'd have come out happily way ahead.

The Gap: A Stock Goes Up for Real Reasons

The stock of this company went up for real reasons. And no, they didn't invent a new Internet widget or software system. They just made clothes that people liked for prices people liked and marketed them better than anyone else. (I personally bought my black velvet holiday pants from The Gap, which I wore over and over again.)

How's that? First of all, The Gap really blankets the casual clothing market. For those of you who didn't know, The Gap also owns Banana Republic and Old Navy. As of May 21, 1999, sales of The Gap clothes had gone up 22% per year for the past ten years (from $1.5 billion to $11.3 billion). Company profits have gone up 24.5% (from $104 million to $1 billion).

There you have it. Something real. Sell more clothes. Make more money. Value of the company goes up. Stock price does too. At one point in 1990, Gap stock sold for less than $3 per share (adjusted backwards for stock splits.) In the first three quarters of 1999, at its height, it sold for $52.69 per share. That's a great price climb.

STOCK PRICES CAN GO UP BECAUSE OF HOPE, HYPE, AND GREED

Stocks can go up for stupid reasons, too.

Just as investors can have fear that leads to stupid selling, the reverse can be true. Investors have been famous, again, in that crazy crowd-like way, for letting hope, hype, and greed get the better of them. They have let the fantasy of a fantastic future cloud their true judgement of the value of a company. Here's an analogy.

Hope, hype, and greed: I admit it. On more than one occasion I have bought one of those really expensive wrinkle goos. I can't help it. I have Irish skin. All those years trying to be a surfing babe . . . and now I've got crow's-feet—or as my dear friend Andy says, a crow's convention. So I put the wrinkle goo on my face before I go to sleep. And, of course, I expect miracles.

Reality check and the morning mirror: Well, I wake up the next day after putting the new wrinkle goo on my face and invariably my pillow is greasy. I go to the mirror full of wild hopes and dreams and what do I get? Crow's-feet! The wrinkles haven't gone away. Those darned crows were supposed to fly away in the middle of the night and take their feet with them. What's up with that? Even after weeks of putting the stuff on my face, the wrinkles don't go away. I have duped myself into believing the impossible.

So it is with some companies. Sometimes, they promise miracles—but a reality check can separate the miracles that last from the miracles caused by hocus-pocus. Once again, a real-life anecdote to explain.

Neoprobe: A Stock Goes Up Because of Hope and Hype and a Miracle Product

Once upon a time, a friend of mine bought stock in a company called Neoprobe. His buddy had told him about this company. Neoprobe, it seemed, had two great new diagnostic medical devices that would really help surgeons remove dangerous cancer cells.

This is how the products worked. A couple of weeks prior to surgery, cancer patients would be injected with the first product, called RIGScan CR 49, a low-energy radioactive drug. The drug would run through the body and attach itself to cancer cells, like mini-magnets glomming onto big iron filings. Then, during the surgery, the surgeon would hold the second product, a pencil-sized probe in hand, wave it over the affected area, and it would emit a *beep beep beep* tone when cancer cells were near. Then the surgeon would know if she had gotten all the cancer cells during the surgery. Awesome, eh?

Things looked promising. The company had a patent on its technology. Clinical trials had shown that the device was effective during surgery in locating otherwise undetectable cancer cells. In fact, surgeons already using the device were swearing by it.

Hope, hype, and greed: Well, let's see. Add all that together: a cool cancer-detecting device based on nuclear technology; a patented technology, at that. This was a product no self-respecting surgeon would want to be without. Why wouldn't you buy it?

Well, my buddy wasn't the only one who was enthused. Lots of other people were, too. The price of Neoprobe's stock reflected that enthusiasm.

The little company had first issued stock to finance its venture in 1992 at around $6 per share. In September 1995, the price per share doubled to $12 per share, and then in October 1995 it tripled to $18 per share. At its height, the stock of the wee little company was bid up to $23.25 per share.

Reality check and the morning mirror: The reality was that the radioactive drug had not been approved by the FDA yet. The company was basing all its growth potential on this product that hadn't even been approved. The company only had like $1 million in sales. The company had never turned a profit. The popularity of the company was based on *hope* and *hype*, not on real things being sold. There was a promise of things being sold, but no big sales were being made. No real profits were rolling in.

Let's have a closer look. This was a little company in Dublin, Ohio. That $23.25 per share multiplied by 23,000,000 shares equals $534,750,000. Whoa. At its most dizzying height, this company was priced at *$535 million*. Was it really worth $535 million? Really?

Let's compare and contrast. My friend Helen runs the restaurant down the street. She pulls in about $1 million in revenue a year. If she sold that shop, she might get $2 million for it, mortgage, location, clientèle, and all. So why were people gonna pay $534 million for a company with smaller profits than Helen's restaurant?

Why? I'll tell you why. The *hope* was so great. Everyone knows someone close to them who died of cancer; it is horrible. Everyone really wanted the product to succeed. And the *hype* was so great. My buddy wasn't the only one who bought into the dream. Then, of course, there was, er, *greed*. Let's face it: Buying stock in a start-up company isn't a donation to the American Cancer Society. People hope to win big and the patent exclusivity is all part of that.

Well, it's a sad story. The little company with high hopes faced one snafu after another. First the Food and Drug Administration had some questions about its clinical trials; so the drug, as of this writing, has not been cleared for mass marketing. Then the company faced competition. Finally, it was such a small company that it had no giant cash reserves to fall back on when its one big product couldn't make it to market in a timely way.

With delays piling up, no real money coming in to speak of, and no profits on the horizon, investors started to get spooked. So they started to sell. They sold and sold and sold.

Today, July 2, 1999, the price of Neoprobe Incorporated is $0.59 per share. You read that right. Not even $1 per share. That's down from $23.25. That's a long way to fall. If you had the cash, and they were willing to sell, today you could buy Neoprobe the company for $13.57 million instead of the $535 million that it went for back in 1996.

I'm not saying Neoprobe's product wasn't useful or good. It was very useful, and still is. The folks at Neoprobe should be downright proud of their work and its contribution to medicine and public health. But as you can see, the stock market can pick a little company up in a whirlwind like a tornado and slam it down just as fast.

A LITTLE BIT OF HISTORICAL PERSPECTIVE ON THE MARKET

Sometimes the stock market goes down and it just stays down. We haven't really seen a bad market for over fifteen years. In fact, the economy has been bubbling along and the stock market has, too. The stocks of the S&P 500 have had a return of 19.2% over the past ten years and 17.7% over the past twenty. But it was not always so. You need to know that. Knowing that the American economy has met with stock market crashes, depressions, inflations and *survived* should give you some comfort. Don't you be the one who bought high and sold at the bottom of the worst bear market in centuries. You hold on to the safety belt during that roller coaster ride. You wait out the bear.

The 1970s: Disco Sucked, but the Economy Sucked Worse

Almost the entire decade of the 1970s was a terrible time for the stock market. In fact, things were so bad throughout the seventies that *BusinessWeek* magazine practically proclaimed the stock business dead in a cover story. On August 13, 1979, *BusinessWeek* magazine published a cover story the title of which was "The Death of Equities: How Inflation Is Destroying the Stock Market."

Nobody was happy with the way things were turning out in the seventies. They'd been bad for such a long stretch that no one except the most dedicated of optimists could imagine how we were going to get out of the mess.

Check this out. From 1969 to 1978, the compounded annual return of the S&P 500 stocks was 3.2%. Yes, you heard me right. Ten years of your hard-earned money could have been mired and waning in the world's greatest investment.

To make matters worse, inflation was chugging right along. From 1969 to 1978, the prices of most goods—bread, cars, diapers—rose by 6.7%. So if you had money in the large company stocks, you likely would have simply lost money in that ten-year period.

Why was this so? Well, there were real economic reasons. In 1973 and 1974, OPEC jacked up the price of oil. Oil, it turned out, was literally the "oil" of the United States economic engine. When the price of oil quadrupled, everything—and I mean everything—that used oil became more expensive. Consumer goods like paint, plastic, baby bottles, and bicycle seats jumped; heating oil, gas and oil for cars and trucks and airplanes (i.e., all commercial transportation), oil to run the big midwestern grain machines and the automobile factories, all skyrocketed.

Add to that inflation, which was already spiking, and corporations were barely making ends meet—they certainly weren't growing very much. It follows that, because stocks just represent pieces of companies that weren't growing very much, the values of the individual stocks weren't growing very much. In 1973, 1974, and 1975, large stocks took a nosedive in price. Forget about growth.

Add to *that* the fact that the federal government still had to raise money to pay off the debts it incurred to finance the Vietnam War. In order to raise that money, they had to come up with interest rates on bonds that would beat inflation; why would you buy a Treasury bond yielding 6% if it were just going to lose value over time? So, in the meantime, bonds offered everyone else a much better return.

Everyone started buying bonds and money market mutual funds and certificates of deposit with fixed high interest rates. They saw that stocks had just inched up 3% per year for the past ten years, but brand new bonds were being issued at inflation-beating prices. In 1979, that was 10.4%. Naturally, many people went to bonds.

The more people bought bonds, the more they sold stocks, the more the overall stock market went down. Simple economics. If nobody wants to buy it, the price will drop until someone *does* want to buy it.

Well, that's what happened in 1974. That was a bear market. There was a real reason for that bear market, real economic problems that made things difficult. It wasn't until inflation was brought under control by the Federal Reserve, and oil prices dropped, and tax laws were reformed, that corporations found that it became profitable again to start making things like bread, bicycles, refrigerators, and computers. When the corporations started to have healthy profits, the stocks that they issued became valuable, and that's when the economy really started booming again.

So, wait out the bear markets and bear days when the stock market looks like it's going nowhere but down forever. For if what goes up must come down, the reverse is also true. People who bought Coca-Cola stock at its bargain basement price in 1974 have been laughing all the way to the bank.

CONCLUSION: TWO AND TWO STILL MAKE FOUR

There is a wonderful book entitled *Extraordinary Popular Delusions and the Madness of Crowds* that details the selling manias and buying frenzies and many other "popular delusions" throughout history. The book was originally published in 1841.

In the aftermath of the stock market crash of 1929, a book entitled "Extraordinary Popular Delusions and the Madness of Crowds" seemed painfully appropriate, and so it was reprinted. Bernard Baruch wrote a new foreword to the re-released book. In it, he wistfully affirmed, "All economic movements, by their very nature, are motivated by crowd psychology. Without due recognition of crowd thinking, which often represents crowd madness, our theories of economics leave much to be desired."

So that, in part, should explain why a perfectly good company can see its value go from $3 billion to $1 billion in one week, and why a company with no profits and hardly any sales can sell for $535 million. Whether it's Tickle Me Elmo, Beanie Babies, tulips, or stock prices, the prices of "things" get separated from their "value." They just do. Because we, as humans, are all too human.

And what to do about it?

Turn on the light before you shoot the coat rack.

Don't expect miracles from wrinkle goo.

Or as Bernard Baruch so aptly put it, as stock prices tumbled all around him, bread lines formed, unemployment soared and the Great Depression swept over the face of the United States:

"I have always thought that if, . . . even in the presence of dizzily spiraling prices, we had all continuously repeated, 'two and two still make four,' much of the evil might have been averted. Similarly, even in the general moment of gloom in which this foreword is written, when many begin to wonder if declines will never halt, the appropriate abracadabra may be, 'They Always Did.' "

Buying
STOCKS
the Smart
Shopper Way

Chapter Fourteen

Warren Buffett, the Billionaire: The Smartest of "Smart" Shoppers

Before we get into the nitty gritty of "how to shop for stocks," there's someone I want you to meet: Warren Buffett, the third-richest man in the United States, one of the greatest investors of all time. I have referred to him before, but it's time you really met him. His commonsense, rational, wise view of the manic investment world makes him not only a great investor but also a great teacher. In the write-up below I've transcribed an interview with him conducted by the illustrious Adam Smith, Emmy award–winning host of *Adam Smith's Money World*.

First, a little background: Warren Buffett lives in Omaha, Nebraska. A regular place, maybe even a little dull. He still lives in the same house that he bought in 1958 for $32,000. A regular kind of guy. He is a man of modest beginnings, but is now the third-richest man in the country, with a net worth of $31 billion as of this writing. His fortune is in the investing company he controls called Berkshire Hathaway, a giant holding company that owns stocks and businesses. *Not* so regular or dull.

How did he do it? He was a smart shopper.

He did the kind of research you do all the time. Think about it:

Let's say you are looking for the cheapest airfare because you have to fly across the country to a childhood friend's wedding. You are looking for a bargain—a flight that gets you where you want to go at half the usual cost, but without adding five extra cities and ten extra hours to your journey. You call your travel agent, you look in the newspaper, and then you call a discount travel agent. Finally, you look on the Internet. Bingo! Delta has slashed its prices again, and you get a special deal if you fly Friday morning. In seconds, you are on the phone, having saved $300 per ticket!

This is the story of how Warren Buffett, a.k.a. the smartest shopper, went bargain hunting.

Buffett was looking to buy bonds.[1] He found two types to his liking: the bonds of the Illinois turnpike and the bonds of the Indiana turnpike. The state governments of Indiana and Illinois both wanted to raise money to pay for the cost of maintaining their turnpikes, so they issued bonds.

The Indiana turnpike bonds sold at $750 per bond and the Illinois turnpike bonds sold at $980 per bond. They both paid the same interest. Buffett figured that the Indiana bonds might be a better deal. He could pay less money for them ($230 less apiece) and get the same amount of interest as he would get on the Illinois bond.

But wait. Why were many people willing to pay more for the Illinois bonds? Buffett decided to find out.

He did some research and was told that the Indiana turnpike bonds were cheaper because the Indiana turnpike might need a lot of repair. To finance repairs, the Indiana state turnpike authority might have to skip an interest payment on the bond. The bonds

[1]Remember, a bond is a loan that you give an institution like a corporation, the state, or federal government. Say you lend the Indiana state government $1,000 for ten years. In return, they give you a percentage, say 5%, every year for ten years. That's $50 per year for ten years. Then they give you your principal back—your $1,000—at the end of the ten years.

supposedly weren't as reliable as the Illinois ones. Kind of like the difference between a Yugo and a Honda.

Buffett was a smart shopper. He wasn't so sure that the Indiana turnpike was a Yugo and the Illinois turnpike was a Honda. After all, he saw for himself that the two turnpikes connected to each other. They were practically the same road. They had much of the same traffic. So Buffett got into his car and drove the length of the Indiana turnpike. He didn't see where a lot of road work was really necessary. So he went to the records of the Indiana turnpike commission and turned over the dusty pages. He found enough financial reserves to repair any potholes. It didn't look like the state of Indiana would have to skip an interest payment to repair the road. It looked like the Indiana turnpike was a Honda, disguised as a Yugo.

Buffett bought a big block of Indiana turnpike bonds. Eventually, everyone else realized the true value of the Indiana turnpike bonds, and the price of those bonds went from $750 to $980—until they matched the Illinois bonds. Buffett had gotten in early and had gotten a *steal* of a deal by being a smart shopper.

A very handsome return, a very simple story, and something *you* could have done, with the same kinds of savvy bargain-hunting tactics you would use to fly across the country to your childhood friend's wedding.

In the following interview, Buffett emphasized four basic points that make up his investment philosophy—the four points for being a smart shopper in the stock market:

- Think of buying stocks as buying businesses.
- Only invest in stocks of the businesses you are familiar with.
- Have faith in your stocks, not the moody stock market.
- Have patience: The stock market is not like the lottery. You don't get rich quick.

THE INTERVIEW

ADAM SMITH: You've said that they could close the New York Stock Exchange for two years and you wouldn't care—can you explain that?

WARREN BUFFETT: We own parts of businesses when we own stocks. And the New York Stock Exchange being open has nothing to do with whether The Washington Post [the business] is getting more valuable over a five-year or a ten-year period. What we want to do is be right on the business. If we're right on the business, the stock market will take care of itself.

The stock exchange closes on Saturday and Sunday and I don't break out in hives. So if it closed for a couple of years and the businesses were doing well, we'd do very well.

ADAM SMITH: I noticed that in your annual report you say, "If you're in a poker game for thirty minutes and you don't know who the patsy is—you're the patsy."

WARREN BUFFETT: You got it.

ADAM SMITH: How do you apply this to the market and to investing?

WARREN BUFFETT: Well, in the market, if you think the market knows more about your business than you do . . . in other words, if your stock goes down 10% and that upsets you, it obviously means that you think the market knows more about the company than you do and in that case you're the patsy. If it [your stock] goes down 10% or more, and you want to buy more because you know the business is worth just as much as when you bought it before, perhaps a little bit more with the passage of time, they're the patsy.

ADAM SMITH: Where do you get these aphorisms?

WARREN BUFFETT: (Laughs) Well, I don't know. They're about the limit of my intellectual capacity. I have to work with one sentence.

Translation: Buffett is saying that when you buy a stock, you are not buying a number on a roulette wheel. You are buying a business. Buying a business is just like buying any other product. If you research the product thoroughly and exhaustively, you'll feel very good about your decision by the time you fork over the cash to buy it.

For example, I needed a computer. So I went to the computer guy in my office and asked him to brief me on the latest models and their functions. Then I asked him to come with me to a couple of different stores to check out the different computers. (I had to bribe him with a large pizza and a Coke.) He was able to explain the differences to me, and help me figure out exactly what I needed. He was able to tell me which salespeople were bluffing and which ones knew their stuff. Finally, I thumbed through Consumer Reports to check up on laptops. When I finally made my decision, I called two other computer geek friends of mine just to double-check. By the end, I was beginning to feel like a computer geek myself.

Finally, I bought the computer. It had enough memory and hard drive space. It was portable. It had a modem. And the price was right. The computer store could have closed the next day and I wouldn't have cared. I bought a computer that I liked and whether it went up or down in price didn't matter to me. I was happy with my purchase.

In six months, the price of my computer did drop substantially as Texas Instruments came out with a newer model. Did I have a twinge of angst? Of course. I'm human. But I also realized that I had gotten six months of work out of my computer, that I would not have been able to do without it.

My little story illustrates two of the rules.

- Only buy businesses you are familiar with. (I did my homework and became a computer geek.)
- Have faith in your stocks. (I didn't rush out and sell my computer when Texas Instruments came out with a new model. The old one was working just fine. Nor did I throw a temper tantrum because computer prices had dropped. I thought back to all

those wonderful days that I'd been able to work at home in my pajamas because I had my own computer and modem.)

BACK TO THE INTERVIEW

ADAM SMITH: If you had to look over the next five or ten years, what do you think would be good businesses [to invest in]?

WARREN BUFFETT: The businesses that have some sort of a franchise to 'em. What makes a business a good business is when . . . if I go into a drugstore and I want a Hershey bar, they can't sell me an unmarked bar. I'm gonna pay 35 cents for a Hershey bar, and they say, "well, wouldn't you like this wonderful unmarked chocolate bar for 30 cents?" But I buy the Hershey bar. And if they don't have it someplace, I'll go across the street to buy it. That's what makes a good business.

I don't feel that way about the carton of milk I buy. I'll take whatever carton of milk is in the grocery store's freezer—er—cooler.

ADAM SMITH: That's the power of the franchise.

WARREN BUFFETT: That's the power of the franchise.

Translation: Part of what makes a stock a good buy is whether or not the business that issues it has brand-name loyalty. I like a double skim latte, and I know that when I go to Starbucks it's going to be made exactly how I like it. Anywhere in the country. Even over in the U.K. It's going to made with skim milk, not whole, and it's going to taste great.

Yesterday, I went to a local coffee shop down the street. The sentiment was to help out the local merchants.

"Double skim latte," I said.

"We don't have skim," the lady behind the counter said.

I did an about-face and headed over to Starbucks. I paid 40 cents more; and so do a lot of other people. If I'd bought Starbucks stock six years ago, I'd have made a handsome little profit!

BACK TO THE INTERVIEW

ADAM SMITH: You've been talking this philosophy for years [the "be patient—do your homework—buy value" philosophy]. It's no secret.
WARREN BUFFETT: It's no secret.
ADAM SMITH: Why doesn't everybody do it?
WARREN BUFFETT: Well—it requires patience, which a lot of people don't have. People would much rather be promised that they're gonna win a lottery ticket next week than that they're gonna get rich slowly.

My colleague used to say that he was long-term greedy, not short-term greedy. If you're short-term greedy, you probably won't get a very good long-term result.
ADAM SMITH: But there's been so much publicity about buying value. Why doesn't everybody concentrate on it?
WARREN BUFFETT: Lots of publicity about exercise and a good diet too, but in the end I think about exercise but I don't do it . . . (laughs). I guess that's what happens with other people buying stocks.

This was just a snippet of wisdom from one of the greatest investors of all time. It's nice to know that he's human. He has days where he skips his workout because he just doesn't feel like it. He likes Hershey bars. He's even self-effacing about his own intellectual capacity. But he is plodding and disciplined in the area of stock picking. He researches what he knows, and he buys bargains.

In the following section, "How to shop for stocks," you'll see how you can put Warren Buffett's principles into practice. Maybe you'll get rich slowly, too, and grow from bargain hunter to billionaire by sticking to the boring basics. After all, being a billionaire isn't *that* boring.

Chapter Fifteen

How to Shop for Stocks the "Smart Shopper" Way

It's time to go shopping. But instead of scouring the sales rack at Nordstroms, you and I are going to go shopping for stocks. Don't know how? Sure you do.

Shopping for stocks is exactly the same as shopping for an outfit for the holiday party. First, you generate a list of what you want to buy. Holiday dress. Shoes to match. Maybe some earrings. The second thing you do is you hit the stores and scour for low prices and great values.

That's exactly how you shop for stocks. You generate a list of what you want to buy. Then you determine whether the stocks are overpriced or whether they are great deals that will really pay off. So let's go shopping for stocks.

GENERATE A LIST OF WHAT YOU WANT TO BUY

How do you decide what kind of stocks, in the whole universe of stocks out there, you want to buy? The best and easiest way is simply to rack your brain for all the successful companies that you can think of.

How do you find these companies? These are the companies that just plain look like they are successful. For example, you could walk into Williams-Sonoma on a busy Saturday and you could see that it was really crowded. You might say, "Man, these people must be making money hand over fist." That would be a good company to research. Or you could go to Starbucks and give them $3 every morning for some bean water, and you might say, "Man, I hope these people like my money because they sure take a lot of it." That would also be a good company to research.

Are you starting to get the picture? *Your list of the type of stocks you want to shop for should come from corporations you encounter (and give your money to) every day.* This is the Peter Lynch approach to investing documented in his wonderful, readable book called *One Up on Wall Street.*

Your list can also include companies that your Uncle Marty told you about. Or that you heard about at a party. Or that a rating service like Value Line gave a high ranking to. (You'll find out about Value Line later.) But to start shopping, you do need to have a list of what you want to buy. Then you can start your research.

RESEARCH THE COMPANIES ON YOUR LIST FOR PRICE AND VALUE

The next step is to research the companies on your list to determine if their price matches their value. How do you find out what the price of the company is? How do you determine the value?

Let's go back to the idea of dress shopping for a minute. It's a great way to think about price and value. Say you go shopping for that outfit for the holiday party, and you spy a little black velvet dress. You are going to look at two things before you buy it. One, you are looking at the *price* of the outfit. And two, you are looking at the *value* of the outfit.

The *value* of the dress is determined by the following questions. Will you wear it more than once? Will it last for a number of years? Do you look completely sassy in that black velvet dress? The answer to those questions will give you a good idea of the dress's value.

Value is subjective. I might buy a dress for $100 that I adore. To me, that dress might be worth every penny. You might try on the same dress and think "Yuck! What an ugly dress! I wouldn't pay 10 cents let alone $100 for this thing."

Price, on the other hand, is not subjective. The price for the dress is fixed and objective. The dress costs $100 whether or not you think it is ugly.

As a smart shopper, you need to look at *price* and *value.* You need to determine whether the *price* of that dress is in line with its *value.* If the dress costs $600 and you think you'll only wear it once, the price is probably out of line with the value. If it costs $49.99 and you think you'll wear it every chance you get (because you look so good!) the price is probably in line with the value.

You know how to determine the price and value of a dress. How do you determine the price and value of a company?

FINDING THE PRICE AND VALUE OF A COMPANY

To start your research, remember: Individual stocks are really just pieces of a company. Looking at an individual stock won't tell you much. You need to look at the whole company. So just pretend that you are Mariah Carey or Madonna or someone very rich, and you want to buy a company.

Let's say that you, rock star that you are, are particularly interested in buying a small clothing company to add to your empire. The first thing you look at is price. How much does the clothing company cost? The second thing you look at is value. Is it worth it to buy the clothing company? Does the clothing company turn a big profit year after year? Are the profits growing? Will the profits of the clothing company add to your empire? Are the sales of the company growing? Are the clothes the company makes getting more or less popular over the years? Those are the questions you need to answer.

Now, just in case you are not familiar with thinking about a business in terms of its sales, profits, and growth potential, I'm going to tell you a story to get you familiar with those ideas. Once you understand these concepts, you'll be ready to start your research.

JILL & CO. — THE STORY OF A COMPANY

Chapter One: Jill Designs Some Clothes and Sells Them for Profit at a Boutique Show

Ahem.

Once upon a time, there was a woman named Jill. Jill was often frustrated when she went shopping. If she found something she liked one year, the designer would have discontinued it the next. If she found a cool, snappy jacket, it didn't go with any of her pants.

So Jill cashed out her savings, sketched out some patterns, hired a pattern maker and a seamstress, and made the very first *Jill* brand sleek black trousers, slimming jacket, and long flowing dress.

She got a boutique at the International Boutique Show where all the great independent boutique owners come to buy stuff for their boutiques. She didn't make that many sales, but she listened to what the boutique owners wanted, and she redesigned her clothes in the way that they had advised.

Chapter Two: Jill's Clothing Line Is a Success with Boutique Owners

In six months, Jill had another booth at another boutique show and it was a success! All the boutique owners flocked to her booth. Her trousers, her jacket, her scarf and her cotton top were hits! Everyone looked sleek and tailored in her clothes. But the clothes were *also comfortable*.

Thirty-two different boutique owners placed orders for five pantsuits apiece. That's 160 orders! Because each pantsuit had a wholesale value of $250, Jill had $40,000 worth of orders!

When Jill got home, she was totally psyched and she called her favorite sister, Melva. "Well the good news is I sold $40,000 worth of clothing orders. The bad news is, I don't have the $15,000 it's gonna take to make them."

Melva was cool-headed. She had an excellent plan for raising the $15,000 needed to fill the clothing orders. She used the conference call button on her phone and got their third sister, Anne, on the line.

Chapter Three: Jill, Melva, and Anne Form the Jill & Co. Clothing Company and Create Three Shares of Stock in the Company

At the end of the conversation, it was decided: Jill would form a company to be owned by the three sisters. The ownership of the company would be divided into three *shares*. Jill would have one share. Melva would have one share. Anne would have one share. Each sister would do what it took to get $5,000 to buy a "share of ownership" or "*share of stock*" in the company. The $15,000 raised would go toward making the clothes to fill the orders.

Anne borrowed against her home. Melva borrowed against her retirement plan. Jill took out a very expensive consumer loan (not something I'd advise).

The company balance sheet looked like this.

Jill—$5,000—1 share of Jill & Co. stock
Melva—$5,000—1 share of Jill & Co. stock
Anne—$5,000—1 share of Jill & Co. stock

Each sister, in a separate arrangement, agreed to take on a responsibility in the beginning. Jill supervised the clothes-making. Melva oversaw the legal and financial operations, paid the bills, and kept the books. Anne communicated directly with the boutique owners to make sure they were happy.

Each sister owned one *share* of *stock* in the company *Jill & Co.*

Chapter Four: Clothing Sales Take Off, Profits Increase, and Jill, Melva, and Anne Hang In There

The next year, *Jill & Co.* clothes were so popular that their *sales* more than doubled to $100,000. That year, all three sisters quit their day jobs and went on the payroll of their newly founded company. The year after that, their sales doubled again to $200,000.

By the fifth year they had *sales of $1,500,000*. After all their bills were paid—such as the pattern maker, the fabric maker, the seamstress team, their salaries—they had $100,000 in *net profits*. (In stock speak, net profits are called *earnings*.) They opened a bottle of champagne to celebrate!

(Note: During this time, Jill and her sisters worked hard to make sure that their company was run ethically. Because clothing manufacturing is an industry rife with labor law abuse, they were very careful about monitoring their subcontractors and they worked with the Social Venture Network to do so.)

Chapter Five: Jill, Anne, and Melva Marshal the Company Into a Huge Success

In the following years, *Jill & Co.* continued to grow at a rapid-fire pace. After six years in business, Melva supervised the opening of the very first *Jill & Co.* specialty retail store. Just like Ann Taylor or The Gap, this was a retail shop dedicated only to selling *Jill & Co.* In three years, there were six *Jill & Co.* shops where "Jill fanatics" could go and buy Jill designs exclusively.

After eight years in business, Anne got big-name department stores to become interested in buying their clothes. Neiman-Marcus, Saks Fifth Avenue, and Nordstrom all began to order clothes from *Jill & Co.* This made their sales skyrocket, especially because two of the department stores created "in-store" boutiques, a section of the department store where only *Jill & Co.* was featured.

Chapter Six: After Ten Years, Jill and Her Sisters Look Into Selling Their Company

After ten years, *Jill & Co.* had done very, very well. Company sales had grown at an astonishing pace and so had profits. In year number 10, *Jill & Co.* had $1,250,000 in *earnings (net profits)* and $25,000,000 in *sales*.

However, the three sisters were very exhausted. They thought seriously about selling the company completely. So they put the word out in the retail/wholesale clothing community that they were interested in selling. Some of the larger clothing companies became sincerely interested in buying the company.

Towbin's, another extremely successful women's clothing company, was very interested.

Chapter Seven: Jill, Melva, and Anne Sell Their Company for $15,000,000

So, Towbin's made an offer. Jill, Melva, and Anne sold their company to Towbin's for a *price* of $15,000,000. In other words, each of the three shares of stock in *Jill & Co.* was worth $5,000,000. I'd say they did pretty well considering they purchased their first stock shares with only $5,000 each.

Here's a chart.

	1982 share price	1992 share price
Jill	$5,000	$5,000,000
Melva	$5,000	$5,000,000
Anne	$5,000	$5,000,000

What the Story of *Jill & Co.* Will Tell You About Shopping for Stocks

Why did I tell you this story? To get you familiar with the concepts that determine the *value* of a company, like profits, sales, and growth rate. When you are shopping for stocks, you have to put yourself in the position of Towbin's—the company that bought out *Jill & Co.* And you have to look at the price of *Jill & Co.* ($15,000,000) and determine if the sales and profits and other factors make the company *Jill & Co.* a good purchase. Let's take a look at *Jill & Co.* Once you can understand how to determine the value of this fictitious company, you can apply your new smarts to real ones and start making the big bucks.

SALES OR REVENUE

Sales is the same as *revenue*. Sales are reported in dollar figures. In the investment world, you say, "Jill's company had $40,000 in sales"—not "Jill's company sold 160 of those way cute pantsuits." Of course, it's the same thing. The fact is, if the pantsuits aren't way cute, they don't sell. But that's how sales is expressed.

What You Want the Sales of Your Company to Look Like

1. Generally speaking, you want to see a sales pattern that has begun to develop. If a company has healthy sales, it's an indication that at least the public wants its product.

Jill & Co. did grow from year to year very nicely. In year one they had $40,000 in sales, and in year 10 they had $25,000,000 in sales. In fact, if you do the math, you'll see that Jill & Co. had sales that went off the charts. Sales grew by 90% per year! That's a faster rate than Microsoft, which in 1999 posted an average sales growth rate 37.5% over the past ten years.

2. You want to see potential for future sales growth. Sure, you can buy a company with a *huge* number of sales, but unless the value of that company goes from huge to huger, your little slice of the company won't get any bigger and your stock won't grow.

While a lot of factors can determine future sales, looking at the kind of history Jill & Co. had can be very encouraging. After all, the growth of Jill & Co. sales could drop in half to a growth rate of 45%. That would still beat the sales growth rate of Microsoft. So the company has a lot of room for failure.

NET PROFITS OR "EARNINGS"

You'll want to look at the company's *earnings*, also known as *net profits*. This is the money left over after everything has been paid for: taxes, rent, salaries, contractors, everything. After ten years, Jill & Co. had $1,250,000 in earnings. Earnings are important because they show how much money the company is actually keeping at the end of the day.

What You Want the Earnings of Your Company to Look Like

As a potential owner of a company, or of a share of stock in a company, you want to see three things with respect to earnings:

1. You want to see net profits or earnings in the first place—or at least you don't want to see a company becoming less profitable. Neoprobe, the little company whose price was way out of line with its value, never posted any positive earnings.

2. You want to see a healthy pattern of earnings growth, proving the company can make a profit. Again, let's look at *Jill & Co.* The net profits for the sale of its clothing were $2,000 in 1982 and $1,250,000 in 1992. You do the math and realize net profits (or earnings) grew by 90%. Again, that beats Microsoft.

3. You want to see potential for earnings growth. As a prospective buyer of *Jill & Co*, you have to realize that growth like 90% per year might not be maintained, but even if it dropped from 90% to 35%, the company would still be a great buy. And you do have to think that as the company got bigger, it would be cheaper to make the clothes, because they could buy fabric in bulk and contract out in bulk. This is what economists call "economies of scale."

NET MARGINS

Net margin is a "bang for your buck" measurement. It's a way to measure how much Jill gets for what she gives. In year number 10, *Jill & Co.* had $1,250,000 in earnings (net profits) and $25,000,000 in sales. According to my calculator, that means that in 1992, for every $100 Jill received making and selling pantsuits, she took home $5. How did I figure that?

The Math:
$$\frac{\$1{,}250{,}000 \textbf{ (earnings)}}{\$25{,}000{,}000 \textbf{ (sales)}} = \frac{5}{100} = 5\% \textbf{ net margin}$$

While that's not a killing as net margins go, it's pretty healthy for the retail clothing industry. In 1998, Ann Taylor had a net margin of 4.6% and The Gap had a net margin of 9.1%. So at a 5% net margin, that's right in the range of two very successful retail clothing businesses.

What You Want the Net Margins of Your Company to Look Like

Generally, you want to see a company that has large net margins. Just to give you a reference point, the net margins of Microsoft run about 30% per year. The more bang for the buck that the company is getting, the better.

BOOK VALUE: A BENCHMARK FOR PRICE

As a prospective buyer of a company, it's generally a good idea for you to know how much the parts of the company would be worth if they had to be sold separately and right away. That's called the *book value*.

For example, say suddenly all three *Jill & Co.* sisters needed to stop working and liquidate the company. They needed to sell off the designs, the customer lists, the boutique owner lists and, of course, the clothes. All the fabric they had bought, whether or not it had been made into clothes, needed to be sold also. The warehouse, the front office, the computers, the fax machine—even the fire extinguishers and flower pots in the front of the showroom had to go.

Say the sisters completely liquidated their company in 1992—sold everything off piece by piece. They would have probably received something like $8,000,000 in cold, hard cash for all the different pieces of the company. That number is the book value. So *Jill & Co.* had a book value of $8,000,000.

What You Want the Book Value of Your Company to Look Like

Book value is a benchmark. Most companies are worth much more than their book value. Just as most things are greater than the sum of their parts. For example, the members of the band the Rolling Stones are worth more together as a band making songs and touring than each of them is worth separately.

Knowing a company's book value will help you determine if the company is priced right. It goes back to that question of *price* and *value*. It's a reference point—a benchmark—that gives you a sense of what a company is worth.

If a company is selling for its book value that means that nobody wants to buy the company—at least not as a whole. That could mean one of two things:

1. The company sucks. It's such a bad company that it should be scrapped and sold for parts. Everyone knows it—and now you know it, too.
2. The marketplace is stupid. Here's a perfectly good company, and nobody wants it. Kind of like stumbling across the most beautiful silk shirt ever on the sale rack for $5. You kind of have to pinch yourself before grabbing it and making a mad dash for the cash register.

PRICE: HOW MUCH THE MAJORITY OF PEOPLE ARE WILLING TO PAY FOR A COMPANY

What determines the price of a company? It's the same thing that determines the price of that black velvet holiday dress. Supply and demand. When you *demand* to buy that dress for $49.99 and the seller agrees to *supply* you with it for $49.99, you've reached a price of $49.99. It's not really any more complicated than that.

The same is true for a company that you want to buy. You are looking to buy a company whose price is in line with its value, according to your calculations.

What You Want to See in the Price of Your Company

You want to see whether the company is priced competitively. You'd do the same thing that you would do when looking to buy a dress. You compare and contrast. How does your company's sales, profits, and net margins compare to those of similar companies? Are they stronger or weaker than their peers?

PRICE-EARNINGS RATIO — THE SASSY STOCKBROKER TERM FOR "VALUE"

This rather scary term—the *P/E ratio*—is really another fancy way of finding out if the price of the company is in line with its value. You compare the price you would pay to buy the company to the years of earning profits it would take to reimburse yourself for that purchase. The *price-earnings ratio*, or *P/E* as it is called, simply denotes the number of years it takes for a company to earn back the money spent on its original purchase.

Say you bought a taxi for $20,000. Working weekends and nights, you net $10,000 per year by charging people for your taxi service. How many years would you have to be in business before you actually made back the original amount it cost to buy the company? Hey—you can do that in your head. You bought the taxi for $20,000. Two years of making $10,000 per year and you would have earned back the original amount that you paid for the cab.

How did you figure it out? You divided the original *price* of the cab ($20,000) by the *earnings* per year ($10,000) and you got two years.

$$\frac{\$20,000 \textit{ (price)}}{\$10,000 \textit{ (earnings)}} = \textbf{2 years}$$

The *P/E* of your taxicab is 2!

Let's go back to *Jill & Co.*

1992—Net Profits (Earnings) are $1,250,000
1992—Price is $15,000,000

So the buyer of *Jill & Co.* has to shell out $15,000,000 in *price* for the company. We know that *Jill & Co.* can *earn* a net profit of at least $1,250,000 a year. How many years would *Jill & Co.* have to earn $1,250,000 to pay for itself? The answer is 12 using the same simple math as above.

$$\frac{\$15,000,000 \textit{ (price)}}{\$1,250,000 \textit{ (earnings)}} = \textbf{12}$$

So you might think about buying *Jill & Co.* And you might think, hmmm, twelve years. That's a pretty long time, but that assumes that profits will stay static at $1,250,000. One look at the rate at which *Jill & Co.*'s profits grow, and it seems that they've gone up every year. So maybe profits will double or even triple over the next six years—and then the number of years it would take to buy back the company would be a lot fewer than twelve.

What You Want the P/E of Your Company to Look Like

This is a tough question. Some very respected money managers don't like to buy companies with a P/E of 17 or higher. They want to make sure they're not paying too much. A lower P/E will indicate that you are not paying too much.

Some money managers don't really care if the P/E of the company is high or not. For example, on September 3, 1999, Microsoft had a P/E of 65.1. That is, it's a very expensive stock to buy; but is it expensive because it's overpriced, or because it's valuable—and worth every penny? The key is to do the research, and look at a variety of factors, especially sales and earnings.

Now you know how to look at *Jill & Co.*'s earnings, sales, price, and price/earnings ratio. Those are the things that are going to help you determine if *Jill & Co.* has a price in line with its value, and whether or not you want to spend your hard-earned money on that company.

WHAT HAPPENS WHEN A COMPANY DECIDES TO "GO PUBLIC"?

When you look at the financial outlook for a company, the information on earnings and sales will also be expressed on a *per share basis*.

Let's say that Jill, Melva, and Anne agreed to "take their company public"—that is, sell their ownership of the company to the general public. Let's say they decided they would still run it, but would divide their three shares into 1,000,000 shares and make those shares available to the general public for sale.

Let's say they got together with an investment underwriter and agreed that the company could fetch a price of $15,000,000, if someone were to buy it. (The price that Towbin's offered to buy it for.)

Together with their underwriter, Melva, Anne, and Jill would conduct an *initial public offering (IPO)*. They would offer up 1,000,000 shares of their company. Because the entire company had a price tag of $15,000,000, each of those 1,000,000 shares would cost $15.

The Math: $\dfrac{\$15,000,000 \textbf{ (price of company)}}{1,000,000 \textbf{ (\# of shares)}} = \textbf{\$15 per share}$

As a public company, *Jill & Co.* ends up first costing the public $15 per share.

Here's something else important to note when a company goes public. All of its major numbers—*earnings, sales,* and *book value* get expressed on a *per-share basis*. In other words, the *Jill & Co.* company would be written up in the following way.

Earnings per share = $1.25 per share

$\dfrac{\$1,250,000 \textbf{ (earnings)}}{1,000,000 \textbf{ (\# of shares)}} = \textbf{\$1.25 earnings per share (eps)}$

Sales per share = $25 per share

$\dfrac{\$25,000,000 \textbf{ (sales)}}{1,000,000 \textbf{ (\# of shares)}} = \textbf{\$25 in sales per share}$

Book Value per share = $8 per share

$\dfrac{\$8,000,000 \textbf{ (book value)}}{1,000,000 \textbf{ (\# of shares)}} = \textbf{\$8 in book value per share}$

Nerd note: The price-earnings ratio and the net margin will be the same because both the numerator and the denominator will be divided by 1,000,000.

Check it out.

P/E Ratio

Price of full company	$\dfrac{\$15,000,000}{\$1,250,000} = 12$
Earnings of whole company	

Price per share	$\dfrac{\$15.00}{\$1.25} = 12$
Earnings per share	

Net Margin

Earnings of whole company	$\dfrac{\$1,250,000}{\$25,000,000} = \dfrac{5}{100} = 5\%$
Sales of whole company	

Earnings per share	$\dfrac{\$1.25}{\$25.00} = \dfrac{5}{100} = 5\%$
Sales per share	

SUMMARY

That was the first lesson in shopping for stocks. As you can see, you already have a knack for it. It really is just like shopping for anything else. All you have to look at is price and value. Are you ready to go shopping? Here is a brief review of the things that will determine the value of a company, below and a word to the wise about shopping for growth.

Sales—How many pantsuits or cars or scarves or toys the company sold, expressed as the total dollar figure of those sales. Not 100,000 of those way cute pantsuits—but $25,000,000 worth of those pantsuits, which is 100,000 x $250 per pantsuit, or $25,000,000.

Sales is also expressed on a per-share basis. In Jill's case, sales are $25 per share.

Earnings—Earnings are net profits. Don't let anyone tell you otherwise. Again, these are usually expressed as earnings per share.

Net Margin—The bang for the buck. Net profits expressed as a percentage of sales.

Price—What someone will pay for the company. Most of the time a company is listed as price per share.

Price-Earnings Ratio or P/E—The number of years it would take to make back the amount you originally paid for the company—given no growth in net profits. The math is the same whether it is expressed per-share or not.

Remember, what all these numbers give you is a way of measuring the data and interpreting it. What you are looking for basically is *growth*: growth of the sales of the company, growth of the net profits of the company, and consequently, growth of your piece of the pie. This style of investing—looking for growth in all areas—is called, guess what? *Growth investing.*

Looking for growth is only one style of investing. Some investors like to buy only stocks that have had some trouble and are consequently out of favor with the investing public. They believe that there is hidden value in the company, and that the company will turn around and become profitable, and they will have bought it cheap. This is called value investing. (When you are doing growth investing you are still looking for value, but it's not your primary focus.) So-called "value" investments are a little more complicated to spot, and you really have to know the industry to distinguish a company that's hit bottom and is going to turn around from a company that's hit bottom and is going to stay there. I'm not going to talk about how to spot value here. Talking about growth is good enough for now.

Let's hit the market.

Chapter Sixteen

How to Research Individual Stocks

Learn how to walk through the financials of a company like The Gap

Now you know what to look for when you buy stocks. But where do you get that kind of information?

I am going to tell you of two great places to get the numbers you need. One, called Value Line, is a print publication. It's in your public library. You can get a ten-week trial subscription for $50. The other, for all you Internet hounds, is the World Wide Web. There are several excellent web sites that will give you the facts and figures that you need (listed at the end of this chapter).

THE VALUE LINE INVESTMENT SURVEY

Value Line, Inc., is a financial publisher that provides research on stocks, bonds, and other financial instruments. Their Value Line Investment Survey is a great resource for beginning and expert stock pickers.

Value Line prints these great one-page summaries of over 6,000 companies. Each of those one-page summaries includes all the information discussed in the preceding chapter: *sales, net earnings, net margins, book value, price,* and *price-earnings ratio.* For 1,700 of the largest companies, Value Line also prints a 400–word analysis of the company in question, a ranking of the company's financial strength, and a prediction of how well the company will fare in the future.

Value Line is very handy. I like it *because* it is a print publication and I can thumb through the physical pages with my fingers. My eyes don't grow screen-weary and my mouse-clicking right hand doesn't start to ache. Also, I don't *have* to be online to look something up.

Below I give you an example of The Value Line Investment Survey of The Gap. Don't be spooked by all the teeny tiny numbers. Give them a chance. They tell a story similar to the story about *Jill & Co.* that I just told.

I've numbered key items of this data-filled sheet that you should pay attention to. Let me go over them.

1. Company name. This is important. Companies can sound alike and look alike. Be sure you've got the right one. Also in this area is the "ticker" symbol of the stock. If you want to look up a stock's price in the newspaper you will need the ticker symbol. See right there? It says "GAP, INC. (THE) NYSE-GPS." GPS is the ticker symbol.

2. Business Summary. This section describes what the company sells or manufactures. Subsidiaries of the company are also listed here. You can see here that it "operated 2611 casual apparel speciality stores." And you can see that The Gap owns Banana Republic, Old Navy, GapKids, and BabyGap in addition to its signature stores. The company's mailing address, phone number, and Web site are also listed here.

GAP, INC. (THE) NYSE-GPS

RECENT PRICE	**39**	
P/E RATIO	**32.5** (Trailing: 39.2 / Median: 19.0)	
RELATIVE P/E RATIO	**1.96**	
DIV'D YLD	**0.2%**	

TIMELINESS 2 Lowered 8/13/99

SAFETY 1 Raised 7/27/90

TECHNICAL 1 Lowered 8/6/99

BETA 1.35 (1.00 = Market)

2002-04 PROJECTIONS

	Price	Gain	Ann'l Total Return
High	70	(+80%)	16%
Low	45	(+15%)	4%

Insider Decisions

	S	O	N	D	J	F	M	A	M
to Buy	0	0	0	0	0	0	0	0	2
Options	0	0	2	0	2	0	3	0	0
to Sell	1	0	6	0	2	2	5	2	0

Institutional Decisions

	3Q1998	4Q1998	1Q1999
to Buy	190	233	247
to Sell	181	195	204
Hld'g(000)	418807	424621	420461

LEGENDS
— 14.0 x "Cash Flow" p sh
···· Relative Price Strength
2-for-1 split 1/86
2-for-1 split 8/86
2-for-1 split 10/90
2-for-1 split 7/91
3-for-2 split 4/96
3-for-2 split 12/97
3-for-2 split 12/98
3-for-2 split 6/99
Options: Yes
Shaded area indicates recession

Target Price Range 2002 2003 2004

% TOT. RETURN 7/99

	THIS STOCK	VL ARITH. INDEX
1 yr.	77.0	15.0
3 yr.	439.5	73.5
5 yr.	754.4	128.5

1983	1984	1985	1986	1987	1988	1989	1990	1991	1992	1993	1994	1995	1996	1997	1998	1999	2000	© VALUE LINE PUB., INC.	02-04
.52	.59	.68	.88	1.10	1.32	1.67	2.03	2.62	3.04	3.36	3.81	4.53	5.70	7.36	10.55	13.65	16.75	Sales per sh A	29.65
.03	.03	.05	.09	.10	.11	.15	.22	.32	.33	.41	.50	.57	.72	.91	1.34	1.70	2.15	"Cash Flow" per sh	3.85
.02	.01	.04	.07	.07	.08	.11	.15	.24	.22	.26	.33	.36	.47	.58	.91	1.20	1.45	Earnings per sh B	2.70
..	..	.01	.01	.02	.02	.03	.03	.04	.05	.06	.07	.07	.09	.09	.09	.09	.09	Div'ds Decl'd per sh C	.15
.13	.14	.16	.22	.28	.29	.36	.49	.70	.91	1.15	1.41	1.69	1.79	1.79	1.83	2.25	3.15	Book Value per sh	7.35
919.80	911.79	947.98	960.42	968.49	948.55	948.72	953.53	962.03	973.25	980.43	977.16	971.15	926.50	884.55	857.96	845.00	830.00	Common Shs Outst'g D	810.00
11.7	14.5	9.2	18.5	24.4	14.6	15.8	14.7	23.6	25.0	18.8	17.9	15.0	19.0	22.3	29.2	Bold figures are		Avg Ann'l P/E Ratio	21.0
.99	1.35	.75	1.26	1.63	1.21	1.20	1.09	1.51	1.52	1.11	1.17	1.00	1.19	1.29	1.53	Value Line estimates		Relative P/E Ratio	1.40
1.4%	2.4%	1.5%	.9%	1.1%	1.8%	1.5%	1.5%	.8%	.9%	1.1%	1.2%	1.1%		.7%	.3%			Avg Ann'l Div'd Yield	.3%

CAPITAL STRUCTURE as of 7/31/99

Total Debt $955.8 mill. Due in 5 Yrs $300.0 mill.
LT Debt $542.3 mill. LT Interest $35.0 mill.

(22% of Cap'l)

Leases, Uncapitalized Annual rentals $511.3 mill.
Pension Liability None—no defined benefit plan
Pfd Stock None

Common Stock 1,250 shs. (78% of Cap'l)
as of 5/29/99
adjusted for 3-for-2 stock split that took place 6/21/99

MARKET CAP: $33.4 billion (Large Cap)

CURRENT POSITION

	1997	1998	7/31/99
Cash Assets	913.2	565.3	435.9
Receivables	.1	..	..
Inventory (FIFO)	733.1	1056.4	1502.3
Other	184.5	250.1	283.2
Current Assets	1830.9	1871.8	2221.4
Accts Payable	417.0	684.1	1372.0
Debt Due	84.8	90.7	413.5
Other	489.7	778.3	57.5
Current Liab.	991.5	1553.1	1843.0

ANNUAL RATES

of change (per sh)	Past 10 Yrs.	Past 5 Yrs.	Est'd '96-'98 to '02-'04
Sales	21.0%	24.5%	
"Cash Flow"	22.5%	25.5%	
Earnings	24.5%	22.0%	26.5%
Dividends	18.0%	12.5%	9.0%
Book Value	21.0%	14.5%	26.5%

QUARTERLY SALES ($ mill.) A

Fiscal Year Begins	Apr.Per	Jul.Per	Oct.Per	Dec.Per	Full Fiscal Year
1996	1113.2	1120.3	1383.0	1667.9	5284.4
1997	1231.2	1345.2	1765.9	2165.5	6507.8
1998	1719.7	1905.0	2400.0	3029.8	9054.5
1999	2278.0	2453.0	3000	3799	11530
2000	2750	2950	3600	4600	13900

EARNINGS PER SHARE A B

Fiscal Year Begins	Apr.Per	Jul.Per	Oct.Per	Dec.Per	Full Fiscal Year
1996	.08	.07	.14	.18	.47
1997	.09	.08	.18	.24	.58
1998	.15	.15	.27	.35	.91
1999	.22	.22	.33	.43	1.20
2000	.27	.25	.40	.53	1.45

QUARTERLY DIVIDENDS PAID C

Cal- endar	Mar.31	Jun.30	Sep.30	Dec.31	Full Year
1995	.018	.018	.018	.018	.07
1996	.022	.022	.022	.022	.09
1997	.022	.022	.022	.022	.09
1998	.022	.022	.022	.022	.09
1999	.022	.022			

1586.6	1933.8	2518.9	2960.4	3295.7	3722.9	4395	6507.8	9054.5	11530	13900	Sales ($mill) A	24000
36.8%	39.0%	41.0%	37.8%	39.9%	41.4%	40.7%	42.3%	44.9%	44.8%	44.6%	Gross Margin	44.5%
13.6%	15.5%	18.1%	15.5%	17.2%	18.4%	17.4%	17.9%	17.2%	18.3%	18.3%	18.3%	Operating Margin	18.5%
960	1092	1216	1307	1307	1508	1680	1370	2130	2426	2875	3325	Number of Stores	4750
104.1	144.5	229.9	210.7	258.4	320.2	354.0	452.9	533.9	824.5	1065	1265	Net Profit ($mill)	2250
40.0%	39.0%	38.0%	38.0%	38.0%	39.2%	39.5%	39.5%	30.5%	37.5%	37.5%	37.5%	Income Tax Rate	37.5%
6.6%	7.5%	9.1%	7.1%	7.8%	8.6%	8.1%	8.6%	8.2%	9.1%	9.2%	9.1%	Net Profit Margin	9.4%
129.1	101.8	235.6	354.7	494.2	555.8	728.4	554.4	839.4	318.7	250	430	Working Cap'l ($mill)	2000
17.5	5.0	77.5	75.0	75.0	..	..	..	496.0	496.5	550	500	Long-Term Debt ($mill)	500
338.0	465.7	677.8	887.8	1126.5	1375.2	1640.5	1654.5	1584.0	1573.7	1925	2635	Shr. Equity ($mill)	5950
29.6%	30.9%	30.9%	22.2%	21.5%	23.3%	21.6%	27.4%	25.7%	40.0%	44.0%	41.0%	Return on Total Cap'l	35.0%
30.8%	31.0%	33.9%	23.7%	22.9%	23.3%	21.6%	27.4%	33.7%	52.4%	55.8%	48.0%	Return on Shr. Equity	38.0%
24.0%	24.7%	27.8%	18.8%	18.2%	18.6%	17.5%	22.3%	28.7%	47.5%	51.5%	44.5%	Retained to Com Eq	36.0%
22%	20%	18%	21%	21%	20%	19%	15%	9%	7%	7%		All Div'ds to Net Prof	5%

BUSINESS: The Gap, Inc. operated 2,611 casual apparel specialty stores with 20.4 million square feet of selling space as of 7/31/99. Gap (1,163 stores) sells updated classics, all include BabyGap depts.) sell jeans, sweatshirts, shirts, sweaters, and other casual apparel. Banana Republic (307 stores) sells upscale casual wear. Old Navy division (442 stores) sells budget-priced casual clothing. All merchandise is private label. Has 331 Gap, GapKids, and Banana Republic foreign units, mostly in Can., U.K., and France. Has about 111,000 empls., 6,645 stkhlds. Off. & dir. own 28.4% of stock John Fisher, 5.9% (4/99 proxy). Chrmn.: Donald G. Fisher. C.E.O. & Pres.: Millard S. Drexler. Inc.: DE. Addr.: One Harrison St., San Francisco, CA 94105. Tel.: 415-952-4400. Internet: www.gap.com.

The Gap's stock has had a rough time as of late. The company's strong performance in fiscal 1998 (which ended January 30, 1999) has made same-store sales comparisons difficult thus far this year. As such, GPS's same-store sales results have fallen somewhat from the lofty levels reached in fiscal 1998. In response to this slight deceleration, investors have begun to take some profits. After hitting a 52-week high at the beginning of July, the issue has retreated close to 25%. Still, the shares are up nearly 50% in the past year, and 150% since the beginning of 1998. This price momentum, coupled with GPS' strong earnings performance during the period, has garnered the stock a 2 (Above Average) Timeliness ranking.

The company's operations continue to perform very well. Despite the tough same-store sales comparisons, "comp" are up 10%, year to date. And total revenues have increased 31%, driven by the "comp" increase and GPS' store expansion program (discussed below). On the expense side, management's aggressive advertising budget and the increased contribution from the lower-margined Old Navy stores have kept overall margins relatively level. All told, we expect earnings to approach $1.20 a share in fiscal 1999, about a 30% year-over-year improvement. (All per-share numbers are adjusted for the 3-for-2 stock split that took place June 21st.)

The Gap is aggressively adding to its store base. Management plans to add close to 450 new stores this year. The greatest percentage increase in stores will be in the Old Navy format. Beyond this year, the number of new stores opened will be based on 20% square footage growth.

The long-term outlook appears bright. We expect management's newer initiatives (Gapbody and e-commerce) and its store expansion plans, both in the United States and abroad, to help generate revenue gains of about 20% annually out to 2002-2004. This growth, combined with some additional share repurchases, should result in average annual share-net gains of close to 25% during the period. However, **the generally stellar performance of this issue over the past 18 months appears to have discounted some of the long-term gains we foresee.**

Bryan W. Keane   August 20, 1999

(A) Fiscal year ends Sat. closest to Jan. 31.
(B) Diluted earnings. Excludes loss on discontinued operations: '85, 2¢; '89, 2¢. '97 & '98 earnings do not add due to change in shares outstanding. Next earnings report due about mid-Nov. (C) Next dividend meeting about Nov. 19th. Next ex-date about Dec. 8th. Dividend payment dates: about Mar. 18, June 13, Sept. 12, Dec. 27. (D) In millions, adjusted for stock splits. (E) 7/31/99 accounts payable includes accrued expenses.

Company's Financial Strength	A+
Stock's Price Stability	35
Price Growth Persistence	70
Earnings Predictability	70

© 1999, Value Line Publishing, Inc. All rights reserved. Factual material is obtained from sources believed to be reliable and is provided without warranties of any kind. THE PUBLISHER IS NOT RESPONSIBLE FOR ANY ERRORS OR OMISSIONS HEREIN. This publication is strictly for subscriber's own, non-commercial, internal use. No part of it may be reproduced, stored or transmitted in any printed, electronic or other form, or used for generating or marketing any printed or electronic publication, service or product.

To subscribe call 1-800-833-0046.

1 — Name of the Company

GAP, INC. (THE) NYSE-GPS

The Stock Exchange

Ticker Symbol

2 Business Summary

BUSINESS: The Gap, Inc. operated 2,611 casual apparel specialty stores with 20.4 million square feet of selling space as of 7/31/99. *Gap* (1,163 stores) and *GapKids* (699 stores, all include *BabyGap* depts.) sell jeans, sweatsuits, shirts, sweaters, and other casual apparel. *Banana Republic* (307 stores) sells upscale casual wear. *Old Navy* division (442 stores) sells budget-priced casual clothing. All merchandise is private label. Has 331 *Gap, GapKids,* and *Banana Republic* foreign units, mostly in Can., U.K., and France. Has about 111,000 empls., 6,645 stkhldrs. Off. & dir. own 28.4% of stock John Fisher, 5.9% (4/99 proxy). Chrmn.: Donald G. Fisher. C.E.O. & Pres.: Millard S. Drexler. Inc.: DE. Addr.: One Harrison St., San Francisco, CA 94105. Tel.: 415-952-4400. Internet: www.gap.com.

3 Annual Rates

ANNUAL RATES	Past	Past	Est'd '96-'98
of change (per sh)	10 Yrs.	5 Yrs.	to '02-'04
Sales	22.0%	21.0%	24.5%
"Cash Flow"	26.0%	22.5%	25.5%
Earnings	24.5%	22.0%	26.5%
Dividends	18.0%	12.5%	9.0%
Book Value	21.0%	14.5%	26.5%

CAPITAL STRUCTURE as of 7/31/99
Total Debt $955.8 mill.   **Due in 5 Yrs** $500.0 mill.
LT Debt $542.3 mill.   **LT Interest** $35.0 mill.

(22% of Cap'l)

Leases, Uncapitalized Annual rentals $511.3 mill.
Pension Liability None—no defined benefit plan
Pfd Stock None

Common Stock 857,493,260 shs.   (78% of Cap'l)
as of 5/29/99
adjusted for 3-for-2 stock split that took place 6/21/99
MARKET CAP: $33.4 billion (Large Cap)

4 Market Capitalization

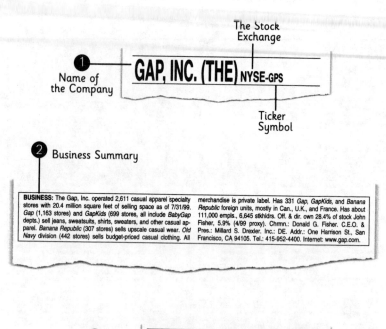

3. Annual Rates. The third item I look for is this tidy little box called "Annual Rates." Remember, when you invest in a company by buying stock, you want that company to grow. When the company grows, your stock becomes more valuable. So understanding how quickly a company has grown in all the vital areas, such as sales, earnings, and book value, can tell you if your company is a fast grower or a slow grower.

This little box basically shows you how much the company has grown in the past five years and ten years. The good people at Value Line also come up with a prediction of what growth rates will be in the next two to five years. No, they are not clairvoyant. But using company estimates, overall industry data, and the company's current financial situation, they make an educated guess.

This is some of the best information on the entire Value Line page. Why? Because by looking at this little box, you will immediately be able to see if your company looks like I told you it ought to look. Let's look here at the *earnings* growth rate for The Gap. Wow. In the past ten years, earnings (i.e. net profits) have grown by 24.5%, and the folks at Value Line think that they will be even higher in the next two years. Same with *sales*. Sales have grown at a rate of 22% per year over the past ten years, and the folks at Value Line predict that they will grow by 24.5% per year in the next two years. This is darn good. (No wonder the company gets an A+ in "financial strength.")

In general, *high numbers* and *estimate of high numbers* in this area means that your company is *growing* in value. Hence, your stock, your little piece of the company, will be growing in value, too—with luck, by the same amount.

One important thing to note is that companies with high projected growth rates are very popular. Everyone wants a piece of the action. Everyone wants to own part of a company that's going to grow a lot. So sometimes people bid the price of a stock way way up. To super-high levels.

That's where the *price-earnings ratio* comes in. If the P/E is around 100—that's an awfully long time to wait for your company to just net the money you spent to buy it. You might want to wait until the price comes down a bit.

4. Market capitalization. Market capitalization tells you how much the overall company would cost if someone were to buy up every last one of its shares. This line item gives you an indication of how large a company is. The very general rule is that giant huge companies like GE and AT&T don't grow as fast as little companies, but they are so big they have many more resources that will help them through bad times. The Gap, at a market capitalization of $33.4 billion, is a "large cap" company (i.e., has a large total market value or capitalization).

5. Financial Strength. Next, I like to look at the bottom right corner to see what kind of grade the folks at Value Line have given a company for financial strength. A financially healthy company is more likely to be able to weather bad times and take advantage of good ones. As mentioned above, The Gap got an A+. A company's financial strength accounts for a combination of things including debt, sales, earnings, and future prospects. The Gap looks great.

6. Company Statistics. Then I like to skip up to the middle of the page and look at those rows and rows of little tiny numbers. On the right-hand side, you can see what those little numbers are for: sales, earnings per share, net profit, etc. They simply post data from previous years. (While this information is interesting, remember it's the overall growth of the company that tells the real story, and that's in the "annual rates" box.)

5 Financial Strength

6 Company Statistics

1989	1990	1991	1992	1993	1994	1995	1996	1997	1998	1999	2000	© VALUE LINE PUB., INC.	02-04
1.67	2.03	2.62	3.04	3.36	3.81	4.53	5.70	7.36	10.55	13.65	16.75	Sales per sh ᴬ	29.65
.15	.22	.32	.33	.41	.50	.57	.72	.91	1.34	1.70	2.15	"Cash Flow"per sh	3.85
.11	.15	.24	.22	.26	.33	.36	.47	.58	.91	1.20	1.45	Earnings per sh ᴮ	2.70
.03	.03	.04	.05	.06	.07	.07	.09	.09	.09	.09	.09	Div'ds Decl'd per sh ᶜ	.15
.36	.49	.70	.91	1.15	1.41	1.69	1.79	1.79	1.83	2.25	3.15	Book Value per sh	7.35
948.72	953.53	962.03	973.25	980.43	977.16	971.15	926.50	884.55	857.96	845.00	830.00	Common Shs Outst'g ᴰ	810.00
15.8	14.7	23.6	25.0	18.8	17.9	15.0	19.0	22.3	29.2	Bold figures are		Avg Ann'l P/E Ratio	21.0
1.20	1.09	1.51	1.52	1.11	1.17	1.00	1.19	1.29	1.53	Value Line		Relative P/E Ratio	1.40
1.5%	1.5%	.8%	.9%	1.1%	1.2%	1.3%	1.0%	.7%	.3%	estimates		Avg Ann'l Div'd Yield	.3%
1586.6	1933.8	2518.9	2960.4	3295.7	3722.9	4395.3	5284.4	6507.8	9054.5	11530	13900	Sales ($mill) ᴬ	24000
36.6%	39.0%	41.0%	37.8%	39.9%	41.4%	40.3%	41.9%	42.3%	44.9%	44.8%	44.6%	Gross Margin	44.5%
13.6%	15.5%	18.1%	15.5%	17.2%	18.4%	17.4%	17.9%	17.2%	18.3%	18.3%	18.3%	Operating Margin	18.5%
960	1092	1216	1307	1307	1508	1680	1370	2130	2428	2875	3325	Number of Stores	4750
104.1	144.5	229.9	210.7	258.4	320.2	354.0	452.9	533.9	824.5	1065	1265	Net Profit ($mill)	2250
40.0%	39.0%	38.0%	38.0%	39.2%	39.5%	39.5%	39.5%	37.5%	37.5%	37.5%	37.5%	Income Tax Rate	37.5%
6.6%	7.5%	9.1%	7.1%	7.8%	8.6%	8.1%	8.6%	8.2%	9.1%	9.2%	9.1%	Net Profit Margin	9.4%
129.1	101.6	235.6	355.7	494.2	555.8	728.4	554.4	839.4	318.7	250	430	Working Cap'l ($mill)	2000
17.5	5.0	77.5	75.0	75.0	--	--	--	496.0	496.5	550	500	Long-Term Debt ($mill)	500
338.0	465.7	677.8	887.8	1126.5	1375.2	1640.5	1654.5	1584.0	1573.7	1925	2635	Shr. Equity ($mill)	5950
29.6%	30.9%	30.9%	22.2%	21.5%	23.3%	21.6%	27.4%	25.7%	40.0%	44.0%	41.0%	Return on Total Cap'l	35.0%
30.8%	31.0%	33.9%	23.7%	22.9%	23.3%	21.6%	27.4%	33.7%	52.4%	55.5%	48.0%	Return on Shr. Equity	38.0%
24.0%	24.7%	27.8%	18.8%	18.2%	18.6%	17.5%	22.3%	28.7%	47.5%	51.5%	44.5%	Retained to Com Eq	36.0%
22%	20%	18%	21%	21%	20%	19%	19%	15%	9%	7%	7%	All Div'ds to Net Prof	5%

7 Recent Price

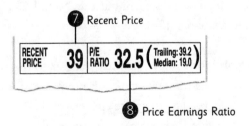

| RECENT PRICE | 39 | P/E RATIO | 32.5 | (Trailing: 39.2 / Median: 19.0) |

8 Price Earnings Ratio

One of the more telling numbers (and one that isn't in the annual ratio box) is the company's *net margin*. Again, this is the "bang for the buck" number. It shows how many dollars of sales are actually coming back into the company as profits.

The Gap has a net margin of around 9%. That's okay, but it's nothing compared to, well, Microsoft. It means that The Gap gets to keep $9 of every $100 it makes. The rest goes to cover costs. Imagine how healthy the company would be, and how much faster it could grow if they kept $35 for every $100 it made?

7. Recent Price. Go back to the very top of the page and look at the row of numbers next to the company name. The first one is the "recent price" of the stock of the company. The price of the stock of the company changes every day, every hour and almost every minute as shares are bought and sold. So it's always wise to check this number against the price of the stock in the morning paper or on the Internet. "Recent price" on Value Line is always dated on the printed Value Line page.

The price of The Gap stock is $39. That doesn't tell you a whole lot, though, because remember, companies like to keep their stock prices in bite-size ranges. If the price of The Gap stock grew to $150 per share, each share would likely "split" in half. There would be twice as many shares then, but they would each cost only $75. That's a little more bite-size.

8. Price-earnings Ratio. The next number to the right of "recent price" is the *price-earnings ratio*. This number will shift almost daily as well, simply because the price element of the price-earnings ratio changes every day. Remember, this number tells you how many years it would take to make back the money spent purchasing it.

The P/E of The Gap in this instance is 32.5. That may seem like a long time, but again, you need to look at the overall picture. If the company generates more and more profits each year, the earnings (net profits) will not remain at $824 million. They will grow every year. So if you were going to buy the whole company, it would take you significantly less than 32.5 years to earn back the money that you spent to buy it. A high annual rate of earnings growth can account for a high P/E.

9. Analysis. After looking at the "numbers," it's time to put some meat on those bones. Look down the page to the 400-word analysis of how the company is faring and will fare. This mini-article on the company is prepared by a researcher at Value Line. One researcher will usually cover companies in related industries to get a good idea of how competitive a company is.

This particular mini-article reviews some of the numbers that appear on the rest of the page and comments on the likelihood of future growth for The Gap. It also mentions qualitative information that the numbers can't tell you. For example, this article reviews store expansion information, plans to build The Gap brand name abroad, plans to open more GapBody (intimate apparel) stores, and plans to market Gap clothes over the Web. Finally, the mini-article comments on the relationship of the "price" of The Gap stock to its "value." The article reads:

> The generally stellar performance of this issue over the past 18 months appears to have discounted some of the long-term gains we foresee.

What that investment-speak means is, "You aren't the only one that noticed how yummy this stock looked with its very healthy

The Gap's stock has had a rough time as of late. The company's strong performance in fiscal 1998 (which ended January 30, 1999) has made same-store sales comparisons difficult for this year. As such, GPS's same-store sales results have fallen somewhat from the lofty levels reached in fiscal 1998. In response to this slight deceleration, investors have begun to take some profits. After hitting a 52-week high at the beginning of July, the issue has retreated close to 25%. Still, these shares are up nearly 50% in the past year, and 150% since the beginning of 1998. This price momentum, coupled with GPS' strong earnings performance during the period, has garnered the stock a 2 (Above Average) Timeliness ranking.

The company's operations continue to perform very well. Despite the tough same-store sales comparisons, "comps" are up 10%, year to date. And total revenues have increased 31%, driven by the "comp" increase and GPS' store expansion program (discussed below). On the expense side, management's aggressive advertising budget and the increased contribution from the lower-margined *Old Navy* stores

have kept overall margins relatively level. All told, we expect earnings to approach $1.20 a share in fiscal 1999, about a 30% year-over-year improvement. *(All per-share numbers are adjusted for the 3-for-2 stock split that took place June 21st.)*

The Gap is aggressively adding to its store base. Management plans to add close to 450 new stores this year. The greatest percentage increase in stores will be in the *Old Navy* format. Beyond this year, the number of new stores opened will be based on 20% square footage growth.

The long-term outlook appears bright. We expect management's newer initiatives (*Gapbody* and e-commerce) and its store expansion plans, both in the United States and abroad, to help generate revenue gains of about 20% annually out to 2002-2004. This growth, combined with some additional share repurchases, should result in average annual share-net gains of close to 25% during the period. However, **the generally stellar performance of this issue over the past 18 months appears to have discounted some of the long-term gains we foresee.**

Bryan W. Keane   August 20, 1999

⑩ Timeliness Rank
(Value Line's own ranking system)

TIMELINESS	2	Lowered 8/13/99
SAFETY	3	New 7/27/90
TECHNICAL	2	Lowered 8/6/99
BETA 1.35	(1.00 = Market)	

annual growth rates and financial strength of A+. The other investors have noticed it, too—and bid up the price accordingly—so you may get that future growth but you'll have already paid for a lot of it." That's basically the same information that you can glean by looking at the P/E of The Gap and at the annual growth rates.

10. Timeliness. One of the last things I look at on this Value Line page is the stock's "Timeliness" ranking. This ranking is a proprietary ranking that the folks at Value Line have made up and have been using for years. The "Timeliness" rank goes from 1 to 5—with 1 being the best. It's Value Line's best indicator of whether the stock is a good buy. As you can see, The Gap got a ranking of "2." The Timeliness ranking is created by factoring a company's earnings history, earnings projections, and financial strength.

11. Stock High and Low. The last thing that I look at on a Value Line page is the actual price of the stock and how it has fared over time. The "recent price" box will tell you the price the stock was at the date at the bottom of the page; but in the little boxes below that first line, Value Line records how high the stock has gone each year and how low it has gone each year. Below that, they include a chart indicating that The Gap sold for $39 per share on August 20, 1999, and that in 1999, The Gap had a high of 52.7 and a low of 35.2.

That's my bare-bones outline of stuff that you should look for 52.7 on a Value Line page. As you can see, while my checklist covers some important fundamentals, it does not cover lots of other information on that stacked page. All of that other information is also interesting, so if you're not overloaded already, I urge you to review it. If you don't understand it, you can refer to Value Line's guide book that goes along with the Value Line publication, called "How to Invest in Common Stocks: the Complete Guide to Using the Value Line Investment Survey."

All of this information is also available on CD-ROM and will be available on the Web. You will probably have to pay a subscription fee similar to the one for the print publication before you can access the entire one-page summary of a stock.

11 High and Low for the Year (adjusted for stock splits)

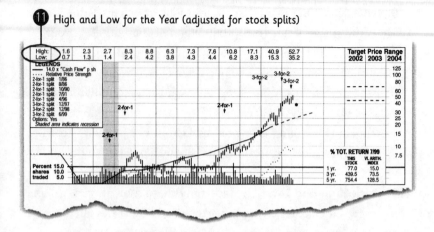

As you begin your foray into investing, I highly recommend that you drop $50 on a ten-week subscription to the Value Line Investment Survey. I'm not on the payroll of Value Line, nor do I own stock in it, I just think that it's a great way to get familiar with the process of scanning a company's numbers.

Once you know how to research a stock, you'll be able to check up on all those possible great buys that you come across every day. You'll be able to research that stock that Uncle Marty says is a "sure winner." You'll be able to *see* whether it makes sense to buy a stock or not, and you won't have to just "hope" that Uncle Marty is right.

WEB SITES

There are many financial Web sites, and more and more seem to be popping up each day. The Web sites are particularly helpful if you are looking up an obscure or tiny stock that trades on the NAS-DAQ.

Currently, my favorite Web site is the Hoovers web page (http://www.hoovers.com). In my humble opinion, it's the most comprehensive, user-friendly Web site out there for researching stocks. A lot of information on that Web site is free, but some of the historical, in-depth information about companies is for "members only." I am a member of Hoovers.com and access that site often to check information or background on a company. It's cheap to be a member—less than $20 per month.

Another excellent Web site is The Motley Fool (http://www.fool.com). This site has great educational material and whimsical wisdom.

Other useful Web sites include the following sites.

Morningstar	www.morningstar.com
Yahoo! Finance	quote.yahoo.com
Big Charts	www.bigcharts.com
Dow Jones	www.dowjones.com
Nasdaq	www.nasdaq.com
Value Line	www.valueline.com

How to Make a
Profit
While Making a
Difference

Chapter Seventeen

How to Invest Without Checking Your Values at the Door

You recycle your cans and bottles. You feel a horrible pang of guilt if the wind grabs your napkin and whirls it across the street, causing you to litter. Factories belching out thick black smoke tend to bum you out. As a rule, you think children should be in school, not sewing stripes on BrandName sneakers fourteen hours a day for pennies an hour. Hey—you are a stand-up kind of gal.

Well, time was, when you invested your money you had to check your values at the door. But no more. "Socially responsible" investing has arrived. And no—you don't have to "give up" the handsome return you could get by just plain old "give me the money" investing.

WHAT IS SOCIALLY RESPONSIBLE INVESTING?

"Socially responsible investing" is simply investing while keeping your values in mind. Yes, the definition of "socially responsible" will vary from person to person, just as individual morals and values vary from person to person. For example, you may be concerned about pollution problems and fair pay for minorities and women;

your sister could be very serious about animal rights; your brother, who is an aspiring Olympian, can't stand the smell or sight of cigarettes. Finally, your best friend's Aunt Mary may be a devout Catholic and only want to invest her money in line with the teachings of the Catholic Church.

In the socially responsible investing world, there are mutual fund managers who must consider such "ethical" criteria when they are investing. How do they do this?

First, the fund manager scouts out companies that she believes will match the financial goals of the fund. For example, if the mandate of the fund is to find small companies that will grow quickly, then those are the companies that the fund manager seeks out. If the goal of the fund is growth and income, then the fund manager will choose mature companies that pay out a dividend.

After these companies are chosen on a financial basis, they go through a second "screening." In this case, the fund manager can choose to exclude certain companies or include certain companies because of the nature and behavior of the company. Because people have different values and therefore different investing needs, there are different types of "socially responsible" mutual funds. I will try to give a broad overview.

"STRAIGHT-UP GOOD GUYS"

This is a catch-all phrase that I've invented. It generally describes funds that:

1. Exclude companies that make their profits by investing in alcohol, tobacco, or gambling, or that have more than 2% of their overall business in military contracting. (Because socially responsible investing on a broad scale started with church money, so-called "sin" stocks [alcohol, tobacco, gambling] are avoided, as are corporations that produce weapons and other means of violence.)

2. Exclude companies that have extremely poor environmental, labor, human rights, or product safety records. (No willful polluters, union busters, or makers of cars that explode when you hit the bumper.)

3. Include companies that have particularly progressive environmental or labor and human rights records.

4. Include companies that may get black marks in some areas of concern, either the environment or labor and human rights, but have been responsive to shareholder activism or simple pressure from mutual fund managers to clean up their act.

"Good guy" mutual fund managers are painfully aware that there are no perfect companies out there, and the bigger the corporation is, the more likely it is to have *some* problems in *some* areas. For example, Merck Co. was cited as one of the ten best places to work by *Working Mother Magazine*, ten years running. The company has on-site child care and has backup care at three locations. Alternative schedules such as telecommuting, job sharing, flextime, and compressed work weeks are available to employees. The company has a very generous pension plan. The company also has some innovative environmental programs.

However, on the down side, Merck has had environmental troubles. According to a report issued by Kinder, Lydenberg and Domini, Merck was potentially the responsible party in twelve Superfund sites (data obtained from the EPA). The report also referred to EPA's 1995 data showing that Merck's Barceloneta facility was the fifth largest emitter of toxic chemicals in Puerto Rico.

Mutual fund managers have to make a choice when reviewing a company that has a mixed track record like this one. Is the company moving ahead in the right direction? Is it responsive to inquiries about its problems? Or does management arrogantly refuse to acknowledge that there are problems? If the management of the company refuses to acknowledge or deal with problems, it is likely that the "straight-up good guy" mutual fund managers will simply sell the stock.

The final tool that a mutual fund manager has for a not-so-great company is voting rights. When a mutual fund manager buys stock in a company that ownership entitles the manager to certain limited voting rights. The fund manager can then vote to change company environmental policy or employment practices. They can even ask that issues be put up for a vote. This is called a shareholder resolution, and mutual fund managers have sponsored many of them over the years. When voting, the mutual fund manager will vote on company-wide policy consistent with the social and economic goals of the fund. (Note: if you want to see what this looks like, the Domini Social Equity Index Fund posts its voting practices on its Web site, www.domini.com.)

So—I'm sure you want to know—who are these straight-up good guy funds? You can get an excellent, up-to-date list by checking out the Web site www.SocialFunds.com—with links to the actual mutual funds. But here's a partial list.

Fund Name	Three-year annualized return	Five-year annualized return	Notes:
Bridgeway Social Responsibility	37.14%	31.11%	
Calvert Social Equity A	17.69%	19.00%	
Citizens Emerging Growth	41.33%	35.25%	
Citizens Index Fund	34.92%	N/A	Invests in an index of 300 companies (200 overlap with S&P 500)
Devcap Shared Return	29.16%	28.37%	Allows investors to automatically donate returns to projects in developing nations
Domini Social Equity Index Fund	30.42%	29.58%	
Dreyfus Third Century	29.90%	29.92%	
Green Century Equity	29.86%	N/A	Invests in the Domini Social Equity Index—percentage of management fee goes to environmental advocacy work
IPS Millennium	55.01%	N/A	Strong focus on technology products. Focus on animal rights. No companies using animals for testing or experimentation. No tobacco, poultry, or fertilizer companies.
Neuberger Berman Socially Responsive	15.27%	20.32%	
Parnassus Fund	24.78%	16.90%	

Source: www.SocialFunds.com. All statistics as of December 31, 1999.

You get the idea. There are a lot to choose from. The good news is that most of these funds are competitive and have fared well compared to the S&P 500 Index.

Moreover, although the company selection criteria are similar from fund to fund, there are differences. Some focus on animal rights. Some do not. Some avoid nuclear power. Some do not. Some of them are no-load funds and some of them you can buy through a full-service broker. (For a greater description of some of the ethical criteria managers of socially responsible mutual funds use, see Appendix IV.)

SPECIALTY SOCIALLY RESPONSIBLE FUNDS

This is a phrase I've invented to deal with funds I couldn't lump into the previous category. These mutual funds pay extra special attention to the advancement of women and minorities, or are designed to reflect the values of a certain religious group or a certain principled agenda.

Examples of these funds follow:

Fund	Fund Directive	Three-year return	Five-year return
Women's Equity Mutual Fund	Invests in companies that advance the social and economic status of women in the work place. Does not invest in companies that have patterns of discrimination or that sell products that adversely affect women.	21.49%	19.15%
Meyers Pride Value	Invests in companies identified as generally having progressive policies toward gays and lesbians.	21.09%	N/A

Fund	Fund Directive	Three-year return	Five-year return
Amana Growth Fund	Invests according to Islamic principles—no liquor, wine, casinos, pornography, gambling. No non-Islamic banks.	40.15%	30.83%
Catholic Values Investment Trust	Invests in companies with products or services that are consistent with the core teachings of the Roman Catholic faith.	Fund is new. Has not been around for three years.	N/A

Source: www.SocialFunds.com. All statistics from 12/31/99.

You can find out much more about each fund by getting on the Internet and doing a little research. Just go to www.social funds.com, click on the fund, hit its Web page, and start reading. You'll want to check out the company's annual report or prospectus. No Web access? Not to worry. You can get the phone number of the company from either a discount broker or full-service broker. Then call the company and ask for them to mail you a prospectus and an annual report.

INVESTING IN A SOCIALLY RESPONSIBLE MANNER IF YOU ONLY OWN INDIVIDUAL STOCKS

If you are inclined to do your own stock picking, you can still keep your values aligned with your stock choices. You can do this in any of the following three ways.

1. You can avoid companies that you don't like. For example, you could refuse to buy stock in corporations that sell cigarettes, or that have a track record of dumping toxins into the water supply. (In Appendix V, I have provided resources that can help you find out this information.)

2. You can buy companies that you do like. For example, you can buy stock in companies that have state-of-the-art pollution prevention programs or very family-friendly benefit policies. (See Appendix V for how to find these companies.)

3. You can buy stock in companies that have a mixed track record and urge them to change their evil ways by casting your vote on company policy.

Yes, *you* can do this. It's called voting your proxy. When you buy a piece of a company, you then also own the right to vote on certain company policies—just like a mutual fund manager has these rights.

For example, if you had owned shares of Home Depot stock in the summer of 1999, you would have received a ballot in the mail. There were seven issues up for a vote by all the shareholders. Most of them were non-controversial. But one of them stated that Home Depot should stop buying timber cut from old growth forests. And right then and there, you could have checked off "yes" and mailed your ballot back to the company. Radical, huh? Just by owning Home Depot stock, you could have helped save the giant redwoods!

Note: If you own individual stocks and your investments are handled by a broker or financial planner, you may have to specifically instruct them to follow your wishes as far as voting proxies.

SUCCESS STORIES

Home Depot

If you wanted mileage for your money, Home Depot was one of the stocks to own in the 1990s. Its profits rose approximately 25% per year in the past five years. The stock price itself soared from a "low" of $12 per share in 1994 to a high of $66 in April 1999. (This figure is adjusted for stock splits.) This means if you'd had $10,000 in Home Depot stock in 1994, you'd have $55,000 on July 16, 1999.

In addition to making a profit from owning your share of a company, you could have had a voice in the business practices of Home Depot. Let me explain.

The Problem: Home Depot Sells Wood from Endangered Forests

Home Depot had concerned environmentalists for a long time because the company bought and sold timber harvested from "old growth" forests. (Picture those beautiful giant redwoods in northern California, the kind that measure eight or ten feet across, and that's what "old growth" means.) Home Depot, is in fact, the nation's biggest lumber retailer. By selling old growth timber, Home Depot had been creating an incentive for loggers to cut down these beautiful trees. This destruction was needless, because ample supplies of second growth and plantation wood made reliance on old growth timber unnecessary.

To make matters worse, less than 20% of the world's old growth forests remain, and the United States has already lost 96% of its old growth trees. These old growth forests are home to nearly 50% of the world's species. Scientists have also discovered an array of plants with vital medicinal features in these forests. For example, rosy periwinkle from the forests of Madagascar has been used to successfully treat leukemia. And the alkaloid d-turbocuarine has been discovered in Latin American rainforests and can be used to treat multiple sclerosis, Parkinson's disease, and other muscular disorders.

The Solution: Stop Home Depot from Buying "Old Growth" Lumber

Environmental groups, led by Rainforest Action Network, began a two-and-a-half-year campaign to urge Home Depot to stop buying wood from old growth forests. The campaign included letter writing, lobbying, pickets, demonstrations, protests, and even letters from rock stars like Michael Stipe of R.E.M. and Dave Matthews of the Dave Matthews Band.

The Shareholder Resolution

As part of their campaign, members of the Rainforest Action Network began to work with the investment firm Trillium Asset Management and the managers of the Domini Social Equity Index and Citizens Funds, all of whom were shareholders of Home Depot stock. Together, they wrote a shareholder resolution and got it placed on the ballot for all the other owners of Home Depot stock to vote on. The resolution stated simply that as part-owners of the company, the investors would like to see their company phase out its policy of purchasing old growth lumber.

VICTORY

After all the votes were tallied, the hard work of the environmentalists paid off. Why? Because almost 12% of Home Depot's owners had asked it to make a plan to stop selling old growth wood! (An additional 6% abstained.) And 12%, while it's not a majority, is a significant minority.

Three months later, Arthur Blank, president and CEO of Home Depot, stated that Home Depot would eliminate its practice of buying some types of wood from endangered forests by 2002. Victory!

It's important to remember that Home Depot's shareholder resolution was part of a three-year campaign including countless demonstrations, letters, phone calls, rallies, and rock concerts. But a resolution from 12% of the very people that owned the company, the shareholders, sent a strong message that something had to be changed.

INTEL

I've got this sticker on my computer that says "Intel Inside." Maybe you have one, too. Intel makes microprocessors, which are basically the brains of a computer. The company really cornered the market in the 1990s.

Intel had an incredible commitment to get its microprocessors in everyone's computers. They made the fastest, most sophisticated microprocessors for years, and they were ruthless about driving down costs.

As a result, the company's profits grew 42% per year in the past ten years, and the stock went from roughly $3 per share in 1990 to approximately $89 per share in 1999 (adjusting for stock splits). If you'd had $10,000 in Intel stock in 1990, then you would have something in the ballpark of $296,640 by now. That was also a stock to own. It's also another place where you could have weighed in on company policy. This is the story.

Intel Associated with Pollution, Health, and Safety Problems

Intel located one of its factories in Rio Rancho, New Mexico, just outside of Albuquerque, in the late 1980s. When Intel moved its plant to Rio Rancho, the local community noticed some problems. A grassroots environmental and economic justice advocacy group called the SouthWest Organizing Project (SWOP) decided to document these problems. They released a report called "Intel Inside New Mexico: A Case Study of Environmental and Economic Injustice." Their complaints were as follows:

1. The air. According to SWOP's report, residents near the Intel factory complained of foul-smelling fumes coming from the factory. In October 1992, the New Mexico Air Pollution Control Bureau found Intel in violation of air emissions standards.

2. Worker safety. To SWOP, it also seemed that Intel wasn't taking adequate precautions to protect workers from hazardous conditions. Eighty workers were hospitalized after a gas leak at the Intel site in June 1993, and thirteen were injured in November 1993 when a pipe exploded at the site.

3. Reporting of hazardous chemicals. Manufacturing microprocessors requires the use of toxic chemicals and also generates a huge amount of toxic waste. Because of a loophole in federal environmental law, Intel was required to report only 11% of the chemicals it used in its production practices. SWOP wanted the company to report on all of the chemicals used and on the disposal of the resulting hazardous waste.

4. Overuse of water. In the desert state of New Mexico, water is a precious resource. Manufacturing microprocessors requires a great deal of water. Intel was granted the right to drill wells to accommodate its needs. However, according to SWOP, Intel was not required to make reparations to local, small farmers if the water table was disrupted and the wells of these farmers dried up as a result of Intel's drilling. SWOP wanted Intel to be held accountable for its adverse impact on these farmers.

The Shareholder Resolution

SWOP was funded in part by the Jessie Smith Noyes Foundation—a foundation with a $70 million endowment, some of it invested in stocks, including Intel stock. The Noyes Foundation worked with SWOP to file a shareholder resolution for the April 1995 ballot. The resolution was very simple: It urged Intel to change its Environmental, Health and Safety Policy to include a commitment to consulting with and sharing information with the communities in which it operated.

VICTORY

The resolution got Intel's attention. And the votes for it (just under 5%) were high enough to allow Noyes to re-file the following year. Intel began to cooperate. Intel and the Noyes Foundation began to talk about the company's lack of accountability to the community of Rio Rancho and started a series of meetings to discuss the problems outlined in SWOP's report.

The next year, when it looked like Intel might be stalling, Noyes—in consultation with SWOP—filed another shareholder resolution. In response, Intel drafted a new environmental, health, and safety policy. SWOP and Noyes reviewed the policy and agreed that it was satisfactory. So the resolution was withdrawn.

"The shareholder strategy allows us to go inside Intel shareholder meetings," said Jeanne Gauna, head of the SouthWest Organizing Project, "and we leveraged over 1 million shares in a coalition of shareholders, investment houses, churches and foundations."

If you had owned Intel stock, you, too, could have had a vote for clean air and water in New Mexico.

No matter what your values are, you can find a way to incorporate them in the way that you invest. These success stories show that investing with your values can certainly make a difference on how corporations behave in the world.

Creating and Implementing Your Grand Master Plan

Chapter Eighteen

Creating Your Grand Financial Plan and Finding a Financial Advisor

With the glint of greed in your eye and fire in your belly you hit the streets. You've maxed out your retirement plan. You're going to set up a Roth IRA—and that's just the beginning. You're not interested in creating a "nest egg" anymore. (Who wants a smelly old egg anyway?) You are are going to build an *empire*. You are going to *implement the master plan*.

Wait. What master plan? Master plan? Who said anything about a master plan?

Guess what? I did. I'll say it again. Plan. Strategem. Outline. Agenda. Blueprint. Whether you want to admit it or not, you already have a plan. It may not be "the grand master plan," but it certainly is *a* plan. It may look something like one of the following:

1. Financial Plan Number One: Pay rent. Go out Saturday night. Have crazy work week. Buy best friend dinner on Thursday because it's her birthday. Spend weekend with Sweetie (buy groceries, watch movie), worry about raising a family. On Monday, wonder what happened to money.

2. Financial Plan Number Two: Transfer high 18% credit card to 3.9% credit card. Wait for paycheck. Buy really cool expensive shoes because hey—you only live once. Worry about future. Take everyone out for brunch on Sunday. Wait for paycheck.

Those, in fact, *are* plans. However, just for the record, you might want to tinker with it a little bit. Maybe modify it to exclude "Worry about future" and include "*Build empire.*"

But where to start? Who's the architect to consult with?

FINDING A FINANCIAL PLANNER

It's not bad to seek the help of a financial professional. The likes of Jennifer Aniston, Queen Latifah, and Mariah Carey all have armies of financial people making sure they maintain their riches. So a good financial advisor is merely a consultant to you and your grand master planning. There are six steps to making a financial plan and finding a financial planner. They are as follows:

1. Write down your goals
2. Cover the basics
3. Start the search: Get names of planners from friends, professional organizations, or financial planning associations themselves
4. Ask your prospective financial advisor the important questions up front
5. Organize your stuff
6. Just do it

STEP ONE: WRITE DOWN YOUR GOALS

First, you have to know *what* you are planning for. So write down your life goals. Go on. Write them down. All of them are legit—even the dreamier ones. So write 'em down. If this exercise spooks you, get your best friend and write them down with him or her. I've written down some items on my own personal list to give you an example. Your list might look something like it.

- Bike across Spain
- Build houses in Central America with Habitat for Humanity
- Scuba dive the Great Barrier Reef
- Nurture relationship with loving supportive spouse
- Buy a house
- Raise two kids
- Educate and play with those children
- Be part of caring, committed community
- Pull together family reunion

Now, many aspects of your life goals may cost money, and many of them don't. But if you don't put them down on paper in black and white, you'll have less chance of getting the emotional, spiritual, and financial support to reach them. I don't cover emotional and spiritual support in this book, but I do cover finance.

A good financial advisor will help you price out your goal and figure out a financial road map for you to reach it. If the issue is retirement, or house buying, or having babies or scuba diving the Great Barrier Reef, a good financial planner will help you see how much money it will cost to get you where you want to go and how much to put away each week towards your various goals.

It's good to be as specific as possible. You might tell them something like the following:

- My spouse and I just got married and we want help figuring out how much we'll need to buy our dream house and how to start saving for it.

- I want help setting up a Roth IRA. And I want to make sure that my money is in a socially responsible mutual fund

- I'm going to have a baby and I plan to stay home with her for a year. I need help designing a cash flow plan that can support that. I also want to buy term insurance. And I want to change my will.

- I read this book telling me I needed a grand master plan. Can you help me create one?

Knowing what you want from a financial advisor is key. It will help you choose a financial advisor from the many different kinds out there.

STEP TWO: COVER THE BASICS

Before you choose an advisor to implement The Plan, you should know what areas of your financial life are lacking. A good financial advisor will help you fill in any holes in your financial life, and a bad one will ignore them. So, to prepare yourself for any good financial advisors you may meet and arm yourself against any bad ones, you should know what the basics of any financial plan are.

1. Be Adequately Insured. I don't want to sound like an insurance salesman, but you may find that you are lacking in this area. One car accident, fire, or theft could wipe out everything you've scrimped and saved for over the years. So at the risk of sounding like a nag, I'm telling you that you *must* have the following types of insurance.

- Health insurance
- Disability insurance
- Renter's insurance, if you rent

- Homeowner's insurance, if you own your home
- Life insurance, if you have kids (term is usually cheaper)
- Automobile insurance, if you own a car

Sorry. There's no discussion here. If you do not have the insurance that you need, you *must, must* go get it.

2. Contribute the Maximum You Can to Your Retirement Plan. As I stated in the retirement plan chapter, this is a no-brainer and you must do it. You'll need something to live on when you can no longer work and all the young whippersnappers have pushed you out of your job. Besides, retirement plans are a no-brainer good deal. If you contribute the maximum you can to your retirement plan, you will reduce the amount you pay in taxes. You may receive "free" money in the form of a matching contribution from your employer. The money inside the retirement plan will grow quickly because it will be sheltered from taxes. You will be creating a very substantial fund for yourself. In most cases, if you want to buy a house or pay for education, you can borrow from this plan. In some cases, you can withdraw money for those purchases penalty-free.

Go back and read Chapter Two and just make sure you are putting the maximum away.

As part of making adequate plans for your retirement, you may also want to set up a Roth IRA. This is a terrific deal. You contribute $2,000 per year ($166 a month) to the stock mutual fund of your choice. If it's inside a Roth IRA, you will not have to pay taxes on this money. You can withdraw your contributions at any time, tax-free and penalty-free. You can withdraw $10,000 for a first-time home purchase or as much as you need for higher education, and you will not be charged a penalty. Go read Chapter Three on why the Roth IRA is such a no-brainer, and then run, don't walk, to set one up.

3. Know the Difference Between Good Debt and Bad Debt and Pay Off Your Bad Debt. Not all debt is bad. A home mortgage is a healthy kind of debt because it's a way for you to own your home, the interest is usually pretty low, and the interest is tax deductible. A student loan is a healthy kind of debt. When you go to school, you are enhancing your marketability or at least your education. The interest rate on student loan debt is comparatively low, and it is also tax deductible.

But there is unhealthy debt. That is usually credit card debt. The interest rate on this kind of debt is usually super-high. So, if you have credit card debt, you want to start paying it off. You can also try to get it refinanced at a lower rate if you do the following:

◆ Borrow money against your house, if you own one, at a low rate and pay your credit card debt off with the borrowed money. The interest rate on your home equity loan should be half the interest rate on your credit card.

◆ Borrow against your retirement plan or any stocks or mutual funds outside your retirement plan at a lower rate and pay off your credit card debt.

If you have a lot of consumer credit card debt, and you don't know how to make ends meet without going into further credit card debt, chances are you need to see a counselor or go to a Debtors Anonymous meeting to get yourself centered and on a positive cash flow plan.

4. Review Your Tax Situation. If you think you are paying too much in taxes, you might be. Review the tax chapter to see if there's anything you are overlooking, and then sit down with a professional tax preparer and review your situation again. Your financial advisor may be able to put you in touch with a tax specialist.

5. Just in Case You Don't Live Forever, It's Good to Draw Up a Will. Who knows? You might live forever. But just in case you have an untimely, inconvenient physical death, you'll want to have drawn up a will. That way, you *can* be the one to decide to whom your assets and sentimental keepsakes can go. A good financial advisor can help you find someone to do that as inexpensively as possible.

Now. That's the list of financial steps you need to take. You can do some of them yourself or you can wait to meet with an advisor to help you do certain things like set up a Roth IRA, write your will, or buy disability insurance. A good financial advisor generally has expertise in one area and can refer you to experts in others.

STEP THREE: START THE SEARCH. GET NAMES OF PLANNERS FROM FRIENDS, PROFESSIONAL ORGANIZATIONS, OR FINANCIAL PLANNING ASSOCIATIONS

Finding a good financial advisor is a little like finding a good doctor. You need to network among your friends and co-workers. The advantage to asking your co-workers for references is that certain planners specialize in certain professions. For example, writers, nurses, and college professors all have different types of tax and financial planning needs.

The following organizations will provide you with a list of financial advisors in your area.

The Social Investment Forum
202-872-5319
http://www.socialinvest.org

If you call the Social Investment Forum at 1-800-58-GREEN, they will send you their Financial Planning Handbook and their Green Pages book for a small fee. The Financial Planning Handbook has useful tips on making your own financial plan and it also lists investment professionals in your area who can help you invest in a socially responsible manner.

If you visit www.socialinvest.org on the Web, and click under "quick links" and on the "Financial Services Directory" icon, you can also get a list of financial professionals who can help you buy stocks or mutual funds in a socially responsible manner. These financial planners can also help you use your rights as a per shareholder to vote on company policy.

SocialFunds
http://www.socialfunds.com
This Web site is sponsored by some of the major socially responsible mutual fund companies. It's very comprehensive. Click on the "Services" icon and the prompts will help you get a list of socially responsible financial planners in your locality.

The National Association of Personal Financial Advisors
at 1-800-366-2732
http://www.napfa.org
NAPFA is the only national organization of *fee-only* financial planners. They earn their money strictly from fees generated in exchange for the advice and service they provide. They do not receive sales commissions or other compensation paid by investment or insurance product suppliers. This organization will provide you a list of financial planners in your local area. You can call them or simply go to their Web site and click on the icon that says "Find a Fee-Only Planner Near You."

Some of these planners will simply meet with you and charge you an hourly fee. Others will act as money managers and will charge you 1% to 2% of your assets to manage your money for you, but usually you have to have more than $100,000 in stocks and bonds to make it worth their while.

The International Association for Financial Planning
1-800-945-4237
http://www.iafp.org

You can call this organization and they will mail you a list of financial advisors in your area. Or you can visit their Web site and click on the "Planning Pays Off" icon. You can then get a complete list of financial advisors in your locality. And the links will take you right to their Web sites.

This Web site is very informative and will also give you good tips on finding a good financial advisor.

This organization is all-inclusive. You will get advisors who are Certified Public Accountants, Certified Financial Planners and just straight-up, full-service stock brokers.

Institute of Certified Financial Planners
1-800-282-7526
http://www.icfp.org

Certified Financial Planners have taken comprehensive classes and training in all areas of personal finance. Contact this organization by phone or on the Web and click on their "Planner Search" icon and you will generate a list of CFPs in your locality. Some of these CFPs work for brokerage services and will charge you a sales commission for products that they sell. Others will only charge you an hourly fee (like $100 per hour) if you want them to generate a plan for you.

STEP FOUR: ASK YOUR PROSPECTIVE FINANCIAL ADVISOR THE IMPORTANT QUESTIONS UP FRONT

1. When you call them, tell them what you want out of the business partnership right away. Tell them about your goals and let them know exactly where you stand financially. They'll let you know if they can help you or if you both will be frustrated by the relationship.

2. Ask them what their areas of expertise are. They may be good at recommending stocks to buy, but lousy at recommendations for estate or tax planning. You'll need to know their strengths.

3. Ask them if they have a working relationship with other professionals in related fields. Your advisor must be ready to recommend another expert if your needs fall outside their area of expertise.

4. Ask them if they've worked with other people whose situation is similar to yours. Ask them to provide references, and then call those references.

5. Find out how much your financial advisor will cost you, up front. Depending on the type of services you want from your financial advisor, the answer may vary, but at the end of the day, there *will* be a dollar figure that *will* go in their pockets. It is only appropriate. Find out *what* that amount will be *before* you invest, or at least a very tight price range of what it will be. This will dispel a lot of confusion on your side.

Keep in mind that financial advisors can be paid in one of four ways or in any combination of these four ways.

♦ A financial advisor can be paid on a "per-task" basis. They draw up a financial plan for you, you pay them $200, for example.

- A financial advisor can be paid by getting a commission on the mutual funds or stocks they sell you. They sell you $3,000 worth of shares in a mutual fund, they get $90 (that's a 3% sales commission on your mutual fund—about average).

- A financial advisor can be paid simply by charging you an hourly fee. They meet with you for an hour, you pay them $150, for example.

- A financial advisor can be paid by charging you a percentage of the money that you give them to manage. You give them $20,000 to invest; they take a yearly cut of $400 (which is 2% of $20,000.)

As long as you know the products and services that you are getting, *and* you know the price, you will be much more comfortable with the whole process. The general rules of thumb in choosing how you are going to pay your financial advisor are as follows:

1. If you don't have much money, you are better off seeing someone who will charge you only on a "per task" basis or on an hourly basis. All you may need them to do is help you get a long-term picture of where you are going. Your best move may be just maxing out your retirement plan and setting up a Roth IRA. You may not be at the stage where buying additional mutual funds is practical or even an option.

2. If you have money, but are a real do-it-yourselfer, you may just want to meet with a financial advisor to get a "check-up." Again, in this case you are better off with a planner that will charge you on a "per-task" or hourly basis.

3. If you have $50,000 or more in assets (not including your house) and you want to work with a financial planner, any of the above might be helpful to you. What you want is to feel like you can

ask all kinds of questions and get really good answers that you understand. If the financial planner is condescending in any way, move on to the next planner. If the financial planner can't admit that she doesn't know something, move on to the next planner. If the answers of the financial planner are muddled or hostile, then move on to the next planner.

You want to choose the planner that you feel is most competent, least intimidating, and most honest.

STEP FIVE: ORGANIZE YOUR STUFF

Lastly, before you venture to your first meeting with your planner, you should organize all of the aspects of your financial life—if it's not already organized. You'll want to bring the following items to your first meeting.

♦ Retirement plan/pension plan statement. You'll want your monthly statement, the plan description, and all the paperwork that came with setting up the plan. You also want your paycheck stub, so that you can see in a dollar amount how much is being withheld each pay period.

When you or you and a financial advisor are reviewing your retirement planning, it will be good to have *everything* about the plan on hand. That way, you will be able to truly make a road map for your future.

If you have a 401(k) or 403(b), you will be able to determine if you've been putting the maximum away and if your employer has been matching. Your retirement plan money should be in stock funds, so you'll be able to see at once, if that's how you've had it allocated.

- Brokerage account statement. If you own stocks or mutual funds, you probably get a monthly statement from the brokerage house you set it up with. If you've set up a Roth IRA or traditional IRA, you probably get a brokerage statement on that once a month.

- Credit card statements. You'll want to hold on to your monthly credit card statements. When you are ready to make a plan, you'll be able to see exactly how much you owe and at what interest rate. If you have different credit card statements, you'll be able to put them all together and see which has the highest interest rate. (That's the one you should get rid of first.)

- Bank statements. You'll want to know exactly how much is in your checking or savings account when you make your plan.

- Student loan. You'll want to have your original student loan agreement and your copy of any statements related to your payments.

- Automobile loan. You'll want to have your loan agreement and a copy of any statements related to your payments.

- Home mortgage loan. You'll want to have copies of your closing statements and all other documents related to your home mortgage and your monthly mortgage payments. If interest rates drop, you may want to refinance your home mortgage loan at a cheaper rate. If you have a car loan or credit card debt, you may want to take out a home equity loan so that you can pay off those debts. The interest on your home equity loan will be deductible, whereas car loan debt and credit card debt interest is not.

- Insurance. You'll want to pull together the various policies that you own and simply review them with the advisor.

- Tax returns. Minimizing your taxes through every means possible is a very important part of making your financial plan. So you'll want to get hold of a couple past year's tax returns.

STEP SIX: JUST DO IT

This last one is tough. Facing our financial issues can be very scary. Who likes to think about retiring or dying or becoming disabled? So sweeten up the process by putting in your dream goals and plan for those as well.

Chapter Nineteen

Introducing One Cool Financial Planner

Just to get you familiar with talking with a financial planner, I'd like to introduce you to one of my favorites. Her name is Sharon Rich. (No really, that *is* her name. I didn't make that up. Neither did she.) She's the author of several books, including *The Challenges of Wealth*, and owns her own fee-only financial planning practice in Boston, called Womoney. She received a diploma in Financial Planning from Boston University, and is registered in Massachusetts as an investment advisor. She also received a Doctorate in Education at Harvard University, focusing on women's psychology.

I interviewed her in her home office in Boston. I drove up there one snowy day and parked on the street in front of her house. I walked in the office entrance, and I could see down the hall to the play room of her house—it was populated with toys, stuffed animals, games, books, and videos—telltale signs that her two daughters were not far away.

We spoke, and I really liked her approach and philosophy about money. She's a financial planner, but she doesn't say, "don't worry your pretty little head—I'll take care of everything." She says the opposite.

She's adamant that her clients understand the fundamentals

and particulars of money management; but she's goofy, has a sense of humor, and lots of desktop toys you can play with.

She's sympathetic to the problems of debting and overspending, but she's no-nonsense in her approach about it. She articulately outlined the three biggest foibles that we women encounter with money:

1. Somehow "money management" is not in the "feminine," or in the domain for womanly responsibilities.
2. That we shouldn't ask basic questions.
3. That we have to tackle our money problems alone.

She counters these foibles by saying that:

1. Money management is something all women eventually will do, so we might as well be prepared.
2. There are no "stupid" basic questions, because we can't learn if we don't ask. Moreover, fear of looking stupid has kept many women from getting the information they need to take control.
3. We don't have to face our money quandaries alone. In fact, we'll do better if we work with a "money buddy," a support group, or a professional financial planner. She says, "This is not fun. A lot of times it's overwhelming both psychologically and technically and so it's just a matter of, 'Let's do it [together].'"

These are snippets from an interview that I had with her on that snowy Boston day. I reprint it here to give you a glimpse of how cool a financial planner can be, and why it's worth it to dig and find one.

SHARON RICH: Basically my theory about money management is that by changing your structures and by changing your behavior, you can make it easy to be successful financially.

As a practical person around money management that's all I can do. Because I'm not a therapist, but if I can say, "Okay, let's make it easy so you don't fail," that's what I think is really important. *Come up with a financial planning system not built for failure.*

The key is to *design something that's doable.* If you find out that you are spending too much eating out, take less cash with you and leave your credit card at home and have an envelope separately for eating out.

Or if you find out you don't know where your cash is going, put everything on your credit card as long as you can pay it off in a month and use that as a way to track.

There are systems you can use to stay on top of things. So that's what I mean by changing the behavior instead of waiting for the psychology to change. *Let's try to change the behaviors first and then the psychology can follow.*

SUSANNAH: Let's talk about credit card debt and overspending. That's a problem that many women, many people in fact, run into.

SHARON RICH: I can think of two clients who are both over-spenders. I'm meeting with them frequently enough that they have feedback on whether they are on track or not. Now, they don't always stay on track. No matter how clear you want to be on your planning, there's always an excuse to fall off on your spending plan. But I think both of them are successful because they are both feeling in control.

On the other hand, I have had some clients that are breaking down, the ones where credit debt comes from a [chronic] spending problem. Those are the clients where you have to say, "Let's come up with some very concrete strategies and review it monthly to see what's working or not."

Sometimes I tell a client to "go do that" [get all their finances in one place, put together a spending plan] and they can't do it.

Do you know what we do at the next meeting? *We do it together.* In other words, *we, as women, don't like to do things alone.* This is not fun.

A lot of times it's overwhelming both psychologically and technically and so it's just a matter of "Let's do it [together]." You try the big steps. And if that doesn't work, you break it down into smaller and smaller and smaller bits.

SUSANNAH: For an overspender, what's the best exercise for you to do?
SHARON RICH: I think a *reality check*. Really having good feedback where their money is going. To use Quicken. To use cash envelopes. In other words, to short-circuit your overspending by not carrying credit cards. Absolutely make it hard to overspend. To not go into stores. To learn other ways to take care of yourself.

And to be checking in on your spending frequently. Debtors' Anonymous is not bad in that you are keeping very close record of where the money is going. That's a support group.

If you're an overspender, let's take away the magical thinking and now let's look at the numbers. Let's list all the debts, look at the interest rates and what you can afford to pay off. A lot of over-spenders try to pay off too much, but then their car breaks the next day and it all goes back on the credit card.

[Here we switched gears to basic financial planning.]

SUSANNAH: Can you tell me some of your success stories?
SHARON RICH: I would say my success stories are my clients who say, "How can we have babies *and* buy the house *and* retire?" And then I see them two or three years later, and they say, "We're in the house. The baby's great." They may be tight on cash, but *I would call success when people are doing what they want to do in the world.*

Or for example, [I would call a "success"] my clients who retire, who weren't retired before. And they are taking woodworking now and classes and doing music. And they are smiling because they are doing what they want to do.

I think we as women want to have it all. In reality some people just can't quit when they want to. But there are others who have substantial money and they still feel that they don't have enough. *Being wealthy is a matter of matching what you have with what you want.*

SUSANNAH: You've been in the business a long time. What do you feel like you need to tell women? It may be something that you also need to tell men, but with women, it seems to pop up over and over.

SHARON RICH: The obvious thing is that you are going to take care of yourself.

SUSANNAH: Really, you mean in terms of . . .

SHARON RICH: You have to assume that you are going to be taking care of yourself *for always*. If you are in a relationship, my bottom line is that all relationships end, and you've got to be prepared for the end of that relationship. Whether it's through death or divorce. You don't have to do it yourself, but you have to know who to hire and what questions to ask.

SUSANNAH: You need to know . . .

SHARON RICH: Enough about your finances so that if you are with somebody and that person died tomorrow you could take over. And you need to know that if you are going to live to be in your late 90s that you have a plan to take care of yourself until then.

Historically, women are starting off with worse retirement assets because they take more time off work to raise a family. When they take more time off a) their careers aren't as far along because they took time off, b) they haven't put as much into retirement, and c) they are earning less so they have less to put there. And often they are spending more on family.

SUSANNAH: So what do you advise?

SHARON RICH: Have a long-term retirement perspective on investments. You've got to worry about taking care of yourself before you worry about taking care of your kids, which is something women don't like to think about.

SUSANNAH: You mean, taking care of yourself in terms of . . .

SHARON RICH: Paying into your own retirement account before you put away for your kid's college fund.

SUSANNAH: That is totally counterintuitive.

SHARON RICH: Uh huh. But in the long run, you've got to be sure you're taken care of first. And kids can pay off their college debt for a long time, but you don't have a long time to make up on a retirement account.

SUSANNAH: Any last words?

SHARON RICH: I think that women feel that we shouldn't be asking the really basic questions. And the short answer is, *there are no stupid questions, only people who give you bad answers. Everything about money is understandable.* If you can't understand something, you shouldn't be investing in it. It's okay to pay someone to do it for you, but you've got to understand what your financial planner is doing and why.

So that's the good news. There are great financial advisors out there. You just have to interview and dig to find them. The bad news is that Sharon isn't taking any new clients right now.

Chapter Twenty

Choosing a Broker to Implement the Grand Financial Plan

You have drawn up your Grand Master Plan. You've written down your Life Goals and you've priced them out. You are ready to start building your empire. You want to buy a stock mutual fund and put it in an IRA. You want to start saving $50 per month in a money market mutual fund. You just might buy some shares of stock you've heard so much about . . . like Microsoft or Coca-Cola. Now that you have a plan, you have my permission to go. But where do you go?

Well, you have to enter the land of the *broker*. A broker is a person who will buy your stocks or mutual funds for you. Unless you are licensed, you can't just march onto the floor of the New York Stock Exchange and wave dollar bills in the air and say, "Gimme thirty shares of Intel!" You would be arrested for doing that. So you need to go through a *broker* or *brokerage service* to make your purchases.

There are three basic types of brokerage services: full-service brokers, discount brokers, and online brokers.

FULL-SERVICE BROKERS

Most full-service brokers double as financial advisors. So, if you met with a financial advisor that you liked, and she were also a full-service broker, then you would be set. She would just implement your grand master plan with you.

But, for those of you who created the grand master plan by yourself, or those of you who just want your own personal broker, here is a brief outline of how a full-service broker works.

You walk into an office. You sit down with a guy in a tie (or a woman in a suit). If they double as a financial advisor, they will want to draw up a financial plan with you. If you already have a plan, they will want to review it with you.

Then it's their job to recommend the stocks or mutual funds that are right for you. *They* sell them to you. You buy them. *They* monitor your purchases. *You* sign the papers. *You* give them the money. If the investment does badly, well, *you* can blame *them*; but if there is an economic downturn or the stock market slides, there's probably little they could do.

I took my friend Eleanor to meet with a full-service broker named Sacha Milstone, who works for Raymond James. Eleanor brought all her financial information in to Sacha—the certificates of deposit from her father, her 401(k) statement, and a statement from a savings account she'd started at her bank. Sacha went through Eleanor's material and worked up a plan with her assistant. When they met again, Sacha made some recommendations to Eleanor—to move the low-interest money in the certificates of deposit and savings account into a solid growth stock mutual fund. Eleanor decided to keep the certificates of deposit, but she did move her savings into a growth stock mutual fund. And she did set up an IRA. Sacha was paid for her services by the commission she received selling Eleanor the mutual fund, and that's basically all there is to the story.

There are some definite benefits and drawbacks to working with a full-service broker.

The Benefits:

1. If you do your research right, you can find a full-service broker who will really take the time to draw up a long-term financial plan with you and make sure that your investments are appropriate for your life goals and your tax situation.

2. If you and your broker see eye to eye investment-wise, they can keep tabs on certain companies and industries for you. For example, I told my broker that I was interested in investing in this fancy closed-end mutual fund when it was open to the public. It was going to go on sale sometime in the summer. I sort of lost track of the mutual fund after that. She's the one who called me up and said, "Hey—that fund that you were interested in just hit the market. You want to buy it?"

3. If you're interested in socially responsible investing, a full-service broker can help you find appropriate investments. She can also find out if there are important issues a company is facing that you need to vote on.

4. If your broker works with a good research team and researches all your stocks and mutual funds, you won't have to.

The Down Side:

1. Most full-service brokers make their income by *selling you something.* That is, every time they make a transaction for you, buying or selling, they get some cash out of the deal. You may not need to buy anything. You may be better off paying off your higher-interest credit cards or just putting more of your paycheck into your retirement plan. But regardless of your needs, a full-service broker may try to sell you something simply because that's what brokers are trained to do—make sales and close deals. That's why you need to have an understanding of your Grand Master Plan from the start. Then when you interview a full-service broker, you will be clear about what you want and don't want from the business partnership.

Note: Some full-service brokers have switched to simply charging their clients annual fees based on a percentage of assets, to avoid this appearance of a conflict of interest.

2. The transaction costs of using a full-service broker to buy stocks or mutual funds are high. To buy 100 shares of Microsoft at a price $95 per share, you might have to pay upwards of $100. (At a discount broker, that would be approximately $40, and online, that would be around $10–$20.)

DISCOUNT BROKERS

You walk into an office. (Charles Schwab, T. Rowe Price, and Fidelity are probably names you've heard before.) You ask to see a broker. You may have to wait a bit if there are people ahead of you. Then you sit down with the broker.

A discount broker will not draw up a financial plan for you. You are supposed to be prepared to tell them what you are interested in doing. You say something like, "I want to open up a Roth IRA," or "I just had a baby and I want to set up an account in her name for college," or "I want to put the $1000 in my checking account into a money market mutual fund. I'm saving up for a down payment on a house."

You are supposed to have a general idea of the funds that you want to invest in or the stocks you want to buy.

Don't get me wrong. You don't have to be a financial whiz to use a discount broker. You don't have to dress nicely. You can wear baggy jeans and tape on the nose of your glasses. And you can ask tons and tons of questions.

When my friend Katherine first went to Charles Schwab to set up an account, she had loads of questions. And the guy at Schwab, we'll call him Chuck-the-Schwab-guy, was very patient and kind to her. He explained exactly what the different Schwab money market mutual funds were. Katherine had done some basic research and already knew that she wanted to invest either in one of two *no-load* funds—the Domini Social Equity Index Fund or the Citizens Index Fund. (She knew that both funds encouraged their chosen companies to engage in responsible environmental and labor practices.) So Chuck-the-Schwab-guy gave her all kinds of background information on the mutual funds that she was interested in buying.

She bothered poor Chuck-the-Schwab-guy for a good two hours. She wasn't afraid to ask "dumb" questions. At the end of the two-hour session, the two of them set up her account—she actually invested in both mutual funds because she couldn't decide between them, and she went home happy.

She did not pay Chuck-the-Schwab-guy a fee, and he did not get a commission from the mutual funds he sold her. Chuck-the-Schwab-guy, discount broker, gets paid by a *salary*. So he did not care what kind of mutual fund she bought or whether she bought one at all, really.

The Benefits:

1. Because discount brokers are paid by salary, they have no desire to sell you any specific mutual funds or stocks. They'll get paid at the end of the day anyway, so they don't have the apparent conflict of interest that beleaguers full-service brokers.

2. The transaction costs for buying stocks or bonds at a discount broker are much lower than at a full-service broker. They are about half the price of a full-service broker.

3. You can still talk to a person if you want to. You can either go into their office and ask lots of questions or get them on the phone and ask lots of questions.

The Downside:

1. Discount brokers do not provide an overall financial plan for you. Some brokers may encourage you to put the maximum into a retirement plan before you open a Roth IRA or something like that, but that isn't their primary job.

One exception: Charles Schwab has started something called Schwab AdvisorSource in which they will refer you to a fee-only financial planner and money manager—but you need to give that financial planner over $100,000 to manage. You are out of luck if you have less than $100,000. And no, they won't refer you if you just want to pay the "advisor" on an hourly basis to draw up a financial plan for you.

2. No one will monitor your stocks or your mutual funds other than you. You are free to make your own choices with a discount broker, but you are also free to make your own mistakes.

3. You won't get any advice about which stocks or mutual funds to invest in. The discount broker may provide you with background information on funds you are interested in, but they won't say "Buy StarTrek Inc. stock. It's a great buy now." You'll have to call those shots yourself. This may change in the future. Discount brokers are moving into the advice-giving area.

ONLINE BROKERAGE SERVICES

Online brokerage services. That's places like E*Trade, DLJ Direct, and Discover Brokerage. You download the application from the Web site. You fill it out and sign it. You send them a check. When your money shows up in the account, you point, click, and voilà! You've just bought yourself something like 300 shares of Microsoft. You've done it all online.

The Benefits:

The transactions costs for buying and selling stocks and mutual funds online are extremely low. Stock trades are usually less than $20 a trade and can be as low as $5 a trade.

The Downside:

If you put an order in wrong, you are accountable. If you slip up and type "5000" instead of "500," there may be no fixing it. You'll just have to undo the trade the next day and incur extra commission costs. You are really on your own when you buy stocks online. Most of the time, there is an "800" number you can call, but they are generally there to provide you with technical assistance.

So that's the world of brokers. The land where you buy all these stocks and bonds and mutual funds. The land where you start implementing the Grand Master Plan.

Money

Makeovers

to

Learn From

Chapter Twenty-one

How Katherine Changed from a Spender to a Saver and How You Can Too!

I had no hand in Katherine's financial makeover. She did it herself over a period of five years. But she was such a success, her secrets bear repeating here.

KATHERINE'S STORY

Katherine wasn't always a saver. In her twenties, she was quite the spender and a debtor. At one point, she owed $4,000 on her Visa bill and $5,000 to her bank in the form of a consumer loan.

Today, Katherine has a retirement plan to which she contributes the maximum. There is about $20,000 in the retirement plan. She has no consumer debt. She has $10,000 in savings *and* she just bought an apartment.

How did she do it? She had three indispensable tools. Two her mother had given her, and one she stole from some guy on a TV talk show, but they all work.

♦ Map out all your bills and income on a calendar
♦ Pay your bills on time
♦ Pay yourself first

This is Katherine's story, and how she used these tools. But first, just so you know that Katherine is not perfect, here's the story of her early disaster days.

Katherine's Early Disaster Days

Right after college, Katherine got a hankering for the mountains and moved to Aspen, Colorado—where, she says, she made her biggest mistake.

"Aspen is like $5 for a slice of pizza, $3 for a bagel. It's insanely expensive for the locals, most of whom need two jobs just to pay rent. And I couldn't pay rent one month. I had no choice. I put rent on my credit card. That is—I took out a $400 cash advance and that was the world's biggest mistake. You rack up interest daily instead of monthly on a cash advance. And if you don't pay it off right away, you get screwed big time."

Katherine also switched jobs a lot in Aspen. In fact, she either got fired from or quit most of her jobs. First, there was the job at the radio station, which she quit. Then there was the job at the T-shirt shop, where she was fired at the end of the season. Then there was the job as a coat-check girl, which Katherine called a good money maker. "That was great—it was lucrative—very lucrative. Hang up 300 coats—get $300 in cash. It was a great job.

"But I got fired from that too. The guy that owned the place was psychotic. He was a psychotic drunk and a horrible mean person.

So one night I threatened to lock all the furs in the coat check and storm off. But I didn't."

Katherine burst into giggles at the memory of her standoff over the fur coats.

Katherine was a fairly typical twenty-something taking time off between college and a career to fullfill her ski bum dreams. In the process, she'd racked up $4,000 of credit card debt and taken out a bank loan for $5,000. (She needed this lump sum to pay her taxes because of all the odd jobs she'd held in Aspen.)

So if you've had a volatile beginning, take heart. With the right job and the right focus, you too can turn your finances and career around.

KATHERINE'S "DO-IT-HERSELF" MAKEOVER

Eventually, Katherine moved back to Boston, where she settled in. She put herself through grad school by taking out a loan for $24,000 and she got a master's degree in public policy. Her early job mishaps were no indication of her ability to build a career. By the time she was 30, she got a job as the public relations director of a major national organization.

But how did she pay down her credit card debt, her bank loan, put away money for retirement, save $10,000 *and* buy an apartment? She used three very valuable tools described below.

TOOL # 1: MAP OUT ALL YOUR BILLS AND INCOME ON A CALENDAR

First, she implemented rule number one: *Map out all your bills and income on a calendar.* Katherine describes how she became familiar with this practice.

"After my parents divorced, my mother took this family financing class. They taught her to take out a calendar and *map* when all her bills were due each month, so that she could have a visual picture of when she would have income coming in versus when she needed money to go out. By mapping, say two or three months of this she could see where she was going to get into a crunch, and exactly how much money she would have for discretionary spending. For example, if rent was due on the first and she got paid on the first, she could see how much would be left over 'til next paycheck."

Katherine comments on the usefulness of this tool.

"Even though it seems like a really obvious thing, unless you really do it visually on a calendar, it's hard to keep track of what you owe and when, week to week, month to month. But if you actually see it, write it down, exactly when you need to have the money to pay bills, then you know, 'Okay, for the last two days of the first two weeks, I have $75.00 to spend on food'—or that kind of thing."

Katherine is a zealot when it comes to the usefulness of this tool. It is the *first* thing she would recommend for anyone trying to sort out their financial life.

Following her careful "mapping" plan, Katherine was able to pay off her credit card and bank loan piecemeal in her late twenties and early thirties. And she was able to keep track of her expenses.

So go ahead and do it. Get out a calendar. Map out your financial life.

If you've never done it before, it may make you anxious. So close your eyes. Again, imagine you are Madonna. You are the chief executive officer of your own brilliant corporation. And you have money coming in and money going out. All you are doing is balancing the books. You are the queen, and the numbers are just that, numbers.

TOOL # 2: PAY YOUR BILLS ON TIME

The second tool that Katherine believes is also simple. *Pay Your Bills On Time.*

Again, because of the urgings of her mother, Katherine has always paid her bills on time, even when she has had debt. This is another thing Katherine is a zealot about:

"I am diligent about paying my bills on time because my mother taught me at a very early age that I had to keep a clean credit history—that that was the most important thing if I ever wanted to buy anything. So she drilled that into my head.

"And I really learned that lesson at one point in graduate school. I went to try to get a car loan or something like that, and they told me 'No' because my debt to income ratio was way too high. I sort of got a concept then. I also watched a lot of my friends unable to get, say, an American Express card, because they were told that their credit history was poor."

Throughout her late twenties and early thirties, even though Katherine was paying down her debts, she *always* paid her bills on time.

This year, that timeliness gave her a necessary boost when she was trying to buy her apartment. "I had the third best credit rating in the bank's history," Katherine bragged. "And that helped me get a mortgage with a really low interest rate."

It's important to note here that *you can always negotiate with your creditors.* A late payment on a credit card or phone bill is more likely to affect your credit history. But with private offices, like your doctor's office or your mechanic, you can usually work out a payment plan. You simply must go to them and be straightforward and honest. Direct and simple.

For example, you could simply talk to the billing person at your doctor's office. You could say something like, "Look, I can't pay you the $160 all at once. I can pay you $40 per month for the next four months. As long as I do this every month, and do it on time, will that be okay with you?"

Chances are they'll be delighted that you are being so responsible, and they'll gladly let you do it. They are used to dealing with much more delinquent accounts and you are making their job easier by being so honest.

TOOL # 3: PAY YOURSELF FIRST

The third and most important tool that Katherine used to amass $10,000 in savings was the simple mantra, *pay yourself first*. She explains how she learned about this mantra.

"I was sitting around lamenting the fact that I was 30. The biggest purchase I had made in my life was a bed. I was working for a non-profit organization, so I wasn't exactly rolling in money. I was single so I didn't exactly have the benefit of a dual income. And I was sitting around the house one day watching this stupid TV talk show. And this guy comes on who's like 30 and he's a self-made millionaire. So he's the kind of guy that everyone loves to hate.

"So he's talking about how everybody in the world can acquire wealth if they follow his few principles. He was just precocious enough to pay attention to. And his simple words were *'pay yourself.'*

"And I thought, 'What a revolutionary idea!' "

"He said, 'What you want to do every month, when you sit down to pay your bills, and *before* you pay anyone else, the most important person to pay is yourself. Because you should be the one to see the fruits of your labor. Not some credit card company. Not some dentist across town. But *you*. You are the most important person that should be paid for your work.'

"And then he also showed those graphs which show what happens when you compound interest."

The concept of paying herself was a novel one for Katherine. She said that she always had the mentality that she needed to pay her bills first, and that whatever was left would go into savings. So just having that little two word instruction to "pay yourself" was a sea change in the way she thought about money management. So it became a priority.

So what did she do?

"I went off to the bank and I set up an automatic deduction savings plan."

After a while, she was putting $300 aside every month.

Although $300 per month may seem like a large payment, she was able to make it work. I asked her about this.

SUSANNAH: But where did you find that extra $300? Did it coincide with a raise?

KATHERINE: I did switch jobs then. And I got a very small raise. But my pay schedule at the new job was different. I was paid once a month instead of biweekly, so there was a much bigger chunk to draw down $300.

SUSANNAH: But suddenly not having $300 didn't you feel the squeeze?

KATHERINE: Definitely. There are still times when I am very squeezed. In fact, I have overdraft protection—there are times when I will spend my budget down to the last nickel. But I don't worry, because I'm still saving every month.

I still have such a small amount to work with that it's never completely stress-free. The good thing about this is that the savings is considered one of the "untouchables." And that has made all the difference.

SUSANNAH: What kind of advice do you have for anyone starting out trying to save?

KATHERINE: Yeah—what you don't want to do is rack up other expensive bills (at a higher interest rate) while you are busy paying yourself. That's what you want to keep your eye on. For example, if it's a doctor's bill that doesn't accrue any interest—yeah—you can space it out over four or five months. He can't come after you. But if your Visa bills are adding up, that's not so smart. So what you want to always do is never spend more on your Visa bill than you can pay off every month. It's a question of priority.

SUSANNAH: Any last words?

KATHERINE: Yes. If I can do it, anyone can do it. (At this she laughs and makes a face, but then becomes serious.)

I would suggest that (prospective savers) take the time, even if they do it one time only, to map out three months, when they expect to get their money coming in versus when their money going out is due. They will get a very clear picture of exactly how much discretionary money there is to spend. And also they'll get an idea of how much they can possibly save.

Because, all of a sudden, within three years time, I have $10,000 sitting there and it's a miracle.

SUMMARY

So, for you to start saving the way Katherine did, you probably have to change the way that you think about your paychecks. That little two word instruction "pay yourself" revolutionized the way she thought about money. She realized that the first person she should pay was herself. All other bills could be negotiated or stretched out over a period of months (as long as there was no adverse effect on her credit rating). And because she made a habit of mapping out all her bills and communicating with people that she owed money to, she never fell far behind or had a drop in her credit rating.

So you go ahead. Use Katherine's tools and you'll be amazed with the results.

Chapter Twenty-two

How Lucy Turned Financial Panic Into Financial Power

And maxed out her retirement plan!

LUCY'S MAKEOVER

Lucy and I sat down to talk about her financial situation. She was convinced that she was a fiscal disaster. She had moved in with her boyfriend—a man she thought she would marry—and now they were having daily fights which all seemed to be about money.

He was very concerned that, at age 35, she had saved nothing at all for retirement. He didn't understand why she didn't have a career plan—at least that would advance her pay. He was worried that he was going to have to shoulder the sole financial burden of their relationship.

He convinced Lucy that she was a poor planner and told her that he was very concerned about spending a lifetime together.

When I started to talk to Lucy, her self-confidence was shattered. Everything her boyfriend said rang true: She felt like she had been completely irresponsible her whole life. She wanted to turn her financial life around.

STEP ONE: REALITY CHECK

The first thing Lucy and I did together was review her current financial situation. It was not surprising to me, but Lucy was not the basketcase that her boyfriend had made her out to be. We wrote it all down in black and white—all Lucy's income, debts, savings, expenses, and investments. And we found that it was, as in almost all cases, a mixed bag of "good" news and "bad" news.

1. Lucy had *no* retirement plant or IRA of any sort.
2. Lucy had a student loan outstanding of $1500 at a 7% annual interest rate.
3. Lucy made $34,000 per year as program director for a non-profit educational program for urban youth.
4. Lucy's expenses were low because all her food and rent were shared between herself and her boyfriend.
5. Lucy had no consumer debt outstanding.
6. Lucy had $5,000 in savings.
7. Lucy's car was about to die—that is, she was about to incur a new expense in the form of a car purchase of some sort.

STEP TWO: THE ANALYSIS

The Bad News

1. Lucy was, in fact, way behind on the "investment for retirement" front. Many people her age have $60,000 to $100,000 in retirement money.

She needed to get started on a retirement plan for two big reasons:

a) Lucy's workplace did have a retirement plan. She was crazy not to contribute to it, because her company would match her contributions. She had essentially been saying "no" to free money by not contributing.

b) A retirement plan is not just for retirement. It's also a safety net. In times of stress, where a large amount of money is suddenly needed, Lucy would be able to borrow against her retirement plan at a cheap rate. Later when she left her job, she could roll it over into an IRA, and then use $10,000 of her money for higher education expenses or for a down payment on a house. (See Chapter 2, "Get Paid for Your Work.")

2. Lucy's salary could use some improvement. It wasn't very high for a 35-year-old woman living in a major metropolitan area. It didn't give her much flexibility.

3. Lucy needed a reliable car, and soon. And cars, unfortunately, only lose value over time.

The Good News:

1. Lucy had no consumer debt. Many people Lucy's age who feel like they are a financial disaster feel that way because they have, say, $40,000 in credit card debt. But Lucy had *no* consumer debt. She lived within her means. She was honest with herself about what she could afford and what she couldn't afford.

To implement *any* financial plan, the first thing you need is honesty.

2. Lucy had managed to save $5,000. This was good for two reasons. One, it proved that she knew how to control her cash flow to meet a goal. Second, the $5,000 would come in handy when her car did die.

3. The debt Lucy did have, a student loan at 7% annual interest rate, was being paid off steadily.

4. Lucy's expenses were low because all her food and rent was shared with her boyfriend. Again, Lucy lived within her means and kept her expenses low.

STEP THREE: THE RECOMMENDATIONS

1. First I recommended that Lucy contribute at least 12.65% of her salary to her 403(b) retirement plan. That would be $4,300 annually, and every cent of it would be tax deductible.

After that, her employer would match 5% of her salary at $1,700.

All told, $6,000 per year would be going to her retirement plan. If she kept that up every year, adjusting the number upward for inflation, she would have enough to retire comfortably, albeit modestly, at age 65.

With one fell swoop, she could go from being retirement plan deficient to being retirement plan proficient.

2. The second thing that I recommended that Lucy do was buy a used car as soon as possible. A good used car is less expensive because insurance is lower, and that's because the overall value of the car is lower. Car payments, if you have them, will not slow you down for long.

3. I recommended that Lucy ask for a raise and consider looking for other work. She had been doing exceptional work at her job and she wasn't being rewarded for it financially. She definitely needed more income.

STEP FOUR: HOW LUCY IMPLEMENTED THE PLAN

1. First, Lucy shared. She was so excited after our financial workshop that she went home and told her boyfriend that she had it all figured out. She was so psyched. She felt empowered.

2. Then Lucy got her employer to make contributions to her retirement plan retroactively! I was totally impressed with this. It hadn't been one of my suggestions—but that Lucy—she went and made it happen. She got her boss to let the organization make a contribution of $850 to her retirement plan. That represented a retroactive 5% of her salary over a 6 month period.

3. Lucy started contributing the maximum to her retirement plan. She did this in a very ingenious way. Because she hadn't made any contributions all year long, and it was already November, she wanted to catch up. She persuaded her employer to put every cent of the net income in her December paycheck, some $2,000, toward her retirement plan. By law, Lucy was allowed to contribute $5,100 per year to her retirement plan—so even contributing $2,000, she was well under her contribution limit.

Then Lucy lived on $2,000 of her savings for the month.

4. Lucy bought a new car. Lucy had to buy a car because her rattletrap old car was always dying on her. I had urged her to buy a used car, but Lucy wanted a safe car that would be extremely reliable, because she did so much driving for work. She also took out a car loan, saddling herself with a $300 monthly payment.

This was not what I had urged her to do, but it is what made her feel most comfortable given the inordinate amount of driving she had to do. She loves the car, but the car payments have weighed her down.

5. Four months later, Lucy broke up with her boyfriend. I had not made this recommendation, but that's what Lucy did. It turned out that even when Lucy finally came up with a financial plan, she and her boyfriend still had many fights and tearful differences. It became apparent that "financial planning" had been a simple peg to hang their relationship troubles on, and that their problems ran much deeper.

So after a four-month period of worry, counseling, and torment, Lucy and her boyfriend agreed to part ways.

6. Lucy had to modify her plan to fit her breakup. Ending a relationship usually costs money, if you've been living together. Lucy had to go from paying very little rent to renting an apartment for $700 per month!

So after four months of maxing out her retirement plan contributions, she had to cut way back. She just needed more take-home pay out of her paycheck.

7. Lucy built up her self-esteem and skills. Lucy had loved her boyfriend very much, but he was bad for her self-esteem. She started to question everything she did and her own self-worth.

After the breakup, she worked hard at rebuilding her life. She spent time with good friends. She started back with activities that she had enjoyed prior to the breakup.

8. Lucy received a huge promotion and raise. Although her plan got derailed a bit with the breakup, Lucy never lost sight of her goals and her desire for financial success. So she started to angle for a raise at work. She was quickly rewarded for her hard work with a raise, and then six months later, she switched over to a much higher-paying job.

9. Lucy got her financial plan back on track. Once she was financially stable enough, she started contributing 15% of her paycheck toward her retirement plan.

SUMMARY

Lucy's primary problem was not that she was a hopeless financial planner. In fact, she didn't really have a major problem. She just hadn't focused on financial planning in her life.

Once she got a game plan, she stuck to it. Sure, it had to be modified to meet major life circumstances. I haven't met anyone who *hasn't* had to change his or her financial plan to fit changes in life. The important thing is not to change your financial goals just because of breakups or babies or other huge life events. The important thing is to stay focused on those goals and find another way to meet them.

The other important lesson I learned working with Lucy is not really a financial lesson. It's a life lesson. No matter how much you love someone, if they have a low opinion of you, for whatever reason, it's probably not a good idea to stay in relationship with them. It's always difficult to succeed when people around you don't support you or believe in you.

Chapter Twenty-three

How Liza Stopped Underearning and You Can Too

Liza's trouble wasn't that she was spending too much—she was earning too little! Find out how she psyched herself up to get a huge promotion and raise.

LIZA'S MAKEOVER

Liza was 35. She was very jumpy about her finances. Liza was just barely making it. Her paycheck was so thinly stretched over her rent, car payment, and college loans that she had panic attacks at bill time. In fact, she started to rack up a little bit of credit card debt just to pay bills. So I sat down with Liza to review her finances and to get the facts straight to see if there was a way to ease the strain on her budget.

STEP ONE: REVIEW THE FACTS AND ANALYZE THEM

First, Liza prepared a detailed accounting of her income, expenses, investments, and debts. Then we reviewed Liza's budget together.

One thing became clear to me: Overspending was not Liza's

problem. She was not extravagant. She lived within her means. She did not have a problem with debt. She covered her bare necessities: a car (which she needed for her forty-minute commute to work), an apartment (which cost $670 per month at the low end of the market), groceries, and a student loan.

Furthermore, from Liza's description of her work, it was clear to me that she was talented and hard-working. She should be making more money. But the Urban Housing Project Inc., where she worked, was paying her only $33,000 per year.

STEP TWO: RECOMMENDATIONS

I had only one recommendation for Liza. Ask for a raise, or get a job that makes more money.

I said, "Look, you can try to cut expenses. But where would you cut? Maybe you wouldn't buy a wedding present for your sister and that would save $200. Maybe you could move into a group house and just rent a room instead of a whole apartment. But do you really want to do that, at age 35?

"You are underpaid. You are 35 years old and only making $33,000. My friend Holly, who is five years younger than you and has less experience in your line of work, is making $50,000. You have extremely valuable energy and experience. You have vision and talent. You are doing a typical woman thing and undervaluing yourself. You should be making at least what Holly is making."

Liza listened to this recommendation with some surprise. It hadn't really occurred to her that the way to make ends meet was to get more means—more money. Usually, reviewing a budget meant looking at where she could "cut"—not where she could "increase."

Also, she agreed with me that she deserved a raise, and that she could probably get one if she made a case for it and presented it to her boss. Liza knew that her boss valued the work that she did.

Furthermore, she decided that she should also start to look for another job. In the event that her boss could not give her a raise, she decided to have other options available. It was time to go out on the open market and explore her options.

STEP THREE: LIZA IMPLEMENTS HER PLAN

Liza asks for a raise. After we had our talk in October 1998, Liza went to her boss and had a discussion. Liza presented her case in a very matter-of-fact way. She outlined all the work she had done, and all the programs she had created, and requested a raise.

Liza's boss agreed that Liza's salary was too low, and he simply asked, "How much do you need?"

Liza said she needed $45,000 to start making ends meet. Her boss was not surprised by this request. He told Liza that he didn't know if he could get her that large a raise, but he would try to work something out by January, when the new budget would start.

Liza also told her boss that she'd be looking for a new job because she simply had to make more money, and he said he understood.

Liza gets a raise and so does everyone else! In January, three months after Liza's initial conversation with her boss, she received a raise to $41,000 per year. It was a start.

Not only that, in a move uncharacteristic of the boss in the "Dilbert" cartoons, Liza's boss decided that everyone's salary was too low. He not only gave Liza a raise, but he increased everyone else's salary too! Good karma all around, and all because Liza had started standing up for herself.

Liza goes out on the job market. Liza still thought she could do better. So she went to a career counselor and explored her skills and values. As she became empowered, Liza decided that she wanted to make $100,000 per year, not $45,000 per year. She wanted to prosper and not just "make it."

She starting interviewing for other jobs. In one interview she stood up right in the interview room and told them politely that she wouldn't take the job because the pay was too low. Eventually, she was offered two other jobs. One job was the executive director position in a nonprofit organization that promised a salary of $50,000 per year!

Liza gets a big promotion. Liza was clearly on a roll. In April 1999, the executive director of the Urban Housing Project Inc. (Liza's boss) announced that he was leaving his job, and he urged Liza to apply for the job. Liza wasn't absolutely sure she wanted the job, but she applied for it anyway. In June, the board of the Urban Housing Project Inc. offered Liza the executive director position for $53,000 per year—$6,000 more than they had paid her boss. She got them to throw in another $2,000 for travel expenses.

SUMMARY

Within *one year* of her initial money panic, Liza had increased her salary by $22,000! The increase was so large because it was clearly long overdue. With this extra salary, Liza did have higher taxes, but she was able to put the maximum amount in her retirement plan and she was able to start saving extra cash in a money market mutual fund at T. Rowe Price. She no longer felt so squeezed, and she also didn't have to rack up any credit card debt just to pay her bills.

ARE YOU AN UNDEREARNER?

Liza's story is true—just the names and jobs have been changed. It can be true for you, too, if you are an underearner. In fact, there's a great book called *Earn What You Deserve*, by Jerrold Mundis, and he lists some of the major characteristics of underearners. Below is a list of common characteristics of people who underearn. This list was taken from Mr. Mundis' book, *Earn What You Deserve*. Take a look. See if any of these characteristics ring true:

♦ Not having a good idea of what your expenses are
♦ Spending time on projects or activities that earn little or no money
♦ Accepting work that you know will pay you less than you need
♦ Failing to request a raise
♦ Not increasing fees
♦ Ignoring or blinding yourself to an opportunity
♦ Not attempting something unless you are positive it will work
♦ Not drawing up a business or personal career plan
♦ Not capitalizing on your skills or abilities
♦ Behaving obnoxiously or offensively on the job or with clients
♦ Equating making money with accepting work you won't like

Do any of those behaviors sound familiar to you? Is it time you asked for a raise? Or switched jobs? Should you generally take yourself more seriously?

Protect

What You've

Got

Chapter Twenty-four

Taxes: The Way to Pay the Least

Find out how Jane could have had to pay $14,152 in taxes—but instead got a refund AND how you can too!

Taxes: They pay for roads, national parks, and schools, but I still WINCE every time tax time comes. Truth is, I don't like giving my money away. *I hate tax time.* But there *is* a good way to get psyched about paying taxes.

The trick is to imagine that you are very, very rich. Close your eyes and put yourself in Madonna's or Oprah's shoes. You are known for your business savvy. You are unabashedly self-made. People may try to mess with you, but you are so smart and resilient that you can't help but come out on top. You keep reinventing yourself. You own an *empire*, and every year it grows because of your savvy and genius.

Now, it's tax time. You don't shrug your shoulders and say, "I'm just a girl. I can't figure this out." What's more, you know you should not pay one penny more than you need to. You sit down and pore over your W-2s and receipts and tax books, maybe seeking the help of a professional tax preparer, and you burn the midnight oil until you are satisfied you're not paying any more than you have to.

Remember the golden rule of taxation:

You have every right as taxpayer to pay the lowest amount of taxes possible—to find every legal deduction, exemption, or credit that you can track down.

You work hard for your money. You want to hold on to it. By learning a few tax fundamentals, you will.

There are many, many smart people with honorable professions (including myself not too long ago) that don't know these basic things because they weren't taught in high school or by some kind, knowledgeable family member.

There are three steps you should take when paying taxes.

1. Take stock in what you own and what's coming to you
2. Figure out what forms to use
3. Track down and use all legal means to reduce your taxes, such as:
   - Exemptions
   - Deductions
   - Credits
   - Tax-deferred retirement plans or annuities
   - Taking capital losses

STEP ONE: TAKE STOCK IN WHAT YOU OWN AND WHAT'S COMING TO YOU

The first thing you do to prepare for tax time is to take stock. You need to know what you have, what you've earned, and what is coming to you. For two reasons:

1. If you don't know, and don't do your homework, the IRS will do it for you, and believe me, you won't like the dollar amount they say you owe.
2. If you do know, and work the system, you can save mega-bucks.

INTRODUCING JANE

Let's go to a real live example to illustrate this point. The story of Jane and Taxes. (This is a live example with a couple details changed to protect the innocent.) Jane is 40 years old and makes $68,584 a year. If she sat back and did nothing—no contributions to her retirement plan, no tax work sheets, no filing—the IRS might send her a bill for **$14,152!**

But Jane decides *not* to do nothing, so instead she gets a refund to the tune of $1,939!

How did she do it? Briefly put, she did her homework. First, she put the maximum amount she could into her retirement account, thus reducing her taxable income. Then she got an exemption for herself and her daughter. Then she itemized her deductions on a Schedule A. Finally, using the new child tax credit, she got $400 knocked off her total bill. That's all it took to save such big bucks.

So, how can you reduce your taxes the way Jane did? First, ask yourself these questions. A "yes" to any of them could mean big savings. I'd like to go over these questions now and then pick back up on Jane's story in a couple of pages.

BASIC QUESTIONS

1. Do you have kids that you support? (eligible for credits, deductions, exemptions)

2. Do you have elderly parents that you support? (eligible for credits, deductions, exemptions)

3. Do you have any sort of retirement plan through your employer? (contributions to certain plans make you eligible for deductions and avoiding capital gains taxes)

4. Do you have an IRA? (eligible for possible deductions and avoiding capital gains tax)

5. Have you taken out student loans in the past five years? (eligible for a deduction)

6. Are you currently a student in college or a vocational training program? (eligible for credits)

7. Have you made substantial gifts to charitable or nonprofit organizations that have tax-deductible status? (eligible for deductions)

8. Do you spend a lot of your "own" money on job-related expenses (eligible for deductions) without getting reimbursed? This can include
   - Job travel expenses
   - Professional and trade association dues
   - Books, subscriptions, and periodicals
   - Union dues
   - Uniforms and special clothing
   - Education expenses to enhance yourself in your line of work
   - Entertainment and travel expenses

9. Do you have a mortgage or home equity loan? This can include a mortgage on a house, condo, or mobile home. (eligible for a deduction)

10. Have you spent a lot of money on *unreimbursed* health care or dental care costs for you or one of your dependents? (eligible for a deduction)

11. Are you paying tuition for college, graduate school, or another education program for yourself or a dependent? (eligible for credits and deductions)

12. Are you self-employed? Do you run a business from your home? Do you own your own business? (eligible for deductions)

13. Do you own stocks or bonds that have lost value in the past year? (eligible for deductions)

STEP TWO: FIGURE OUT WHICH TAX FORMS YOU WILL NEED

Now, you have to figure out what forms to use. Jane had to use a Form 1040 and a Schedule A. Below, I explain the different forms so you can figure out which ones to use. There are only three basic tax forms to worry about: the 1040EZ, the 1040A, or the 1040.

You can use form 1040EZ if:

◆ You are single or are married filing jointly and have no kids, are under 65, and are not blind.

◆ You have income only from your job, unemployment compensation, or taxable scholarships, fellowships, and grants, and you have no more than $400 in interest income.

◆ Your taxable income is less than $50,000.

◆ You are not receiving the Earned Income Credit.

◆ You are not itemizing deductions.

◆ You do not owe any household employment taxes on wages you paid to a household employee.

◆ You do not have a student loan interest deduction or an education credit.

You can use form 1040A if:

- You have income only from your job, unemployment compensation, pensions, annuities, interest, dividends, or taxable scholarships, IRAs, taxable Social Security, or railroad retirement benefits.
- Your taxable income is less than $50,000.
- You are not itemizing deductions.
- Your only adjustments to income are
  a. Deduction for contributions to an IRA
  b. Student loan interest deduction

Basically, if you can't use the 1040EZ or the 1040A, you must use the form 1040. Also, you must use a form 1040 and attach certain additional tax forms called schedules if

- You answered "yes" to questions 7–13 above under "basic questions."
- Your taxable income is $50,000 or more.
- You owe household employment taxes.
- You itemize deductions.
- You have income from capital gains, a business, a farm, rental property, royalties, or alimony.

In order to qualify for all the goodies—the credits, the deductions, the tax breaks—you need to spell out in detail your financial situation. You do this by attaching tax forms called "schedules" to your return. A brief primer on the "ABC's" of schedules.

Schedule A is the form you attach if you are going to itemize your deductions.

Schedule B is the form you attach to determine the tax you owe on interest- and dividend-bearing accounts.

Schedule C is the form you attach to report income and expenses from your business if you are self-employed.

Schedule D is the form you attach to report losses and gains from the sale of stocks, bonds, other securities and properties.

Schedule E is the form you attach to report income and expenses from sources other than your job, such as rent, royalties, and from K-1 forms, which also detail income and expenses from trusts, partnerships, S corporations, and estates.

Schedule SE is the form you attach if you are self-employed and need to pay self-employment tax.

Form 2441 is the form you attach to detail child and dependent care expenses for purposes of receiving a tax credit.

STEP THREE: TRACK DOWN AND USE ALL LEGAL MEANS DESIGNED TO REDUCE YOUR TAXES

Remember, you have every right as a taxpayer to find every deduction and exemption that you can. That's what Jane did, and it served her well. We'll get to her in a minute, but here are four of the most basic ways to reduce your taxable income.

1. Deductions and exemptions
2. Credits
3. Putting savings in tax-deferred retirement accounts or annuities
4. Taking capital losses

WHAT ARE DEDUCTIONS AND EXEMPTIONS?

The IRS will allow you to reduce your taxable income if you spend some of it on worthy causes. You can reduce your taxable income by taking legal deductions and exemptions.

Exemptions

The IRS thinks self-sufficiency is a good thing. It also wants to reward you for supporting yourself and anyone else who is dependent on you. You get to "exempt" a part of your income from taxation—$2,700[1] if you support yourself, and $2,700 for each additional person that you "support" (i.e., you pay more than half of their support).

Deductions

The government wants to encourage you to do good things, like plan for the future by setting up a retirement account or paying your student loans. So it does its part by not taxing the part of your income that goes to your retirement plan or to paying the interest on your student loans.

There are five basic types of deductions:

1. Deductions that require no special forms. These deductions include retirement account contributions and interest on student loans.
2. Deductions that must be itemized on a Schedule A, such as charitable contributions, mortgage interest, property and real estate taxes, state and local income taxes, unreimbursed business expenses, and medical costs.
3. Deductions that must be listed on a Schedule C, including deductions for the self-employed.
4. Deductions that must be listed on a Schedule D, such as those related to the loss of capital in the sale of stocks, bonds, and other kinds of property.
5. Deductions that must be listed on a Schedule E, such as those relating to your rental or royalty or expenses.

[1] This is a 1998 number—tax year 1999 numbers came out in December 1999.

BACK TO JANE'S STORY

Remember, if Jane sat back and did nothing—no contributions to her retirement plan, no tax work sheets, no filing—the IRS might send her a bill for $14,152!

Jane is way smart. First, she always makes a contribution to her 401(k). This year, she contributed $5,465 (almost 8% of her salary). So right away, she reduces her taxable income from $69,158 to $63,693. She does this without looking, because it is automatically taken out of each paycheck by her employer and stashed in her retirement account. The W-2 she gets from her employer for tax season already reflects that only $63,693 of her income is taxable.

How I got Jane's Total Income without 401(k) contribution:

Jane's salary	$68,584
Add in last year's tax refund	$574
Jane's total income	$69,158
Subtract Jane's 401(k) contribution	$5,465
Jane's adjusted gross income	$63,693

This $63,693 is called Jane's *adjusted gross income*. Adjusted gross income is a formal way of referring to the amount of your income after the first tax adjustments have been made. In Jane's case, her adjusted gross income is equal to her income, plus her tax refund, minus her retirement plan contributions. Now, if Jane didn't do any of her tax work, she might owe taxes of $14,524, but Jane is smart. She fills out her tax forms. She uses her exemptions. She gets to reduce her taxable income by one large chunk because she supports herself, and a second chunk because she supports her six-year-old daughter. Each chunk of income is called an "exemption," and is worth $2,700. So right off of the bat, Jane gets to reduce her taxable income by $5,400.

Jane's adjusted gross income	$63,693
Jane's exemption	$2,700
Jane's exemption because her daughter is a dependent	$2,700
Jane's new taxable income	$58,293

So, if she reported to the IRS that her taxable income was $58,293 then she would owe $11,831. But Jane can reduce her taxable income further with *more* deductions. Now comes the part where taking stock is really important.

DEDUCTIONS TAKEN FROM ITEMIZING EXPENSES ON SCHEDULE A

Let's say Jane answered the above questionnaire. It turns out she has made a couple of charitable contributions and owns a house with a mortgage. So she looks into detailing these possible deductions on a Schedule A. To do this, Jane needs to list her possible deductions individually—item by item, a process called *itemizing*—and add them up. I've done this below.

First, she can deduct the state and local income tax that was withheld from her paycheck during the year; then she can deduct real estate taxes and personal property taxes. She can deduct also the interest and points on her mortgage payments.

Here's something "divine": She can deduct the contributions she gives to her church, plus her charitable contributions.

All of these add up to $15,438. (See Jane's tax return at the end of the chapter to follow how she itemizes her deductions.)

The IRS has a guesstimate of how much a person like Jane could deduct if she took the trouble to itemize. And their guesstimate is called a *standard deduction*. The standard deduction that you can take will depend upon your own economic status:

- $4,250 for a single person
- $6,250 for a head of household
- $7,100 for a couple who is married filing jointly or qualifying widow(er) with dependent child
- $3,550 for each member of a couple if they are married filing separately.[2]

Jane qualifies for the head of household deduction of $6,250.

However, because Jane's itemized deductions total $15,438, they are greater than her standard deduction of $6,250. She should go ahead and list each deduction separately on a Schedule A form.

Jane's taxable income is now only $42,855. How did I get that? Just follow along.

Jane's adjusted gross income	$63,693
Jane's exemption	$ 2,700
Jane's exemption because her daughter is a dependent	$ 2,700
Jane's itemized deductions on her Schedule A	$15,438
Jane's taxable income	$42,855

Jane now owes $7,592 on her taxes. (We're still not done with Jane, because she is still eligible for a tax credit discussed later.)

Details on how you can itemize your possible deductions on a

---

[2] These figures are for 1998.

Schedule A and taking advantage of some great money-saving opportunities are covered in Appendix VII.

DEDUCTIONS WHEN YOU ARE SELF-EMPLOYED

If you are self-employed (e.g., a writer, artist, independent contractor), you own your own business. You are entitled to additional deductions and you will need to fill out a Schedule C. All your "income" from your business must be reported on this form, as well as all your legitimate business expenses. You then deduct (subtract) your business expenses from your business income to arrive at your profit.

If you've ever been accused of being—shall we say—compulsively organized, this is your day to shine. If not, it's time to get that way.

You need to go down the Schedule C and look at every type of expense and ask yourself, "Do I have any of that?" It will save you federal tax, self-employment tax, and the state tax.

There is one very serious caveat. Your business has to be a *real* business, not a hobby. Generally speaking, if you don't show a profit in at least three of every five consecutive years, the IRS may decide that your business is just a hobby. You need to show that your "intent" is to make a profit and that you are treating it like a business. For example, the IRS looks for certain things to see whether you have set up a business checking account and a business credit card account, separate from your personal accounts.

Here are some of the legitimate business expenses you'll find on the Schedule C:

♦ Advertising
♦ Car and truck expenses

- ◆ Insurance (other than health)
- ◆ Legal and professional service
- ◆ Rent or lease
- ◆ Mortgage interest on building owned for the business
- ◆ Wages
- ◆ Utilities
- ◆ Repairs and maintenance
- ◆ Supplies
- ◆ Travel, meals, and entertainment
- ◆ Employee benefit programs

WHAT ARE TAX CREDITS?

Tax credits rank right up there with Lycra and Velcro in the pantheon of welcome ideas. A credit is another way the IRS lets you know it wants to reduce your taxes if your money is going for something worthy. But a credit is different from a deduction in that it is a dollar-for-dollar subtraction from your overall tax bill. *After* you figure out what you owe the IRS in taxes, you subtract a *credit* from your tax bill.

For example, let's go back to Jane. In 1997, Congress passed a law giving parents a $400 credit per child under age 17 who is claimed as their dependent. (In 1999, this credit was bumped up to $500.) Jane is eligible for this credit. She gets to knock the full $400 off her total tax bill. So instead of her tax liability being $7,592, it is now $7,192 ($7,592 minus $400).

Now Jane's tax liability is only $7,192, down from the original $16,218.

Because she took the trouble to look hard at all her expenses and all the credits, Jane was able to reduce her tax liability by 56%, or by $9,026.

Jane, in the end, gets a refund. During the tax year, $9,131 was withheld from her combined paychecks, and her tax liability was only $7,192 after all her homework was done. So it turns out she will be getting a refund of $1,939!

The following is a list of credits that you may be eligible for:

- The New Child Credit: Starting in tax year 1998, you can receive a $400 credit towards your tax bill for *each* child claimed as a dependent up to $800. You may also be able to take an additional tax credit if you have three or more qualifying children.
- The Adoption Expense Credit: You can subtract the first $5,000 of unreimbursed qualified adoption expenses per child. The limit is $6,000 for children with special needs.
- The Dependent Care Credit: The dependent care credit is available to parents or guardians who work, or are full-time students, or are disabled, and need to pay for child care. The actual credit can be as much as $720 for one child and as much as $1440 for two or more children.
- The Earned Income Tax Credit: If you make no more than $26,473 and have one child, *or* you make no more than $30,095 and have two or more children, you will qualify for the Earned Income Tax Credit. This credit is great. If this credit is more than the tax you owe, or you don't owe tax, which is often the case—the IRS will send you a check for the amount of the EIC.
- The Hope Scholarship Credit: This credit is designed to cover 100% of the first $1,000 and 50% of the next $1,000 of first- and second-year tuition and fees in a program leading to any undergraduate degree or vocation certificate. The student must attend school at least on a half-time basis.
- The Lifetime Learning Credit: This credit covers 20% of the first $5,000 of tuition and fees each year, with respect to any

course of instruction at an eligible educational institution; this is available for undergraduate, graduate, or professional courses such as acquiring job skills.

These are some of the most common credits. For a more extensive list (or more details), contact the IRS at 1-800-829-1040 or visit the IRS Web site at http://www.irs.gov.

HOW TO TAKE A CAPITAL LOSS

When you own stocks or bonds or other financial instruments and you sell them, you can either make a profit or lose money. If you make a profit by selling a stock or bond for more than you paid for it, you have to tell the IRS you made a profit. This profit is called a *capital gain*. You have to pay a tax on your capital gain, called a *capital gains tax*.[3] If you sell a stock for less than you paid for it, you have a loss. That is called a *capital loss*.

Before you report a capital gains profit to the IRS and pay the tax, you can subtract your capital losses from your capital gains. For example, say your technology stock mutual fund posted $1,000 in

---

[3] There are two types of capital gains taxes: long-term and short-term.

Long-term: When you sell stocks, bonds, coin collections, or any property that you have owned for more than one year you have to pay a "long-term capital gains tax" of 20% on the profit. That means that 20% of the profit you make will go to Uncle Sam. There's only one exception—and that is if you have so little income that you are in the 15% tax bracket. In that case, only 10% of the profit from your capital gains would be taxed.

Short-term: When you sell stocks or bonds that you have owned less than one year, you have to pay a "short-term capital gains tax" on the profit. Generally speaking, the profit is just added to your income and taxed along with the rest of your income. The good news is if you are in a tax bracket above 28%, the most you will have to pay is 28%. So, even if you earn lots of money and your income tax bracket is 39.6%, you'll only have to pay 28% tax on any "capital gains."

capital gains because it bought and sold Microsoft and made you $1,000 profit. On the other hand, your Health Care Products stock mutual fund posted $1,000 in capital losses because it bought Bilbo's Gauze Patches and sold them for less, losing $1,000.

You could subtract your losses of $1,000 from your gains of $1,000 and *you wouldn't have to pay any capital gains tax*, because your net capital gains would be zero. Your capital loss is deducted from your capital gain.

To explain this concept further, I have included a full illustration in Appendix VIII.

The Year-End Capital Loss Tax Trick: The Old Switcheroo

You like the idea of offsetting your gains with losses to avoid paying a capital gains tax, but what if one of your assets goes down in value and you haven't sold it? What if, say, the year were 1998 and you had a mutual fund or stock that went down with a shift in the world economy, but you thought that you still wanted to own the stock or mutual fund—because, after all, it might go back up. What do you do? You can sell it, look the other way for 31 days, and then buy it back. That way you take the loss, but you don't have to be without the stock or the mutual fund long term.

It's kind of a bait-and-switch tax trick, but the IRS allows you to do that. They say that you can sell a stock, and you can count it as a loss as long as you wait 31 days to buy it back.

This way of offsetting losses is the least the government can do to comfort a poor investor who could not foresee a serious downturn in events. It is the only silver lining in losing money, and it is relatively small. After all, if you have a capital gain, you get to keep 80% of your newfound money. If you have a capital loss, you lose 100% of your money. Lowering the amount of gain against the losses is only fair.

Selling stocks that have gone down for tax purposes is also a valuable exercise. Once you have sold the stock, you have to look carefully at what you own and think carefully about whether you *do* in fact *want* to buy the stock back. Suddenly not owning the stock, but having the cash from having sold it, puts you in a good position to truly evaluate your situation.

Caveat: Be sure that you can be without your investment for 31 days. If the stock of a company is in a volatile period, you may want to wait until it has settled down in price. Ideally, you want to be able to sell the stock and then buy it back at the same price or lower—provided that you still want to buy it.

SAVING MONEY ON CAPITAL GAINS TAXES BY PUTTING INVESTMENTS INSIDE RETIREMENT ACCOUNTS

Want to avoid paying a capital gains tax *and* set some money aside for when you're old and gray? Uncle Sam lets you do both with one slick move. You can avoid paying capital gains tax by putting your savings and investments underneath the protective shield of a retirement account. If your money is in a retirement account or annuity, all profits or "capital gains" from the sale of stocks, bonds, or other things *are not taxed*.

So consider this: You hold some stocks and bonds, either in a mutual fund or just individually, and over time, they are sold at a profit. You'd like to reinvest *all* of the profits. When your investment is not inside a retirement plan, however, you do have to pay capital gains tax on the proceeds that come from the sale. So only *some* of your money can be reinvested.

When *all* of your profits are reinvested, your return is higher over time and your money grows faster.

Let's compare.

BLUE CHIP STOCK FUND

Remember Sarah and Joan from the chapter on retirement? A reminder, in case you don't: They each put $2,000 per year into a stock mutual fund called the Blue Chip Stock Fund. Joan put her money into the fund inside an IRA; Sarah put her money in the fund without putting it inside an IRA.

	Sarah's Money NOT Inside the IRA	Joan's Money Inside the IRA
	Grows by 12%	Grows by 15%
10 years	$35,097.47	$40,607.44
15 years	$74,559.43	$95,160.82
30 years	$482,665.37	$869,490.29

Joan has almost twice as much money as Sarah, thirty years later. Just because she sheltered her investments under an IRA and they grew faster under that shelter.

Here's the catch: There are two things that you need to remember.

1. Under most circumstances, money under a retirement plan can't be withdrawn until you are age 59½ unless certain conditions are met or special needs arise. (See IRA and retirement chapters.) So, sheltering your stocks from capital gains taxes, whether they are in a mutual fund or not, is a fine thing—but only if you won't need the money for a long, long time. The general rule is, if you want to cash your stocks out for short-term use, that's fine, but you shouldn't use any type of retirement vehicle.

2. Unless the investment is inside a Roth IRA you will be taxed when it is withdrawn. The money will be taxed right along with your regular income tax.

A NOTE ON DEATH AND TAXES

What you don't know will hurt you in matters of death and taxes.

It works like this. When someone dies and they leave you more than $625,000 of anything, their estate must pay taxes on the amount over $625,000 starting with a rate of 37% and going up.

So if your relatives left you the family farm or the Picasso collection, the estate would have to pay taxes on it. Those taxes are substantial. And unless they left cash in their estate earmarked for the payment of taxes, the family farm itself or some priceless original might have to be sold to generate enough cash to pay those taxes.

Although you may not be inheriting valuable art or a petunia farm, you should still have a conversation with your family about estate planning.

SUMMARY

This chapter is not meant to be comprehensive by any stretch of the imagination, but I want you to imagine the kind of tax savings that you can get if you really do your homework.

Also, I strongly suggest you sit down with a tax planner and just go through the fundamentals. It's one thing to read a book, and it's another to put that information to work where you'll come up against questions. After you're done, I truly hope that you get the biggest tax refund of your life. In the words of Oprah, "You go, girl!"

Form 1040 U.S. Individual Income Tax Return 1998

(99) IRS use only — Do not write or staple in this space.

For the year Jan 1–Dec 31, 1998, or other tax year beginning , 1998, ending , 19   OMB No. 1545-0074

Label (See instructions.)

Your First Name: **JANE**   MI   Last Name: **GOODE**

Your social security number: **123-45-6789**

Use the IRS label. Otherwise, please print or type.

If a Joint Return, Spouse's First Name   MI   Last Name

Spouse's Social Security Number

Home Address (number and street). If You Have a P.O. Box. See instructions.   Apartment No.

▲ **Important!** ▲
You must enter your social security number(s) above.

City, Town or Post Office. If You Have a Foreign Address. See instructions.   State **VA**   ZIP Code

Presidential Election Campaign (See instructions.)

	Yes	No	Note: Checking Yes will not change your tax or reduce your refund.
Do you want 3 to go to this fund?		X	
If a joint return, does your spouse want 3 to go to this fund?			

Filing Status

Check only one box.

1. ☐ Single
2. ☐ Married filing joint return (even if only one had income)
3. ☐ Married filing separate return. Enter spouse's SSN above & full name here ... ▶
4. ☒ Head of household (with qualifying person). (See instructions.) If the qualifying person is a child but not your dependent, enter this child's name here .. ▶
5. ☐ Qualifying widow(er) with dependent child (year spouse died ▶ 19   ). (See instructions.)

Exemptions

6a ☒ Yourself. If your parent (or someone else) can claim you as a dependent on his or her tax return, do not check box 6a

No. of boxes checked on 6a and 6b: **1**

b ☐ Spouse

No. of your children on 6c who:

c Dependents:

(1) First name Last name	(2) Dependent's social security number	(3) Dependent's relationship to you	(4) ✓ if qualifying child for child tax credit (see instructions)	
CLEO GOODE	033-98-7654	Daughter	X	

• lived with you: **1**
• did not live with you due to divorce or separation (see instructions)

If more than six dependents, see instructions.

Dependents on 6c not entered above

Add numbers entered on lines above ▶ **2**

d Total number of exemptions claimed

Income

Attach Copy B of your Forms W-2, W-2G, and 1099-R here.

If you did not get a W-2, see instructions.

Enclose, but do not staple, any payment. Also, please use Form 1040-V.

7 Wages, salaries, tips, etc. Attach Form(s) W-2	7	63,119.
8a Taxable interest. Attach Schedule B if required	8a	
b Tax-exempt interest. Do not include on line 8a 8b		
9 Ordinary dividends. Attach Schedule B if required	9	
10 Taxable refunds, credits, or offsets of state and local income taxes (see instructions)	10	574.
11 Alimony received	11	
12 Business income or (loss). Attach Schedule C or C-EZ	12	
13 Capital gain or (loss). Attach Schedule D	13	
14 Other gains or (losses). Attach Form 4797	14	
15a Total IRA distributions 15a	b Taxable amount (see instrs)	15b	
16a Total pensions & annuities 16a	b Taxable amount (see instrs)	16b	
17 Rental real estate, royalties, partnerships, S corporations, trusts, etc. Attach Schedule E	17	
18 Farm income or (loss). Attach Schedule F	18	
19 Unemployment compensation	19	
20a Social security benefits 20a	b Taxable amount (see instrs)	20b	
21 Other income. List type & amount — see instrs	21	
22 Add the amounts in the far right column for lines 7 through 21. This is your total income ▶	22	63,693.

Adjusted Gross Income

If line 33 is under 30,095 (under 10,030 if a child did not live with you), see EIC in the instructions.

23 IRA deduction (see instructions)	23	
24 Student loan interest deduction (see instructions)	24	
25 Medical savings account deduction. Attach Form 8853	25	
26 Moving expenses. Attach Form 3903	26	
27 One-half of self-employment tax. Attach Schedule SE	27	
28 Self-employed health insurance deduction (see instructions)	28	
29 Keogh and self-employed SEP and SIMPLE plans	29	
30 Penalty on early withdrawal of savings	30	
31a Alimony paid. b Recipient's SSN ... ▶ 31a		
32 Add lines 23 through 31a	32	
33 Subtract line 32 from line 22. This is your adjusted gross income ▶	33	63,693.

BAA For Disclosure, Privacy Act, and Paperwork Reduction Act Notice, see instructions.

FDIA0112 11/02/98

Form 1040 (1998)

Tax and Credits	34	Amount from line 33 (adjusted gross income)	34	63,693.
	35a	Check if: ☐ You were 65/older, ☐ Blind; ☐ Spouse was 65/older, ☐ Blind. Add the number of boxes checked above and enter the total here ▶ 35a		
Standard Deduction for Most People	b	If you are married filing separately and your spouse itemizes deductions or you were a dual-status alien, see instructions and check here ▶ 35b ☐		
	36	Enter the larger of your **itemized** deductions from Schedule A, line 28, **Or** standard deduction shown on the left. But see instructions to find your standard deduction if you checked any box on line 35a or 35b or if someone can claim you as a dependent	36	15,438.
Single: 4,250	37	Subtract line 36 from line 34	37	48,255.
Head of household: 6,250	38	If line 34 is $93,400 or less, multiply $2,700 by the total number of exemptions claimed on line 6d. If line 34 is over $93,400, see the worksheet in the instructions for the amount to enter	38	5,400.
	39	Taxable income. Subtract line 38 from line 37. If line 38 is more than line 37, enter -0-	39	42,855.
Married filing jointly or Qualifying widow(er): 7,100	40	Tax. See instructions. Check if any tax from a ☐ Form(s) 8814 b ☐ Form 4972 ▶	40	7,592.
	41	Credit for child and dependent care expenses. Attach Form 2441 ... 41		
	42	Credit for the elderly or the disabled. Attach Schedule R ... 42		
Married filing separately: 3,550	43	Child tax credit (see instructions) ... 43	400.	
	44	Education credits. Attach Form 8863 ... 44		
	45	Adoption credit. Attach Form 8839 ... 45		
	46	Foreign tax credit. Attach Form 1116 if required ... 46		
	47	Other. Check if from ... a ☐ Form 3800 b ☐ Form 8396 c ☐ Form 8801 d ☐ Form (specify) ... 47		
	48	Add lines 41 through 47. These are your total credits	48	400.
	49	Subtract line 48 from line 40. If line 48 is more than line 40, enter -0-	49	7,192.
Other Taxes	50	Self-employment tax. Attach Schedule SE	50	
	51	Alternative minimum tax. Attach Form 6251	51	
	52	Social security and Medicare tax on tip income not reported to employer. Attach Form 4137	52	
	53	Tax on IRAs, other retirement plans, and MSAs. Attach Form 5329 if required	53	
	54	Advance earned income credit payments from Form(s) W-2	54	
	55	Household employment taxes. Attach Schedule H	55	
	56	Add lines 49-55. This is your total tax	56	7,192.
Payments	57	Federal income tax withheld from Forms W-2 and 1099 ... 57	9,131.	
	58	1998 estimated tax payments and amount applied from 1997 return ... 58		
	59a	Earned income credit. Attach Schedule EIC if you have a qualifying child.		
	b	Nontaxable earned income: amount ▶ and type ▶ _____ 59a		
Attach Forms W-2 and W-2G to page 1. Also attach Form 1099-R if tax was withheld.	60	Additional child tax credit. Attach Form 8812 ... 60		
	61	Amount paid with Form 4868 (request for extension) ... 61		
	62	Excess social security and RRTA tax withheld (see instrs) ... 62		
	63	Other payments. Check if from ... a ☐ Form 2439 b ☐ Form 4136 ... 63		
	64	Add lines 57, 58, 59a, and 60 through 63. These are your total payments ▶	64	9,131.
Refund Have it directly deposited! See instructions and fill in 66b, 66c, and 66d.	65	If line 64 is more than line 56, subtract line 56 from line 64. This is the amount you Overpaid	65	1,939.
	66a	Amount of line 65 you want Refunded to You	66a	1,939.
	▶ b	Routing number ... ▶ c Type: ☐ Checking ☐ Savings		
	▶ d	Account number		
	67	Amount of line 65 you want Applied to Your 1999 Estimated Tax ▶ 67		
Amount You Owe	68	If line 56 is more than line 64, subtract line 64 from line 56. This is the Amount You Owe. For details on how to pay, see instructions ▶	68	
	69	Estimated tax penalty. Also include on line 68 ... 69		

Sign Here
Joint return? See instructions.
Keep a copy for your records.

Under penalties of perjury, I declare that I have examined this return and accompanying schedules and statements, and to the best of my knowledge and belief, they are true, correct, and complete. Declaration of preparer (other than taxpayer) is based on all information of which preparer has any knowledge.

Your Signature	Date	Your Occupation	Daytime Telephone Number (optional)
		PUBLIC RELATIONS	
Spouse's Signature. If a Joint Return, Both Must Sign.	Date	Spouse's Occupation	

Paid Preparer's Use Only	Preparer's Signature ▶	Date 04/26/99	Check if self-employed ☐	Preparer's Social Security No. 033-36-0627
	Firm's Name (or yours if self-employed) and Address ▶	TAX PROFESSIONALS INC 5824 BRIDGETOWN COURT BURKE	VA	EIN 52-1374489 ZIP Code 22015

Schedule A
(Form 1040)

Itemized Deductions

OMB No. 1545-0074

1998

Department of the Treasury
Internal Revenue Service (99)

► Attach to Form 1040.
► See Instructions for Schedule A (Form 1040).

07

Name(s) Shown on Form 1040

JANE GOODE

Your Social Security Number

123-45-6789

Medical and Dental Expenses		Caution: Do not include expenses reimbursed or paid by others.			
	1	Medical and dental expenses (see instructions)	1		
	2	Enter amount from Form 1040, line 34	2		
	3	Multiply line 2 above by 7.5% (.075)	3		
	4	Subtract line 3 from line 1. If line 3 is more than line 1, enter -0-		4	
Taxes You Paid (See instructions.)	5	State and local income taxes	5	3,170.	
	6	Real estate taxes (see instructions)	6	1,407.	
	7	Personal property taxes	7	419.	
	8	Other taxes. List type and amount ►	8		
	9	Add lines 5 through 8		9	4,996.
Interest You Paid (See instructions.) **Note: Personal interest is not deductible.**	10	Home mortgage interest and points reported to you on Form 1098	10	10,102.	
	11	Home mortgage interest not reported to you on Form 1098. If paid to the person from whom you bought the home, see instructions and show that person's name, identifying number, and address ►	11		
	12	Points not reported to you on Form 1098. See instructions for special rules	12		
	13	Investment interest. Attach Form 4952 if required. (See instructions.)	13		
	14	Add lines 10 through 13		14	10,102.
Gifts to Charity If you made a gift and got a benefit for it, see instructions.	15	Gifts by cash or check. If you made any gift of 250 or more, see instructions	15	240.	
	16	Other than by cash or check. If any gift of 250 or more, see instructions. You Must attach Form 8283 if over 500	16	100.	
	17	Carryover from prior year	17		
	18	Add lines 15 through 17		18	340.
Casualty and Theft Losses	19	Casualty or theft loss(es). Attach Form 4684. (See instructions.)		19	
Job Expenses and Most Other Miscellaneous Deductions (See instructions for expenses to deduct here.)	20	Unreimbursed employee expenses — job travel, union dues, job education, etc. You Must attach Form 2106 or 2106-EZ if required (See instructions.) ►	20		
	21	Tax preparation fees	21		
	22	Other expenses — investment, safe deposit box, etc. List type and amount ►	22		
	23	Add lines 20 through 22	23		
	24	Enter amount from Form 1040, line 34	24		
	25	Multiply line 24 above by 2% (.02)	25		
	26	Subtract line 25 from line 23. If line 25 is more than line 23, enter -0-		26	
Other Miscellaneous Deductions	27	Other — from list in the instructions. List type and amount ►		27	
Total Itemized Deductions	28	Is Form 1040, line 34, over 124,500 (over 62,250 if married filing separately)? **No.** Your deduction is not limited. Add the amounts in the far right column for lines 4 through 27. Also, enter on Form 1040, line 36, the **larger** of this amount or your standard deduction. **Yes.** Your deduction may be limited. See instructions for the amount to enter.		► 28	15,438.

Chart of Sam and Jane

Sam and Jane turn 18:

Score:

Sam: 0

Jane: 0

Sam and Jane turn 19:

Score:

Sam: Puts in $2,000

No interest earned because money is put in at the end of the year

Total = **$2,000**

Jane: 0

Sam and Jane turn 20:

Score:

Sam: Subtotal from last year $2,000

10% interest on $2,000 = $200

Puts in another $2,000

$200 + $2000 + $2000 = $4,200

Total = **$4,200**

Jane: 0

Sam and Jane turn 21:

Score:

Sam: Subtotal from last year $4,200

 10% interest on $4,200 = $420

 Puts in another $2,000

 $4,200 + $420 + $2,000 = $6,620

 Total = **$6,620**

Jane: 0

Sam and Jane turn 22:

Score:

Sam: Subtotal from last year $6,620

 10% interest on $6,620 = 662

 Puts in another $2,000.00

 $6,620 + $662 + $2,000 = $9,282

 Total = **$9,282**

Jane: 0

Sam and Jane turn 23:

Score:

Sam: Subtotal from last year $9,282

 10% interest on $9,282 = $928

 Puts in another $2,000

 $9,282 + $928 + $2,000 = $12,210

 Total = **$12,210**

Jane: 0

Sam and Jane turn 24:

Score:

Sam: Subtotal from last year $12,210

10% interest on $12,210 = $1,221

Puts in another $2,000

$12,210 + $1,221 + $2,000 = $15,431

Total = **$15,431**

Jane: 0

Sam and Jane turn 25:

Score:

Sam: Subtotal from last year $15,431

10% interest on $15,431 = $1,543

Puts in another $2,000

$15,431 + $1543 + $2,000 = $18,974

Total = **$18,974**

Jane: 0

Sam and Jane turn 26:

Score:

Sam: Subtotal from last year $18,974

10% interest on $18,974 = $1,897

Puts in another $2,000

$18,974 + $1,897 + $2,000 = $22,871

Total = **$22,871**

Jane: 0

Sam and Jane turn 27:

Score:

Sam: Subtotal from last year $22,871

10% interest on $22,871 = $2,287

Puts in another $2,000

$22,871 + $2,287 + $2,000 = $27,158

Total = **$27,158**

Jane: 0

Sam and Jane turn 28:

Score:

Sam: Subtotal from last year $27,158

10% interest on $27,158 = $2,715

Puts in another $2,000

$27,158 + $2,715 + $2,000 = $31,874

Total = **$31,874**

Jane: 0

Sam and Jane turn 29:

Score:

Sam: Subtotal from last year $31,874

10% interest on $31,874 = $3,187

Does not put in $2,000

$31,874 + $3,187 = $35,061

Total = **$35,062**

Jane: Puts in $2,000

No interest earned because money is put in at the end of the year

Total = **$2,000**

Sam and Jane turn 30

Score:

Sam: Subtotal from last year $35,062

10% interest on $35,062 = $3,506

$35,062 + $3,506 = $38,568

Total = **$38,568**

Jane: Subtotal from last year $2,000

10% interest on $2,000 = $200

Puts in another $2,000

$200 + $2,000 + $2000 = $4,200

Total = **$4,200**

How to Figure Out Whether It's Worth It for You to Buy a Municipal Bond

Imagine there is a municipal bond with a tax rate of 5% and you want to figure out if you should cash it in and buy a corporate bond with a return of 7%.

If you are in the 28% tax bracket, it makes sense to cash in your municipal bond and invest in a corporate bond returning 7%. To arrive at that conclusion, I had to figure out the actual tax rate of the municipal bond. That is, given that no taxes would have to be paid on coupon payments accrued, what would be the actual return on the bond? To figure that out I would divide 5% by 100, minus the 28% tax rate.

$$\frac{\text{Municipal bond yield}}{100 \text{ minus your tax rate}} \qquad \frac{5\%}{100-28} \quad = \quad \frac{0.05}{72} \quad = \quad 6.9\%$$

So, it's a little bit better for you to invest in a bond returning 7%. With the tax break, you get a return of only 6.9%—0.1% less then what you can get with the corporate bond.

Now if your tax rate was 38%, it would be a different story. The actual rate of return for the municipal bond would be higher than that of the corporate bond.

Municipal bond yield	$\dfrac{5\%}{100-38}$	=	$\dfrac{5}{62}$	=	8.06%
100 minus your tax rate					

Clearly, it's better for you to invest in the municipal bond. It only appears to be returning 5%—but with the tax break, your return is 8.06%! A nice taxable corporate bond doesn't really hold up.

A Description of Some of the Major Stock Exchanges of the World

THE NEW YORK STOCK EXCHANGE

The New York Stock Exchange is the largest stock exchange in the United States. Close to 63,070 stocks are listed on the NYSE. Its trading floor is the size of a football field, with hundreds of designated buyers and sellers watching computer screens, answering phones, and shouting out orders. Generally speaking, the NYSE lists the largest and soundest corporations.

THE AMERICAN STOCK EXCHANGE

The stocks traded on the American Exchange tend to be medium-sized companies and not as well established as the companies on the New York Stock Exchange. As of April 1999, there were 779 companies listed on the American Exchange.

THE NASDAQ EXCHANGE (NATIONAL ASSOCIATION OF SECURITIES DEALERS AUTOMATED QUOTATION) SYSTEM

The NASDAQ is not located in an actual physical place. It is a network of 11,500 computer terminals that provide up-to-the-minute prices for stocks. In stock language, that is called "real time automated quotations." Brokers then buy and sell securities by telephone with other brokers. In 1971, NASDAQ was created to provide up-to-date information to the dealers who traded shares of smaller companies that were not listed on the New York Stock Exchange or any of the other major exchanges. Companies like Apple, Microsoft and Intel began trading on the NASDAQ, and even after having grown to be large companies they still trade on this exchange. As of July 1999, there were approximately 4,900 companies listed on the NASDAQ exchange.

OVER THE COUNTER (OTC)

"Over the counter" stocks are so small that they aren't even listed on the NASDAQ. Like NASDAQ, OTC stocks are traded via telephone or computer. The OTC market displays pricing information daily for these small companies, but you have to subscribe to a financial service like Bloomberg to get this information on a daily basis. Otherwise the prices and information about these OTC stocks are listed with the National Quotation Bureau and published and released daily to subscribers of their information service.

When a company whose stock is listed with the OTC exchange becomes successful enough to meet certain criteria set by the National Association of Securities Dealers, it can be listed with the NASDAQ companies.

In-Depth Description
of Certain Social Screens
for Socially Responsible
Mutual Funds

EXCLUSIONARY SCREEN: "SIN" STOCKS

Sin stocks are stocks from companies that profit from selling alcohol, tobacco, or gambling products. In the early part of the twentieth century, as churches built up wealth to fund their schools, mission programs, and other activities, more and more chose to invest this money in stock portfolios. Keep in mind, this was the time that the anti-alcohol and anti-smoking "temperance" movement was sweeping the country, most often led by the religious community. The clergy did not want to profit from the very industries they spent Sunday mornings preaching against. So they told their money managers to avoid these "sin" industries. As a result, most socially responsible mutual funds avoid alcohol, tobacco, or gambling products as a matter of course.

EXCLUSIONARY SCREEN: WEAPONS

Because certain religious organizations opposed violence as a means of dispute resolution, corporations that produced weapons, guns, and bombs were added to the list of industries to be avoided. During the Vietnam War, the ranks of both secular and religious organizations opposing the war grew, and so the number of portfolio managers using the anti-military screens also grew. Consequently, the stocks of companies like Boeing, Lockheed Martin, Raytheon, and Northrop Grumman are not considered viable investment opportunities for many socially responsible mutual funds.

QUALITATIVE SCREEN: ENVIRONMENT

In many socially responsible mutual funds, the fund manager will also consider the environmental practices of the corporations they are investing in. Unlike with alcohol or tobacco, it's not the product or the industry itself that the fund managers are told to object to. Indeed, the company may manufacture something desirable like drugs to combat AIDS or airbags for automobiles. This screen concerns the kinds of processes the company uses to take care of any pollution it creates, how responsive it is to the EPA or communities that criticize its practices.

For example, in the Domini Social Equity Index Fund, a company will be excluded from the index and the fund if:

♦ The company's current liabilities for hazardous waste sites exceed $50 million.
♦ The company has recently paid substantial fines or civil penalties for violations of air and water regulations.
♦ The company has a pattern of regulatory controversy under the Clean Air Act, Clean Water Act, or other environmental regulations.

On the other hand, the managers of the Domini Social Equity Index and the mutual fund will try to invest in companies that make positive contributions to the environment by having a commitment to the following kinds of practices:

◆ The company has notably strong pollution prevention programs including both emissions reductions and toxics reduction programs.

◆ The company either uses recycled materials in its manufacturing processes or is a major player in the recycling industry.

◆ The company makes profits from alternative fuels such as natural gas, wind power, and solar energy.

◆ The company has demonstrated a commitment to energy efficiency.

Over the past decade, shareholders have lobbied corporations to adopt a specific set of environmental principles to guide corporate environmental impacts. These principles, called the CERES principles (for Coalition for Environmentally Responsible Economies) state that the corporations must conduct all aspects of their business as responsible stewards of the environment. As a result, corporations that have adopted these principles have created senior positions responsible for environmental management.

Furthermore, many companies have discovered ways of doing business that significantly reduce their impact on the environment while saving money. Some of the larger companies that have adopted the CERES principles include Coca-Cola, General Motors, and Sunoco, Inc. For more information, check out the Web site http://www.ceres.org.

QUALITATIVE SCREEN: EMPLOYEE RELATIONS

In SRI funds, the mutual fund manager also looks at employee relations and diversity in the workplace. The mutual fund manager will look for positive practices, for example:

♦ The company has made notable progress in the promotion of women and minorities.
♦ The company has strong union relations.
♦ The company encourages worker involvement through participation in management decision-making.
♦ The company has an expansive profit-sharing program or stock ownership program.
♦ The company has strong retirement benefits.
♦ The company has a progressive policy for gay and lesbian employees providing for benefits for the same-sex domestic partners of its employees.
♦ The company has outstanding employee benefits or other programs addressing work/family concerns such as child care, elder care, and flextime.

A manager of a socially responsible mutual fund will likely look down on the following kinds of negative practices:

♦ The company recently has paid substantial fines for violations of employee health and safety standards.
♦ The company has paid substantial fines or civil penalties with regard to affirmative action controversies or has faced discrimination lawsuits.
♦ The company has a substantially under-funded pension plan or an inadequate retirement program.

QUALITATIVE SCREEN: PRODUCT SAFETY

Socially responsible mutual fund managers will look favorably on corporations that have a good product safety record. For example, the fund manger will look favorably on the following kinds of practices:

♦ The company has a long-term, well-developed company-wide quality program.
♦ The company has as part of its mission the provision of products or services for the economially disadvantaged.

The fund manager will look down on corporations that have experienced the following kinds of events:

♦ The company has recently faced lawsuits or paid fines or civil penalties because its products and services were harmful to consumers.
♦ The company has recently paid substantial fines for practices such as price fixing, collusion, or predatory pricing.

QUALITATIVE SCREEN: LABOR AND HUMAN RIGHTS

Corporate conduct, especially the conduct of corporate subcontractors worldwide, that results in labor and human rights violations of workers is highly problematic. The apparel industry in particular is rife with problems around the world.

Following reports of child labor, forced overtime work without pay, dangerous working conditions, and inadequate wages, shareholders have urged huge corporations like Nike, The Gap, and Wal-Mart to adopt corporate codes of conduct that apply not only to them but to everyone they subcontract to as well. However, these codes are meaningless if they are not enforced.

A current strategy of socially responsible investors to promote the enforcement of these codes of conduct has been to request that corporations publicly disclose all factory locations where clothing and products are made worldwide so that independent monitoring on a factory-by-factory basis may take place.

Investing in Individual Stocks Without Checking Your Values at the Door

If you want to invest on your own in individual stocks, you can do this without taking leave of your social senses. You can do your responsible investing with or without the help of an investment advisor.

SOCIALLY RESPONSIBLE INVESTING WITH THE HELP OF A SOCIALLY RESPONSIBLE INVESTMENT ADVISOR

The easiest way for socially responsible investors to invest in individual stocks is to work with an investment advisor dedicated to this kind of investing. These advisors have access to all kinds of expensive software products and services that provide details on the corporate practices of publicly held companies. These products are expensive for the individual investor because they were designed for million-dollar stock portfolios such as those held by pension funds, foundations, mutual funds, or in retirement plans. The work that goes into creating and maintaining these databases and services is labor-intensive. Purchasing the software and services of Kinder, Lydenberg and Domini or the Investor Responsibility Research Center costs in the ballpark of $10,000.

The good news is that a socially responsible financial advisor usually has subscribed to these services and products simply as part of the cost of doing business. You can find this type of advisor by checking out the financial advisors listed at the following web sites.

www.socialfunds.com
www.socialinvest.org
www.naturalinvesting.com

SOCIALLY RESPONSIBLE INVESTING WITHOUT AN ONGOING RELATIONSHIP WITH A FINANCIAL ADVISOR

If you want to choose your own stocks and don't want to have an ongoing relationship with a financial advisor, you can still find necessary information on the business practices of your companies.

1. You can contact a socially responsible investment advisor and ask if they will consult with you on an hourly basis. The investment advisors at Natural Investing Services advertise that they do this simple hourly consulting. They can be reached at 1–800–793–7512 or contacted through their Web site www.naturalinvesting.com. It is likely that other investment advisors offer hourly consulting services as well.
2. You can invest in the companies listed in either the Citizens Index or Domini Social Equity Index. You can check out how to be a shareholder activist and vote on company policies by looking at how the managers of the Domini Social Equity Index vote their proxies. Currently, they post how they vote on company policies on their Web site www.domini.com.

3. You can also find out if the socially responsible investing community is pushing for changes in the business practices of corporations whose stock you own. You can do this by contacting the following organizations.

SocialFunds.Com
www.socialfunds.com
A comprehensive list of shareholder resolutions backed by members of the socially responsible investing community is available on a company by company basis on the SocialFunds.com Web site under "activism."

The Interfaith Center on Corporate Responsibility
All the shareholder resolutions filed and supported by the Interfaith Center on Corporate Responsibility are listed on the Social-Funds.com Web site. If you don't have Web access, you can contact them at 212-872-2215.

The Social Investment Forum
www.socialinvest.org
202-872-5319
The Social Investment Forum is a membership organization that provides all kinds of comprehensive information on socially responsible investing including activist updates, academic research, professional contacts, and shareholder resolutions.

A Partial List of Full-Service, Discount, and Online Brokers

FULL-SERVICE BROKERS

Legg Mason
www.leggmason.com
800-822-5544

Merrill Lynch
www.ml.com
800-637-7455
201-557-1000

Morgan Stanley Dean Witter
www.deanwitter.com
800-869-3326
212-392-7767

Paine Webber
www.painewebber.com
800-382-9989

Raymond James Financial Services
www.raymondjames.com
800-647-7378

Salomon Smith Barney
www.salomonsmithbarney.com
800-556-7008
212-723-6000

A.G. Edwards & Sons Inc.
1-800-351-4488

Discount and Online Brokers

These companies provide both discount brokerage and online services.

Brown & Company
www.brownco.com
800-822-2021

Charles Schwab & Co.
www.schwab.com
800-435-4000

Fidelity Investments
www.fidelity.com
800-544-7272

Olde Discount Corporation
www.oldediscount.com
313-961-6666

ScotTrade
www.scottrade.com
800-619-7283

T. Rowe Price
www.troweprice.com
800-225-5132

ONLINE BROKERS

Almost all of these online brokerage services also provide touch-tone phone services. Some also provide over the phone "live" brokerage services. A few have offices where you can speak to a broker face-to-face, but are limited geographically.

AB Watley
www.abwatley.com
888-229-2853

Ameritrade
www.ameritrade.com
800-454-9272

BCL Online
www.bcl.net.com
800-621-0392

Bull & Bear Securities
www.bullbear.com
800-262-5800

Datek
www.datek.com
888-463-2835

DLJdirect
www.dljdirect.com
800-825-5723

Empire Financial Group
www.empirenow.com
800-569-3337

E*Trade
www.etrade.com
800-387-2331

Firstrade
www.firstrade.com
800-869-8800

InvestExpress Online
www.investexpress.com
800-392-7192

InvesTrade
www.investrade.com
800-498-7120

JB Oxford & Co.
www.jboxford.com
800-782-1876

Morgan Stanley Dean Witter Online
www.online.msdw.com
800-584-6837

My Discount Broker
www.mydiscountbroker.com
888-882-5600

National Discount Brokers Online
www.ndb.com
800-888-3999

Quick & Reilly
www.quick-reilly.com
800-837-7220

SiebertNet
www.siebertnet.com
800-872-0711

SureTrade
www.suretrade.com
401-642-6900

TradeOptions
www.tradeoptions.com
888-781-0283

Trading Direct
www.tradingdirect.com
800-925-8566

Waterhouse Securities
www.waterhouse.com
800-934-4410

Web Street Securities
www.webstreetsecurities.com
800-932-8723

FINANCIAL PLANNING

First Affirmative Financial Network
www.firstaffirmative.com
800-422-7284
719-636-1045

Deductions for a Schedule A

WHAT QUALIFIES AS A LEGITIMATE DEDUCTION AND HOW DO YOU ITEMIZE EACH ONE?

Schedule A is quite straightforward. This is a list of some of the more common items that can be deducted from your taxable income and how to figure out if you qualify for the deduction.

1. Medical Expenses (Lines 1–4 on Schedule A). I'd use Jane as an example here, but *she* didn't get hit by a car. My friend Phil, however, was not so lucky. He was in a really, really bad accident. He spent the better part of the year in the hospital and almost lost his right foot. The IRS has decided that if something this expensive were to happen to you, taxing money that would go to pay for your hospital bills is really not cool. But they only let you slip away from taxes if your hospital expenses were quite dramatic. They determine "dramatic" to be anything *above* 7.5% of your adjusted gross income.

Remember: Anything you got reimbursed for by insurance doesn't count as an expense.

You have to pay all medical expenses up to 7.5% of your adjusted gross income. They don't feel sorry. For example, say you earned $50,000 per year, and you got run over by a truck, accruing

$10,000 in health care costs. Your insurance company might pay for $2,000 because they are cheap and stingy. So you are really out of pocket only $8,000. After that, you still have to shovel out 7.5% of your adjusted gross income before Uncle Sam even begins to feel sorry.

$50,000 income per year
$42,000 adjusted gross income
$10,000 truck accident
$2,000 paid by insurance
$8,000 out of pocket
($42,000 x 0.075) = $3,150 *out of pocket and no deduction*

$4,850 is what Uncle Sam will let you knock off your taxable income. What a pal. This isn't much of a break. I mean, after you get run over by a truck, it really is adding insult to injury to have to shovel out $3,150 of your own money to pay for hospital bills.

Conclusion: Getting run over by a truck is not a good way to reduce your taxable income.

2. State and local taxes (that you already paid) (Lines 5–9). When itemizing, you can deduct the following:

♦ State and local taxes that were taken out of your paycheck during the year. (Look at your W-2. In boxes 18 and 21 of your W-2 you'll see that your employer withheld money from your pay to make your tax payments for you. You get to deduct that from your taxable income.)
♦ Taxes that you paid to your state and local government last year. (Look at last year's tax return, and you will see what you paid to the state.)

Example:

Coco Labelle lives in a tony Upper East Side apartment and is an extremely successful advertising executive. She also has lots of income from "other sources"—a stash of stocks and bonds.

She pays her state taxes in two ways. First, she has a chunk of her income withheld by the state of New York every paycheck. Second, she writes a check to the State of New York for the income tax she owes on all the other income she receives throughout the year.

Here comes the deduction part. The federal government lets her deduct *both* the money withheld from her paycheck during the year *and* the check she wrote to the State of New York the preceding year. (Yes, there is a time lag there—it's last year's check written to New York State that she gets to deduct.)

3. Real estate taxes and property taxes Real estate taxes that you already paid to your state and local government are also deductible, as are any state or local property taxes that you already paid to your state or local government. For example, I live in the state of Virginia. Virginia has property tax on automobiles. They've been phasing it out, but nonetheless, I still have to pay tax on my 1988 Chevy Nova to the government. That amount is deductible on this year's tax return. Personal property taxes usually cover big ticket items: car, mobile home, boat—the kinds of things that sit in your driveway.

4. Interest you paid on a home mortgage If you own a house and still have a mortgage, you get to deduct the interest on that mortgage from your taxable income. As a matter of fact, any time you use your house as collateral and take out a loan on it, be it a first mortgage, home equity loan, or line of credit, you get to deduct the interest on the mortgage.

If you take out a loan on your investments (that is, borrow money against the value of securities held in a brokerage account, sometimes called buying *on margin*) you can deduct the interest on that loan.

5. Interest you paid on student loans For 1999, you will be able to deduct $1,500 of interest even if you don't itemize your deductions. If you're single, your income can't exceed $55,000 or this deduction is phased out.

6. Gifts to qualifying charitable organizations (Lines 15–18). The government wants to encourage you to be generous to good causes. Many contributions to charitable organizations are tax-deductible. To find out if your contributions are tax-deductible, *ask* the organization and make sure that they have 501(c)(3) status. (If they raise a substantial portion of their money from people like you, chances are that your contributions are tax deductible.) The following is a list of the types of organizations that are tax deductible:

—The Environmental Defense Fund
—The American Cancer Society
—The YMCA
—Save the Children
—Any church, synagogue, or religious organization

You can also deduct the fair market value of anything that you *give* to the charity. If you donate your $1,000 1988 Chevy Nova to the Beth Israel synagogue, you can deduct that $1,000 from your taxes.

7. Casualty and theft loss (Line 19). If a hurricane hits your house or a burglar breaks into your home and steals *everything*, then you may be able to deduct your losses. But the IRS has some pretty high bars that you must jump over. First, any casualty must be "sudden, unexpected or unusual." Any theft must be reported to the police. And then, the value of the property stolen must be at least 10% above your adjusted gross income after insurance reimbursements. So you still get stuck paying tax on the first 10% of your income that goes to repairing your home or replacing your stolen items.

8. Miscellaneous. The IRS allows you to deduct miscellaneous expenses—these have to be over 2% of your AGI. They can include the following: job travel expenses, professional and trade association dues, books, subscriptions and periodicals, union dues, uniforms and special clothing, education expenses to enhance yourself in your line of work, and entertainment and travel expenses.

That about sums it up for itemizing. The key here is to document each item well. When it's done, tally up your total and make sure the total of your itemized deductions is greater than your standard deductions. If your itemized deductions are not greater than your standard deduction, take the standard deduction.

How to Offset Capital Gains with Capital Losses

"Capital Gain" Defined: There are two types of capital gains taxes: long-term and short-term.

Long-Term: When you sell stocks that you have owned over 12 months you have to pay a "long-term capital gains tax" of 20%. That means that 20% of the profit you make will go to Uncle Sam.

Example: In 1995, I had a long-term capital gain. I bought stock in a company called Checkpoint Systems. It's a company that makes burglar and security systems. I bought $863 worth of Checkpoint Systems on September 2, 1994. Then on June 11, 1996—21 months later—I sold my shares in Checkpoint Systems for $3,728. (Pretty good.) In a little under two years, I had made a profit of $2,865.

The Math: 9/2/94 bought Checkpoint Systems for $863

6/11/96 sold Checkpoint Systems for $3,728

Profit of $2,865 realized

Under today's laws, I would have owed 20% of that $2,865 to the IRS—coming to a grand total of $573.

Short-Term: When you sell stocks that you have owned for less than twelve months, the profit counts just as ordinary income. Say my salary was $35,000 per year. On 1/23/96 I bought shares of Vans Inc. equaling $3,128. On 8/7/96, I sold shares of Vans Inc. for $4,163.

My profit over this seven-month period was $1,035.

The Math: 1/23/96 bought   Vans Inc. for $3,128

8/7/96 sold   Vans Inc. for $4,163

Profit of $1,035 realized

That $1,035 is added to my salary of $35,000 per year as taxable income. So I start out reporting that my taxable income is $36,035.

"Capital Loss" Defined: If you buy stocks or bonds and then they decrease in value, you have a capital loss. There are no long-term or short-term capital losses.

For Example: On October 31, 1995 I bought $4,125 of Syquest. On May 8, 1996 I sold Syquest for $1,908. I incurred a loss of $2,217.

The Math: 10/31/95 bought   Syquest for $4,125

5/8/96 sold   Syquest for $1,908

Loss of $2,217 incurred

Other than making you feel like an idiot, a capital loss is good for you to offset your capital gains dollar for dollar. So you pay less tax. To do this, you simply subtract your losses from your gains.

Short-term gain: $1,035 Vans Inc.

Short-term loss: –$2,217 Syquest:

(Vans at $1,035 plus Syquest at –$2,217 = Net Loss of –$1,182)

Net Short-Term Loss of –$1,182

Long-term gain: $2,865 Checkpoint Systems:

Long-term loss: $0 (no stock sold at long-term loss)

(Checkpoint Systems at $2,865 plus 0 = Net gain of $2,865)

Net Long-Term Gain $2,865

To reduce my capital gains tax I add my loss and my gain together.

Net Short-Term Loss of –$1,182

plus Net Long-Term Gain of $ 2,865 =

Net Long-Term Gain of $ 1,683

In 1996, the amount that I would pay for capital gains taxes is $336.60. That's 20% of the capital gain of $1,683.

If I hadn't had any short-term losses, my capital gains tax would have been higher. It would have been **$573.** Because the whole net long-term gain of $2,865 would have been subject to tax. ($2,865 × 0.20) = $573.

Index